Study Guide for the *Middle School* Tests

▶ ▶ ▶ ▶ ▶ ▶ ▶ ▶ ▶ ▶ ▶ ▶

A PUBLICATION OF EDUCATIONAL TESTING SERVICE

Table of Contents

Study Guide for the *Middle School* Tests

► ► ► ► ► ► ► ► ► ► ►

TABLE OF CONTENTS

Chapter 1
Introduction to the *Middle School* Tests and Suggestions for Using This Study Guide

▶   ▶   ▶   ▶   ▶   ▶   ▶   ▶   ▶   ▶   ▶   ▶

Introduction to the *Middle School* Tests and Suggestions for Using This Study Guide

Introduction to the *Middle School* Tests

The Praxis *Middle School* tests assess test takers' understanding of the essential knowledge required for a beginning teacher at the middle school level. Four of the tests each focus on one specific content area: English Language Arts, Mathematics, Social Studies, and Science. A fifth test covers all four content areas. In developing assessment material for these tests, ETS works in collaboration with teacher educators, higher education content specialists, and accomplished practicing teachers to keep the tests updated and representative of current standards.

The *Middle School English Language Arts* test (0049) consists of 90 multiple-choice questions and 2 constructed-response questions, and covers 4 major areas in the following proportions:

Content Category	Approximate Number of Questions	Approximate Percentage of Total Score
▪ Reading and Literature	37	31%
▪ Language and Linguistics	16	13%
▪ Composition and Rhetoric	37	31%

▪ Short Essays
    ▪ Literary Analysis
    ▪ Rhetorical Analysis
	2
	(constructed response)
		25%

Test takers have 120 minutes to complete the test.

The *Middle School Mathematics* test (0069) consists of 45 multiple-choice questions and 3 constructed-response questions, and covers 4 major areas in the following proportions:

Content Category	Approximate Number of Questions	Approximate Percentage of Total Score
▪ Arithmetic and Basic Algebra	16-18	26-30%
▪ Geometry and Measurement; Coordinate Geometry, Functions and Graphs	14-18	22-30%
▪ Data, Probability, Statistical Concepts; Discrete Mathematics; and Computer Science	11-16	18-26%
▪ Problem-Solving Exercises (including Content-Specific Pedagogy)	3 (constructed response)	25%

Test takers have 120 minutes to complete the test. A four-function, scientific, or graphing calculator without a QWERTY keyboard is permitted.

The *Middle School Social Studies* test (0089) consists of 90 multiple-choice questions and 3 constructed-response questions, and covers 7 major areas in the following proportions:

Content Category	Approximate Number of Questions	Approximate Percentage of Total Score
▪ United States History	22-24	18-20%
▪ World History	16-19	14-16%
▪ Government/Civics	13-15	11-13%
▪ Geography	14-16	11-14%
▪ Economics	12-14	10-12%
▪ Sociology and Anthropology	0-6	0-5%

▪ Short Content Essays
    ▪ United States History – Government/Civics
    ▪ World History – Geography
    ▪ U.S. History – Economics or Geography or World History – Economics or Government/Civics
	3 (constructed response)	25%

Test takers have 120 minutes to complete the test.

The *Middle School Science* test (0439) consists of 90 multiple-choice questions and 3 constructed-response questions, and covers 7 major areas in the following proportions:

Content Category	Approximate Number of Questions	Approximate Percentage of Total Score
▪ Scientific Methodology, Techniques, and History	9	8%
▪ Basic Principles	14	11%
▪ Physical Sciences	22	18%
▪ Life Sciences	18	15%
▪ Earth Sciences	18	15%
▪ Science, Technology, and Society	9	8%

▪ Short Content Essays
    ▪ Physical Sciences
    ▪ Life Sciences
    ▪ Earth Sciences
	3 (constructed response)	25%

Test takers have 120 minutes to complete the test. Calculators are not permitted.

The *Middle School: Content Knowledge* test (0146) consists of 120 multiple-choice questions and covers 4 major areas in the following proportions:

Content Category	Approximate Number of Questions	Approximate Percentage of Total Score
▪ Literature and Language Studies	30	25%
▪ Mathematics	30	25%
▪ History/Social Studies	30	25%
▪ Science	30	25%

Test takers have 120 minutes to complete the test. A four-function or scientific calculator is permitted.

How to Use This Study Guide

This study guide gives you instruction, practice, and test-taking tips to help you prepare for taking one or more of the *Middle School* tests. In chapter 2 you will find a discussion of The Praxis Series™—what it is and how the tests in The Praxis Series are developed. In chapter 3 you will find information on how to answer multiple-choice questions. In chapter 4 you will find information on answering constructed-response questions and on how constructed-response questions are scored. Then chapters 5, 6, and 7 (for the *Middle School English Language Arts* test), 8, 9, and 10 (for the *Middle School Mathematics* test), 11, 12, and 13 (for the *Middle School Social Studies* test), and 14, 15, and 16 (for the *Middle School Science* test) will help you prepare for the test, give you the chance to take a practice test, and show you answers and sample responses and how they were scored.

If you are using this study guide to prepare for the *Middle School: Content Knowledge* test, you will want to look at the multiple-choice sections of chapters 5 through 16 because the test contains multiple-choice questions in all four of the content areas. Refer to chapter 17 for more information about using this study guide to prepare for the *Middle School: Content Knowledge* test.

So where should you start? Well, all users of this book will probably want to begin with the following two steps:

- **Become familiar with the test content.** Note what the appropriate chapter of the book (5, 8, 11, or 14) says about the topics covered in the test you plan to take.

- **Consider how well you know the content in each subject area.** Perhaps you already know that you need to build up your skills in a particular area. If you're not sure, skim over the chapter that covers test content (5, 8, 11, or 14) to see what topics the test covers. If you encounter material that feels unfamiliar or difficult, fold down page corners or insert sticky notes to remind yourself to spend extra time in these sections.

Also, all users of this book will probably want to end with these two steps:

- **Familiarize yourself with test taking.** Chapter 3 contains information to help you sharpen your skills in reading and answering multiple-choice questions. Succeeding on multiple-choice questions requires careful focus on the question, an eye for detail, and patient sifting of the answer choices. Chapter 4 explains how constructed-response tests are scored and contains valuable tips on how to succeed on test questions in this format.

When you feel you understand the question formats, you can simulate the experience of the test by taking a practice test (chapter 6, 9, 12, or 15) within the specified time limits. Choose a time and place where you will not be interrupted or distracted. After you complete the test, look at the appropriate chapter (7, 10, 13, or 16) to find the correct answers, explanations of those correct answers, and sample responses that scored well, scored poorly, or scored in-between. Score your responses to the multiple-choice questions and then examine the sample responses to the constructed-response questions to help you focus on the aspects of your own practice responses that were successful and unsuccessful. This knowledge will help you plan any additional studying you might need.

- **Register for the test and consider last-minute tips.** Consult http://www.ets.org/praxis/index.html to learn how to register for the test, and review the checklist in chapter 18 to make sure you are ready for the test.

What you do between these first steps and these last steps depends on whether you intend to use this book to prepare on your own or as part of a class or study group.

Using this book to prepare on your own

If you are working by yourself to prepare for a *Middle School* test, you may find it helpful to fill out the Study Plan Sheet in appendix A. This work sheet will help you to focus on what topics you need to study most, identify materials that will help you study, and set a schedule for doing the studying. The last item is particularly important if you know you tend to put off work.

Using this book as part of a study group

People who have a lot of studying to do sometimes find it helpful to form a study group with others who are preparing toward the same goal. Study groups give members opportunities to ask questions and get detailed answers. In a group, some members usually have a better understanding of certain topics, while others in the group may be better at other topics. As members take turns explaining concepts to each other, everyone builds self-confidence. If the group encounters a question that none of the members can answer well, the members can go as a group to a teacher or other expert and get answers efficiently. Because study groups schedule regular meetings, group members study in a more disciplined fashion. They also gain emotional support. The group should be large enough so that various people can contribute various kinds of knowledge, but small enough so that it stays focused. Often, three to six people is a good size.

Here are some ways to use this book as part of a study group:

- **Plan the group's study program.** Parts of the Study Plan Sheet in appendix A can help to structure your group's study program. By filling out the first five columns and sharing the work sheets, everyone will learn more about your group's mix of abilities and about the resources (such as textbooks) that members can share with the group. In the sixth column ("Dates planned for study of content"), you can create an overall schedule for your group's study program.

- **Plan individual group sessions.** At the end of each session, the group should decide what specific topics will be covered at the next meeting and who will present each topic. Use the topics in the chapter that covers the test you will take.

- **Prepare your presentation for the group.** When it's your turn to be presenter, prepare something that's more than a lecture. Write two or three original questions to pose to the group. Practicing writing actual questions can help you better understand the topics covered on the test as well as the types of questions you will encounter on the test. It will also give other members of the group extra practice at answering questions.

- **Take the practice test together.** The idea of the practice test is to simulate an actual administration of the test, so scheduling a test session with the group will add to the realism and will also help boost everyone's confidence.

- **Learn from the results of the practice test.** For each test, score each other's answer sheets. For the constructed-response questions, read the chapter that contains the sample responses to those questions and shows how they were scored (7, 10, 13, or 16), and then try to follow the same guidelines that the test scorers use.

  - *Be as critical as you can.* You're not doing your study partner a favor by letting him or her get away with an answer that does not cover all parts of the question adequately.

  - *Be specific.* Write comments that are as detailed as the comments made in chapter 7, 10, 13, or 16 by the scoring leader. Indicate *where and how* your study partner is doing an inadequate job of answering the question. Writing notes in the margins of the answer sheet may also help.

  - *Be supportive.* Include comments that point out what your study partner got right and that therefore earned points.

  Then plan one or more study sessions based on aspects of the questions on which group members performed poorly. For example, each group member might be responsible for rewriting one paragraph of a response in which someone else did an inadequate job of answering the question.

Whether you decide to study alone or with a group, remember that the best way to prepare is to have an organized plan. The plan should set goals based on specific topics and skills that you need to learn, and it should commit you to a realistic set of deadlines for meeting these goals. Then you need to discipline yourself to stick with your plan and accomplish your goals on schedule.

Chapter 2

Background Information on The Praxis Series Subject Assessments

▶   ▶   ▶   ▶   ▶   ▶   ▶   ▶   ▶   ▶   ▶

What Are The Praxis Series Subject Assessments?

The Praxis Series Subject Assessments are designed by ETS to assess your knowledge of the subject area you plan to teach, and they are a part of the licensing procedure in many states. This study guide covers assessments that test your knowledge of the actual content you hope to be licensed to teach. Your state has adopted The Praxis Series tests because it wants to be certain that you have achieved a specified level of mastery of your subject area before it grants you a license to teach in a classroom.

The Praxis Series tests are part of a national testing program, meaning that the tests covered in this study guide are used in more than one state. The advantage of taking Praxis tests is that if you want to move to another state that uses The Praxis Series tests for licensure, you can transfer your scores to that state. Passing scores are set by states, however, so if you are planning to apply for licensure in another state, you may find that the passing scores there are different. You can find passing scores for all states that use The Praxis Series tests online at www.ets.org/praxis/prxstate.html or in the *Understanding Your Praxis Scores* pamphlet, available at your college's School of Education or by calling ETS at 609-771-7395 or 800-772-9476.

What Is Licensure?

Licensure in any area—medicine, law, architecture, accounting, cosmetology—is an assurance to the public that the person holding the license has demonstrated a certain level of competence. The main premise of licensure is that the person holding the license *will do no harm.* In the case of teacher licensing, a license tells the public that the person holding the license can be trusted to educate children competently and professionally.

Because a license makes such a serious claim about its holder, licensure tests are usually quite demanding. In some fields licensure tests have more than one part and last for more than one day. Candidates for licensure in all fields plan intensive study as part of their professional preparation: some join study groups, others study alone. But preparing to take a licensure test is, in all cases, a professional activity. Because it assesses your entire body of knowledge or skill for the field you want to enter, preparing for a licensure exam takes planning, discipline, and sustained effort. Studying thoroughly is highly recommended.

Why Does My State Require The Praxis Series Subject Assessments?

Your state chose The Praxis Series Subject Assessments because the tests assess the breadth and depth of content—called the "domain"—that your state wants its teachers to possess before they begin to teach. The level of content knowledge, reflected in the passing score, is based on recommendations of panels of teachers and teacher educators in each subject area. The state licensing agency and, in some states, the state legislature ratify the passing scores that have been recommended by panels of teachers. You can find out the passing score required for The Praxis Series Subject Assessments in your state online or by looking in the pamphlet *Understanding Your Praxis Scores,* which is free from ETS (see above). If you look through this pamphlet, you will see that not all states use the same test modules, and even when they do, the passing scores can differ from state to state.

What Kinds of Tests Are The Praxis Series Subject Assessments?

The Praxis Series Subject Assessments generally include two types of test questions: multiple choice (for which you select your answer from a list of choices) and constructed response (for which you write a response of your own). Tests composed of multiple-choice questions can survey a wider domain because they can ask more questions in a limited period of time. Tests using constructed-response questions have far fewer questions, but the questions require you to demonstrate the depth of your knowledge in the area covered. Some tests, such as the Praxis Middle School tests, include both multiple-choice and constructed-response questions, allowing them to test both the breadth and depth of your knowledge.

What Do the Tests Measure?

The Praxis Series Subject Assessments are tests of content knowledge. They measure your understanding of the subject area you want to teach. The multiple-choice tests measure a broad range of knowledge across your content area. The constructed-response tests measure your ability to explain in depth a few essential topics in your subject area. The content-specific pedagogy tests, most of which are constructed-response, measure your understanding of how to teach certain fundamental concepts in your field. The tests do not measure your actual teaching ability, however. They measure your knowledge of your subject and of how to teach it. The teachers in your field who help us design and write these tests, and the states that require these tests, do so in the belief that knowledge of subject area is the first requirement for licensing. Your teaching ability is a skill that is measured in other ways; observation, videotaped teaching, or portfolios are typically used by states to measure teaching ability. Teaching combines many complex skills, only some of which can be measured by a single test. The Praxis Series Subject Assessments are designed to measure how thoroughly you understand the material in the subject area(s) in which you want to be licensed to teach.

How Were These Tests Developed?

ETS began the development of The Praxis Series Subject Assessments with a survey. For each subject, teachers around the country in various teaching situations were asked to judge which knowledge and skills a beginning teacher in that subject needs to possess. Professors in schools of education who prepare teachers were asked the same questions. These responses were ranked in order of importance and sent out to hundreds of teachers for review. All of the responses to these surveys (called "job analysis surveys") were analyzed to summarize the judgments of these professionals. From their consensus, we developed the specifications for the multiple-choice and constructed-response tests. Each subject area had a committee of practicing teachers and teacher educators who wrote these specifications (guidelines). The specifications were reviewed and eventually approved by teachers. From the test specifications, groups of teachers and professional test developers created test questions.

When your state adopted The Praxis Series Subject Assessments, local panels of practicing teachers and teacher educators in each subject area met to examine the tests question by question and to evaluate each question for its relevance to beginning teachers in your state. This is called a "validity study." A test is considered "valid" for a job if it measures what people must know and be able to do on that job. For the test to be adopted in your state, teachers in your state must judge that it is valid.

These teachers and teacher educators also performed a "standard-setting study"; that is, they went through the tests question by question and decided, through a rigorous process, how many of the questions a beginning teacher would be able to answer correctly. From this study emerged a recommended passing score. The final passing score was approved by your state's licensing agency.

In other words, throughout the development process, practitioners in the teaching field—teachers and teacher educators—have determined what the tests would contain. The practitioners in your state determined which tests would be used for licensure in your subject area and helped decide what score would be needed to achieve licensure. This is how professional licensure works in most fields: those who are already licensed oversee the licensing of new practitioners. When you pass The Praxis Series Subject Assessments, you and the practitioners in your state can be assured that you have the knowledge required to begin practicing your profession.

Chapter 3
Don't Be Defeated by Multiple-Choice Questions

▶   ▶   ▶   ▶   ▶   ▶   ▶   ▶   ▶   ▶   ▶   ▶

Understanding Multiple-Choice Questions

When you read multiple-choice questions on the Praxis *Middle School* tests, you will probably notice that the syntax (word order) is different from the word order you're used to seeing in ordinary material that you read, such as newspapers or textbooks. One of the reasons for this difference is that many test questions contain the phrase "which of the following."

In order to answer a multiple-choice question successfully, you need to consider carefully the context set up by the question and limit your choice of answers to the list given. The purpose of the phrase "which of the following" is to remind you to do this. For example, look at this question.

> Which of the following is a flavor made from beans?
>
> (A) Strawberry
>
> (B) Cherry
>
> (C) Vanilla
>
> (D) Mint

You may know that chocolate and coffee are also flavors made from beans, but they are not listed, and the question asks you to select from the list that follows ("which of the following"). So the answer has to be the only bean-derived flavor in the list: vanilla.

Notice that the answer can be substituted for the phrase "which of the following." In the question above, you could insert "vanilla" for "which of the following" and have the sentence "Vanilla is a flavor made from beans." Sometimes it helps to cross out "which of the following" and insert the various choices. You may want to give this technique a try as you answer various multiple-choice questions on the practice tests.

Looking carefully at the "which of the following" phrase helps you to focus on what the question is asking you to find and on the answer choices. In the simple example above, all of the answer choices are flavors. Your job is to decide which of the flavors is the one made from beans.

The vanilla bean question is pretty straightforward. But the phrase "which of the following" can also be found in more challenging questions. Look at this question:

> Which of the following methods of producing electricity contributes most of the incidence of acid rain in North America?
>
> (A) Generators that use windmills
>
> (B) Nuclear generators that utilize fission
>
> (C) Power plants that burn fossil fuels
>
> (D) Hydroelectric power plants

The placement of "which of the following" tells you that the list of choices is a list of methods (in this case, these are methods of producing electricity). What are you supposed to find as an answer? You are supposed to find the choice that contributes most of the incidence of acid rain in North America.

ETS question writers and editors work very hard to word each question as clearly as possible. Sometimes, though, it helps to put the question in your own words. Here, you could paraphrase the question as "Which of these methods is most responsible for acid rain in North America?" The correct answer is (C). (Acid rain is caused by the reaction of sulfur oxides and nitrogen oxides with water in the atmosphere to form acids. The burning of fossil fuels is a major source of these oxides.)

You may also find that it helps you to circle or underline each of the critical details of the question in your test book so that you don't miss any of them. It's only by looking at all parts of the question carefully that you will have all of the information you need to answer it. Circle or underline the critical parts of what is being asked in this question.

>   According to the United States Constitution, the President has the power to
>
>   (A) negotiate treaties
>   (B) amend the Constitution
>   (C) impeach members of Congress
>   (D) raise and support an army

Here is one possible way you may have annotated the question:

>   According to the United States Constitution, the President has the power to
>
>   (A) negotiate treaties
>   (B) amend the Constitution
>   (C) impeach members of Congress
>   (D) raise and support an army

After thinking about the question, you can probably see that you are being asked to identify a power given to the President by the United States Constitution. The correct answer is (A). The important thing is understanding what the question is asking. With enough practice, you should be able to determine what any question is asking. Knowing the answer is, of course, a different matter, but you have to understand a question before you can answer it correctly.

Understanding Questions Containing "NOT," "LEAST," or "EXCEPT"

The words "NOT," "LEAST," and "EXCEPT" can make comprehension of test questions more difficult. They ask you to select the choice that *doesn't* fit. You must be very careful with this question type because it's easy to forget that you're selecting the negative. This question type is used in situations in which there are several good solutions, or ways to approach something, but also a clearly wrong way. These words are always capitalized when they appear in The Praxis Series test questions, but they are easily (and frequently) overlooked.

For the following test question, determine what kind of answer you need and what the details of the question are.

> All of the following river valleys are densely populated EXCEPT the
>
> (A) Yangtze
> (B) Amazon
> (C) Nile
> (D) Indus

You're looking for a river valley that is NOT densely populated. (B) is the correct answer—all of the other choices *are* densely populated river valleys.

 TIP

It's easy to get confused while you're processing the information to answer a question with a NOT, LEAST, or EXCEPT in the question. If you treat the word "NOT," "LEAST," or "EXCEPT" as one of the details you must satisfy, you have a better chance of understanding what the question is asking.

Be Familiar with Multiple-Choice Question Types

You will probably see more than one question format on a multiple-choice test. Here are examples of some of the more common question formats.

1. Complete the statement

In this type of question, you are given an incomplete statement. You must select the choice that will make the completed statement correct.

> My sister and I always loved <u>sledding</u> down the hill behind our house.
>
> The underlined word in the sentence above is an example of
>
> (A) a conjunction
> (B) a participle
> (C) a gerund
> (D) an adverb

To check your answer, reread the question and add your answer choice at the end. Be sure that your choice best completes the sentence. The correct answer is (C).

2. Which of the following

This question type is discussed in detail in a previous section. The question contains the details that must be satisfied for a correct answer, and it uses "which of the following" to limit the choices to the four choices shown, as this example demonstrates.

Which of the following is a way to find 420 percent of 39.7?

(A) $\frac{39.7}{42}$

(B) (0.42)(39.7)

(C) (4.2)(39.7)

(D) (420)(39.7)

[handwritten: 4.2 × 39.7 ~ 4 × 40 ≈ 160]

The correct answer is (C).

3. Roman numeral choices

This format is used when there can be more than one correct answer in the list. Consider the following example.

For the greater part of the time humankind has existed on Earth, people have obtained their food by which of the following means?

I. Hunting *[handwritten: ✓]*

II. Gathering *[handwritten: ✓]*

III. Agriculture *[handwritten: – later]*

(A) I only

(B) III only

(C) I and II only

(D) I and III only

One useful strategy for this type of question is to assess each possible answer before looking at the answer choices and then evaluate the answer choices. The oldest known remains of *homo sapiens* have been dated at 75,000 to 115,000 years old. The earliest evidence from agriculture dates from 10,000 years ago. Until then, humans survived only by hunting animals and gathering plants for food. Therefore, the correct answer is (C).

4. Questions containing NOT, LEAST, EXCEPT

This question type is discussed at length in a previous section. It asks you to select the choice that doesn't fit.

5. Other formats

New formats are developed from time to time in order to find new ways of assessing knowledge with multiple-choice questions. If you see a format you are not familiar with, read the directions carefully. Then read and approach the question the way you would any other question, asking yourself what you are supposed to be looking for and what details are given in the question that help you find the answer.

Other Useful Facts about the Test

1. You can answer the questions in any order. You can go through the questions from beginning to end, as many test takers do, or you can create your own path. Perhaps you will want to answer questions in your strongest area of knowledge first and then move from your strengths to your weaker areas. There is no right or wrong way. Use the approach that works best for you.

2. There are no trick questions on the test. You don't have to find any hidden meanings or worry about trick wording. All of the questions on the test ask about subject matter knowledge in a straightforward manner.

3. Don't worry about answer patterns. There is one myth that says that answers on multiple-choice tests follow patterns. There is another myth that there will never be more than two questions with the same lettered answer following each other. There is no truth to either of these myths. Select the answer you think is correct based on your knowledge of the subject.

4. There is no penalty for guessing. Your test score for multiple-choice questions is based on the number of correct answers you have. When you don't know the answer to a question, try to eliminate any obviously wrong answers and then guess at the correct one.

5. It's OK to write in your test booklet. You can work out problems right on the pages of the booklet, make notes to yourself, mark questions you want to review later, or write anything at all. Your test booklet will be destroyed after you are finished with it, so use it in any way that is helpful to you. But make sure to mark your answers on the answer sheet.

Smart Tips for Taking the Test

1. Put your answers in the right "bubbles." It seems obvious, but be sure that you are filling in the answer "bubble" that corresponds to the question you are answering. A significant number of test takers fill in a bubble without checking to see that the number matches the question they are answering.

2. Skip the questions you find extremely difficult. There are sure to be some questions that you think are hard. Rather than trying to answer these on your first pass through the test, leave them blank and mark them in your test booklet so that you can come back to them later. Pay attention to the time as you answer the rest of the questions on the test, and try to finish with 10 or 15 minutes remaining so that you can go back over the questions you left blank. Even if you don't know the answer the second time you read the questions, see if you can narrow down the possible answers, and then guess.

3. Keep track of the time. Bring a watch to the test, just in case the clock in the test room is difficult for you to see. You will probably have plenty of time to answer all of the questions, but if you find yourself becoming bogged down in one section, you might decide to move on and come back to that section later.

4. Read all of the possible answers before selecting one—and then reread the question to be sure the answer you have selected really answers the question being asked. Remember that a question that contains a phrase such as "Which of the following does NOT ..." is asking for the one answer that is NOT a correct statement or conclusion.

5. Check your answers. If you have extra time left over at the end of the test, look over each question and make sure that you have filled in the "bubble" on the answer sheet as you intended. Many test takers make careless mistakes that they could have corrected if they had checked their answers.

6. Don't worry about your score when you are taking the test. No one is expected to answer all of the questions correctly. Your score on this test is *not* analogous to your score on the SAT, the GRE, or other similar-looking (but in fact very different!) tests. It doesn't matter on this test whether you score very high or barely pass. If you meet the minimum passing scores for your state and you meet the state's other requirements for obtaining a teaching license, you will receive a license. In other words, your actual score doesn't matter, as long as it is above the minimum required score. With your score report you will receive a booklet entitled *Understanding Your Praxis Scores*, which lists the passing scores for your state.

7. Use your energy to take the test, not to get angry at it. Getting angry at the test only elevates test anxiety, decreasing the likelihood that you will do your best on the test. Highly qualified educators and test development professionals (all with backgrounds in teaching) worked diligently to make the test the best it could be. Your state had the test painstakingly reviewed before adopting it as a licensure requirement. The best thing to do is concentrate on answering the questions as well as you can. Take the test, do your best, pass it, and get on with your career.

Chapter 4
Succeeding on Constructed-Response Questions

▶ ▶ ▶ ▶ ▶ ▶ ▶ ▶ ▶ ▶ ▶ ▶

This chapter provides advice for maximizing your success on the constructed-response questions on the *Middle School* tests, with special focus on the scoring guides and procedures used by the scorers. Chapters 5, 8, 11, and 14 offer step-by-step strategies for working through constructed-response questions, lists of the topics covered, and lists of sources you can use to prepare.

Advice from the Experts

Scorers who have scored hundreds of real tests were asked to give advice to teacher candidates preparing to take the *Middle School* constructed-response questions. The scorers' advice boiled down to the practical pieces of advice described below.

1. **Read and answer the question accurately.** Be sure to dissect the parts of the question and analyze what each part is asking you to do. If the question asks you to describe or discuss, keep those requirements in mind when composing your response—do not just give a list.

2. **Answer everything that is asked in the question.** This seems simple, but many test takers fail to provide a complete response. If a question asks you to do three distinct things in your response, don't give a response to just two of those things. No matter how well you write about those two things, the scorers will not award you full credit.

3. **Give a thorough and detailed response.** Your response must indicate to the scorers that you have a thorough understanding of the applicable principles and guidelines related to teaching middle school. The scorers will not read into your response any information that is not specifically stated. If something is not written, they do not know that you know it and will not give you credit for it.

   A word of caution: Superfluous writing will obscure your points and will make it difficult for the scorers to be confident of your full understanding of the material. Be straightforward in your response. Do not try to impress the scorers. If you do not know the answer, you cannot receive full credit, but if you do know the answer, provide enough information to convince the scorers that you have a full understanding of the topic.

4. **Do not change the question or challenge the basis of the question.** Stay focused on the question that is asked. You will receive no credit or, at best, a low score if you choose to answer another question or if you state, for example, that there is no possible answer. Answer the question by addressing the fundamental issues. Do not venture off-topic to demonstrate your particular field of expertise if it is not specifically related to the question. This undermines the impression that you understand the concept adequately.

5. **Reread your response to check that you have written what you thought you wrote.** Frequently, sentences are left unfinished or clarifying information is omitted.

The General Scoring Guides for the *Middle School* Tests

The scorers' advice above corresponds with the official scoring criteria used at scoring sessions. It is a good idea to be familiar with the scoring rubrics so that you can maximize your success and spend your time on things that matter (e.g., demonstrating understanding of a topic and providing good examples) rather than spending time on things that don't matter (e.g., writing a very long essay, making copious citations).

The following scoring rubrics provide the overarching framework for scoring the questions in each of the *Middle School* tests.

The General Scoring Guide for the *Middle School English Language Arts* Test

Score	Comment
3	The response is successful in the following ways:

- It demonstrates an ability to analyze the stimulus material thoughtfully and in depth.
- It demonstrates a strong knowledge of the subject matter relevant to the question.
- It responds appropriately to all parts of the question.
- It demonstrates facility with conventions of standard written English.

2 The response demonstrates some understanding of the topic, but it is limited in one or more of the following major ways:

- It may indicate a misreading of the stimulus material or provide superficial analysis.
- It may demonstrate only superficial knowledge of the subject matter relevant to the question.
- It may respond to one or more parts of the question inadequately or not at all.
- It may contain significant writing errors.

1 The response is seriously flawed in one or more of the following ways:

- It may demonstrate weak understanding of the subject matter or of the writing task.
- It may fail to respond adequately to most parts of the question.
- It may be incoherent or severely underdeveloped.
- It may contain severe and persistent writing errors.

0 ■ Response is blank, off-topic, totally incorrect, or merely rephrases the question.

The General Scoring Guide for the *Middle School Mathematics* Test

Score	Comment

3
- Responds appropriately to all parts of the question
- Where required, provides a strong explanation that is well supported by relevant evidence
- Demonstrates a strong knowledge of subject matter, concepts, theories, facts, procedures, or methodologies relevant to the question
- Demonstrates a thorough understanding of the most significant aspects of any stimulus material presented

2
- Responds appropriately to most parts of the question
- Where required, provides an explanation that is sufficiently supported by relevant evidence
- Demonstrates a sufficient knowledge of subject matter, concepts, theories, facts, procedures, or methodologies relevant to the question
- Demonstrates a basic understanding of the most significant aspects of any stimulus material presented

1
- Responds appropriately to some part of the question
- Where required, provides a weak explanation that is not well supported by relevant evidence
- Demonstrates a weak knowledge of subject matter, concepts, theories, facts, procedures, or methodologies relevant to the question
- Demonstrates little understanding of significant aspects of any stimulus material presented

0
- Blank, off-topic, or totally incorrect response
- Does nothing more than restate the question or some phrases from the question
- Demonstrates very limited understanding of the topic

The General Scoring Guide for the *Middle School Social Studies* Test

Score	Comment

3
- Shows a thorough understanding of the stimulus (where appropriate)
- Provides an accurate and complete response
- Provides the analysis required by the question
- Applies appropriate subject matter knowledge
- May contain minor errors

2
- Shows an adequate understanding of the stimulus (where appropriate)
- Provides a mostly accurate and complete response
- Provides most of the analysis required by the question
- Applies mostly appropriate subject matter knowledge
- May contain significant errors

1
- Shows little understanding of the stimulus (where appropriate)
- Provides a basically inaccurate and incomplete response
- Provides little of the analysis required by the question
- Applies mostly inappropriate subject matter knowledge

0
- Blank, off-topic, or totally incorrect response; rephrases the question

The General Scoring Guide for the *Middle School Science* Test

Score	Comment

Score   **Comment**

3
- Demonstrates a thorough understanding of the most significant parts of any stimulus material presented
- Responds appropriately to all parts of the question
- Where required, provides a strong explanation that is well supported by relevant evidence
- Demonstrates a strong knowledge of concepts, theories, facts, procedures, or methodologies relevant to the question

2
- Demonstrates basic understanding of the most significant aspects of any stimulus material presented
- Responds appropriately to most aspects of the question
- Where required, provides an explanation that is sufficiently supported by relevant evidence
- Demonstrates a sufficient knowledge of concepts, theories, facts, procedures, or methodologies relevant to the question

1
- Demonstrates misunderstanding of significant aspects of any stimulus material presented
- Fails to respond appropriately to most parts of the question
- Where required, provides a weak explanation that is not well supported by relevant evidence
- Demonstrates a weak knowledge of concepts, theories, facts, procedures, or methodologies relevant to the question

0
- Blank, off-topic, or totally incorrect response; rephrases the question

What You Should Know About How the *Middle School Constructed-Response* Questions Are Scored

As you build your skills in writing answers to constructed-response questions, it is important to have in mind the process used to score the questions. If you understand the process by which experts determine your scores, you may have a better context in which to think about your strategies for success.

How the Tests are Scored

After each test administration, test books are returned to ETS. The test booklets in which constructed-response answers are written are sent to the location of the scoring session.

The scoring sessions usually take place over two days. The sessions are led by scoring leaders, highly qualified middle school or high school teachers who have many years of experience scoring test questions. All of the remaining scorers are experienced middle school or high school teachers or teacher-educators. An effort is made to balance experienced scorers with newer scorers at each session; the experienced scorers provide continuity with past sessions, and the new scorers ensure that new ideas and perspectives are considered and that the pool of scorers remains large enough to cover the test's needs throughout the year.

Preparing to Train the Scorers

The scoring leaders meet several days before the scoring session to assemble the materials for the training portions of the main session. Training scorers is a rigorous process, and it is designed to ensure that each response gets a score that is consistent both with the scores given to other papers and with the overall scoring philosophy and criteria established for the test when it was designed.

The scoring leaders first review the "General Scoring Guides," which contain the overall criteria, stated in general terms, for awarding the appropriate score. The leaders also review and discuss—and make additions to, if necessary—the "Question-Specific Scoring Guides," which serve as applications of the general guide to each specific question on the test. The question-specific guides cannot cover every possible response the scorers will see, but they are designed to give enough examples to guide the scorers in making accurate judgments about the variety of answers they will encounter.

To begin identifying appropriate training materials for an individual question, the scoring leaders first read through many responses to get a sense of the range of answers. They then choose a set of benchmarks, one paper at each score level. These benchmarks serve as solid representative examples of the kind of response that meets the scoring criteria at each score level and are considered the foundation for score standards throughout the session.

The scoring leaders then choose a larger set of test-taker responses to serve as sample papers. These sample papers represent the wide variety of possible responses that the scorers might see. The sample papers serve as the basis for practice scoring at the scoring session, so that the scorers can rehearse how they will apply the scoring criteria before they begin.

The process of choosing a set of benchmark responses and a set of sample responses is followed systematically for each question to be scored at the session. After the scoring leaders are done with their selections and discussions, the sets they have chosen are photocopied and inserted into the scorers' folders in preparation for the session.

Training at the Main Scoring Session

At the scoring session, the scorers are placed into groups according to the question they are assigned to score. New scorers are distributed equally across all groups. One of the scoring leaders is placed with each group. The "Chief Scorer" is the person who has overall authority over the scoring session and plays a variety of key roles in training and in ensuring consistent and fair scores.

For each question, the training session proceeds in the same way:

1. All scorers carefully read through the question they will be scoring.

2. All scorers review the "General Scoring Guide" and the "Question-Specific Scoring Guide" for the question.

3. For each question, the leader guides the scorers through the set of benchmark responses, explaining in detail why each response received the score it did. Scorers are encouraged to ask questions and share their perspectives.

4. Scorers then practice on the set of sample responses chosen by the leader. The leader polls the scorers on what scores they would award and then leads a discussion to ensure that there is a consensus about the scoring criteria and how they are to be applied.

5. When the leader is confident that the scorers for that question will apply the criteria consistently and accurately, the actual scoring begins.

Quality-Control Processes

A number of procedures are followed to ensure that accuracy of scoring is maintained during the scoring session. Most importantly, each response is scored twice, with the first scorer's decision hidden from the second scorer. If the two scores for a paper are the same or differ by only one point, the scoring for that paper is considered complete, and the test taker will be awarded the sum of the two scores. If the two scores differ by more than one point, the response is scored by a scoring leader, who has not seen the decisions made by the other two scorers. If this third score is midway between the first two scores, the test taker's score for the question is the sum of the first two scores; otherwise, it is the sum of the third score and whichever of the first two scores is closer to it.

Another way of maintaining scoring accuracy is through back-reading. Throughout the session, the leader for each question checks random samples of scores awarded by all the scorers. If the leader finds that a scorer is not applying the scoring criteria appropriately, that scorer is given more training.

At the beginning of the second day of reading, additional sets of papers are scored using the consensus method described above. This helps ensure that the scorers are refreshed on the scoring criteria and are applying them consistently.

Finally, the scoring session is designed so that several different scorers (usually four to six) contribute to any single test taker's total score. This minimizes the effects of a scorer who might score slightly more stringently or generously than other scorers.

The entire scoring process—general and specific scoring guides, standardized benchmarks and samples, consensus scoring, adjudication procedures, back-reading, and rotation of test questions to a variety of scorers—is applied consistently and systematically at every scoring session to ensure comparable scores for each administration and across all administrations of the test.

Chapter 5

Preparing for the *Middle School English Language Arts* Test

▶ ▶ ▶ ▶ ▶ ▶ ▶ ▶ ▶ ▶ ▶ ▶

The *Middle School English Language Arts* test is designed to measure the subject-area knowledge and competencies necessary for a beginning teacher of English Language Arts in a middle school. The test contains both multiple-choice and constructed-response questions.

The first part of this chapter focuses on the multiple-choice section of the test. The second part of the chapter contains information about the constructed-response section of the test.

Part One: Multiple-Choice Questions

This part of the chapter is intended to help you organize your preparation for the multiple-choice portion of the test and to give you a clear indication about the depth and breadth of the knowledge required for success on the multiple-choice questions.

The *Middle School English Language Arts* test contains 90 multiple-choice questions that constitute approximately 75 percent of the test taker's total test score. It is expected that about 90 minutes will be spent on the multiple-choice questions.

> **Here is an overview of the areas covered on the test, along with their subareas:**

Reading and Literature
> Major works and authors of adolescent literature
> Interpreting, paraphrasing, and comparing text
> Figurative and technical language and other literary elements
> Literary forms and text structures
> Historical and cultural contexts
> Critical approaches to interpreting text
> Teaching reading

Language and Linguistics
> Traditional grammar
> Syntax and semantics
> Language acquisition and development

Composition and Rhetoric
> Teaching writing
> Thesis statements and supporting evidence
> Audience and purpose
> Types of discourse and strategies for development
> Coherence and organization
> Critical reasoning

Using the topic lists that follow

You are not expected to be an expert on all aspects of the topics that follow. You should understand the major characteristics of each topic, recognize the minor topics, and have some familiarity with the subtopics. Virtually all accredited undergraduate English programs address the majority of these topics, subtopics, and even minor topics.

Here, for instance, is one of the topic lists in "Reading and Literature," under "Literary forms and text structures":

- Some questions will ask you to recognize the form of a poem or prose excerpt or to recognize the definition of a poetic or prose form. These include, but are not limited to,

  ▶ Biography
  ▶ Drama
  ▶ Epic poem
  ▶ Essay
  ▶ History
  ▶ Lyric
  ▶ Novel
  ▶ Prose poem

Referring to textbooks, state standards documents, or other sources as needed, make sure you can describe in your own words what each literary form is. For example, you should be able to think to yourself that "An epic poem is a long narrative recounting the deeds of legendary heroes" or "A prose poem is a short composition employing the devices and rhythms of free verse but formatted as prose." It is also very important to be able to recognize the poetic or prose form of an excerpt of literature.

You are likely to find that the topics below are covered by most introductory literature textbooks, but these general survey textbooks may not cover all of the subtopics. Consult materials and resources, including lecture notes and portfolio items from all your English coursework. You should be able to match up specific topics and subtopics with what you have covered in your courses.

Try not to be overwhelmed by the volume and scope of content knowledge in this guide. An overview such as this that lists English topics does not offer you a great deal of context. Although a specific term may not seem familiar as you see it here, you may find you can understand it when it is applied to a real-life situation. Many of the items on the actual Praxis test will provide you with a context in which to apply these topics or terms, as you will see when you look at the practice questions in chapter 6.

Special questions marked with stars

Interspersed throughout the list of topics are questions that are outlined in boxes and preceded by a star (★). These questions are intended to help you test your knowledge of fundamental concepts and your ability to apply fundamental concepts in particular content areas. Most of the questions require you to combine several pieces of knowledge in order to formulate an integrated understanding and response. If you spend time on these questions, you will gain increased understanding and facility with the subject matter covered on the test. You might want to discuss these questions and your answers with a teacher or mentor.

Note that the questions marked with stars are not short-answer or multiple-choice, and this study guide does not provide the answers. The questions marked with stars are intended as *study* questions, not practice questions. Thinking about the answers to them should improve your understanding of fundamental concepts and will probably help you answer a broad range of questions on the test.

Study Topics

Reading and Literature

This section of the test focuses on knowledge of concepts relevant to reading and literature study, including comprehension, interpretation, and analysis of literary works. Some specific factual knowledge is required, but for most questions, no previous experience with the supplied passages is required. However, you should have familiarity with major works and authors of literature appropriate for adolescents and the ability to locate and interpret such literature within historical and cultural contexts. In addition, you will need to draw upon your knowledge of literary elements, figurative language, and literary forms as you interpret, paraphrase, and compare various types of texts. You will also be asked to identify critical approaches to interpreting texts and strategic approaches to teaching reading.

Major works and authors of adolescent literature

- Some of these questions will expect you to have familiarity with the authors and titles of specific literary works commonly taught to adolescents. The following authors are *representative* of those you may be asked to identify:

  - ▶ Louisa May Alcott
  - ▶ Maya Angelou
  - ▶ Ray Bradbury
  - ▶ Stephen Crane
  - ▶ Daniel Defoe
  - ▶ Emily Dickinson
  - ▶ Frederick Douglass
  - ▶ Ralph Waldo Emerson
  - ▶ F. Scott Fitzgerald
  - ▶ Anne Frank
  - ▶ Robert Frost
  - ▶ S. E. Hinton
  - ▶ Zora Neale Hurston
  - ▶ John Keats
  - ▶ Helen Keller
  - ▶ Harper Lee
  - ▶ Madeleine L'Engle
  - ▶ C. S. Lewis
  - ▶ Jack London
  - ▶ Lois Lowry
  - ▶ Herman Melville
  - ▶ George Orwell
  - ▶ Edgar Allan Poe
  - ▶ J. D. Salinger
  - ▶ William Shakespeare

- ▶ Mary Shelley
- ▶ Percy Bysshe Shelley
- ▶ Amy Tan
- ▶ J. R. R. Tolkien
- ▶ Mark Twain
- ▶ Alice Walker
- ▶ H. G. Wells
- ▶ Walt Whitman

★ What novels, poems, and essays might you teach in a middle school Language Arts class, and why?

Interpreting, paraphrasing, and comparing text

- Some of the questions will present a poem or passage and ask you to demonstrate comprehension and interpretation by asking about a specific word or phrase in the selection. For example,

  - ▶ "In the poem, the phrase 'the dreaded horseman' refers to..."
  - ▶ "The poet's use of the word 'timorous' emphasizes which of the following themes?"
  - ▶ "The contrast between the landscape and the narrator's 'sweet musings' is appropriate to the context of the excerpt because..."

- Some of the questions will ask you to develop a conclusion based on your comprehension and interpretation of the passage as a whole rather than just a single word or phrase. For example,

  - ▶ "The protagonist's attitude toward her travels can best be described as..."
  - ▶ "Which of the following best describes the theme of the poem?"
  - ▶ "This passage portrays the narrator's mother as..."
  - ▶ "The author asserts that art can compensate for loss only if..."
  - ▶ "The content of the poem can best be described as..."

Figurative and technical language and other literary elements

- Some of the questions will test your ability to interpret and analyze such elements as

  - Alliteration
  - Allusion
  - Analogy
  - Characterization (through a character's words, thoughts, actions, etc.)
  - Cliché
  - Dialect or slang
  - Diction
  - Figurative language (e.g., metaphor, simile, hyperbole, personification)
  - Foreshadowing
  - Imagery
  - Irony
  - Mood
  - Point of view (e.g., first person, third-person objective, third-person omniscient)
  - Setting (established through description of scenes, colors, smells, etc.)
  - Style
  - Symbolism
  - Tone
  - Voice

Literary forms and text structures

- Some questions will ask you to recognize the form of a poem or prose passage or to recognize the definition of a poetic or prose form. These include, but are not limited to,

  - Biography
  - Drama
  - Epic poem
  - Essay
  - History
  - Lyric
  - Novel
  - Prose poem

- Some questions will ask you to identify a passage by literary type. These include, but are not limited to,

  - Bildungsroman/coming of age story
  - Comedy
  - Gothic
  - Pastoral
  - Romance
  - Satire
  - Tragedy

- Some questions may ask you to interpret meters and rhyme schemes in poems. You will need to analyze patterns and either connect them with a traditional scheme or determine an unconventional use or effect achieved through meter or rhyme.

Historical and cultural contexts

- Some questions will ask you to apply your knowledge of various schools of writers and to identify the period in which they worked, and/or the titles of important representative works. The schools covered on the test include, but are not limited to,

  - Harlem Renaissance (Zora Neale Hurston, Langston Hughes, Countee Cullen)
  - British Romantics (John Keats, Percy Bysshe Shelley, Lord Byron)
  - Transcendentalism (Ralph Waldo Emerson, Henry David Thoreau)

- Some questions will ask you to identify particular literary and historical periods. The periods covered on the test include, but are not limited to,

  - Old English period
  - Middle English period
  - British Renaissance
  - British Neoclassical period
  - British Romantic period
  - American Colonial period

▶ American Renaissance

▶ British Victorian period

▶ American naturalistic period

▶ British and/or American modernism

▶ British and/or American postmodernism

Critical approaches to interpreting text

■ Some questions will test your ability to recognize specific critical approaches, which may include, but are not limited to,

▶ Formalism

▶ Historicism

▶ Reader response

▶ Shared inquiry

★ What set of reading skills is introduced to students with each different critical approach?

■ Some questions may ask you to identify a critical approach as expressed through a commentary. Other questions may ask you to identify how a specific critical approach informs a described assignment or classroom activity. For example,

▶ "This passage of literary criticism best reflects what critical approach?"

▶ "This assignment draws primarily on what critical approach?"

▶ "Which classroom activity reflects a formalist approach to poetic interpretation?"

Teaching reading

■ Some questions will test your ability to recognize specific terms related to teaching reading. These may include, but are not limited to,

▶ Anticipation guides

▶ Contextual analysis

▶ Informal Reading Inventories (IRIs)

▶ Metacognition

▶ Phonics

▶ Reading workshops

▶ Reciprocal teaching

▶ Semantic feature analysis

★ What specific and practical classroom activities can you envision using to teach a text such as Jack London's *The Call of the Wild*? For teaching Gwendolyn Brooks' "We Real Cool"?

■ Some questions may ask you to identify a reading strategy based on a description of a classroom activity. Other questions may ask you to identify a reading strategy that would address a specific teaching objective. For example,

▶ "Based on the description above, which of the following comprehension strategies did the teacher use?"

▶ "Which of the following strategies is most likely to help students understand the historical context of the novel?"

▶ "Semantic feature analysis is an appropriate reading strategy when..."

Exercises Related to the "Reading and Literature" Study Topics

The following exercises and annotated samples are intended to give you practice in the kinds of interpretive and analytical thinking about literature that are expected in the "Reading and Literature" study questions described above. Although the format of the annotation exercises is not like that of the multiple-choice questions on the test, the types and levels of understanding and evaluation needed to complete them are comparable. For each of these two exercises, read the passage and the questions in the heading and then try to annotate the passage in response to those questions. Then, for each, read the annotated version on the following page and compare your analysis.

★ Read the following fiction selection, from Ellen Glasgow's story "The Professional Instinct." Describe in your own words the characteristics of Dr. Estbridge. How does the author build this characterization? Why does the author compare Dr. Estbridge's career with a tree? What happens in terms of the narrative in the two sentences beginning with "Long ago..."?

As he unfolded his napkin and broke his toast with the precise touch of fingers that think, Doctor John Estbridge concluded that holidays were becoming unbearable. Christmas again, he reflected gloomily, and Christmas in New York, with a heavy snowstorm that meant weeks of dirt and slush and back-breaking epidemics of influenza and pneumonia! Beyond the curtains of rose-colored damask the storm locked the boughs of an ailanthus tree which grew midway out of the high-fenced backyard. Long ago, in the days of his youth and mania for reform, Estbridge remembered that he had once tried to convert the backyard into an Italian garden. For a brief season box had survived, if it had not actually flourished there, and a cypress tree, sent by an ex-patient from Northern Italy, had lived through a single summer and had died with the first frost of winter. That was nearly twenty years ago, for Estbridge had relinquished his garden with the other dreams of his youth, and today the brawny ailanthus stood there as a symbol of the prosperous failure of his career.

★ Here is the same paragraph with annotations that relate to the questions asked on the previous page.

As he unfolded his napkin and broke his toast with the precise touch of fingers that think, Doctor John Estbridge concluded that holidays were becoming unbearable. Christmas again, he reflected gloomily, and Christmas in New York, with a heavy snowstorm that meant weeks of dirt and slush and back-breaking epidemics of influenza and pneumonia! Beyond the curtains of rose-colored damask the storm locked the boughs of an ailanthus tree which grew midway out of the high-fenced backyard. Long ago, in the days of his youth and mania for reform, Estbridge remembered that he had once tried to convert the backyard into an Italian garden. For a brief season box had survived, if it had not actually flourished there, and a cypress tree, sent by an ex-patient from Northern Italy, had lived through a single summer and had died with the first frost of winter. That was nearly twenty years ago, for Estbridge had relinquished his garden with the other dreams of his youth, and today the brawny ailanthus stood there as a symbol of the prosperous failure of his career.

A metaphor vividly depicts the doctor's manual dexterity.

In these sentences, Estbridge is not described directly, but through his attitudes toward the holiday and the storm.

The narrative turns to the past, and a significant memory further characterizes Estbridge.

A major theme of the story is that Estbridge is materially successful, but has not led the life he truly wanted to live.

The ailanthus tree gripped in the snow becomes a symbol of Estbridge's career—apparently substantial ("brawny") but nothing like the fulfilling, romantic garden of his dreams.

An oxymoron captures the essence of the characterization.

★ Read the following excerpt from Ted Hughes's poem "The Badlands." What images and techniques does the poet use to depict the landscape of the Badlands National Park? Where does he shift from describing the landscape to describing the Sun? What technique is used to depict the Sun? Is word repetition important? If so, how? Is there a traditional rhyme scheme? If not, what patterns of sounds are apparent to you?

In the Badlands

We got deeper. A landscape

Staked out in the sun and left to die.

The Theodore Roosevelt National Park.

Long ago dead of the sun. Loose teeth, bone

Coming through crust, bristles.

Or a smashed industrial complex

For production

Of perpetual sacrifice, of canyons

Long ago disemboweled.

When Aztec and Inca went on South

They left the sun waiting,

Starved for worship, raging for attention,

Now gone sullenly mad.

As it sank it stared at our car.

Middle distance, yellow, the Missouri

Crawled, stagnated, crawled.

★ Here is the same excerpt with annotations that relate to the questions asked on the previous page.

In the Badlands

We got deeper. A landscape

Staked out in the sun and left to die.

The Theodore Roosevelt National Park.

Long ago dead of the sun. Loose teeth, bone

Coming through crust, bristles.

Or a smashed industrial complex

For production

Of perpetual sacrifice, of canyons

Long ago disemboweled.

When Aztec and Inca went on South

They left the sun waiting,

Starved for worship, raging for attention,

Now gone sullenly mad.

As it sank it stared at our car.

Middle distance, yellow, the Missouri

Crawled, stagnated, crawled.

The landscape of the park is depicted as dead from violent exposure to the Sun.

The poet uses modern industrial images to describe the barren landscape.

The poet turns to the sluggish movement of the Missouri river, using three verbs, "Crawled, stagnated, crawled." The repetition of "crawled" hints that the alternation in the river's movement is endlessly repeated.

The description of the landscape is intensified because it precedes the name of the actual location—it is as if the poet rushes to present the dramatic description, then remembers to give the name.

The poet uses body elements to evoke the desiccated, crumbling landscape.

The hard initial c's and the soft internal s's predominate in these lines and resonate in other lines.

The focus shifts from the landscape to the Sun. The poet personifies the Sun as a god/person, abandoned by its former worshippers, who remains behind, fierce and demented.

The four images—the decaying body in the desert, the "smashed industrial complex," the angry, ruthless, abandoned sun, and the stagnating and crawling river—together create intense feelings of pain and alienation.

Language and Linguistics

This section of the test focuses on knowledge of concepts relevant to reading comprehension at the level of the word and sentence. Some specific factual knowledge is required, particularly the terms for the elements of grammar. In addition, you will need to draw upon your knowledge of syntax and semantics and your knowledge of theories of language acquisition and development, and how those theories inform common classroom practices for teaching English Language Arts.

Traditional grammar

- Elements of grammar that may be tested include
  - Parts of speech
    - Noun: proper, common, collective
    - Pronoun
    - Verb
    - Adjective
    - Adverb
    - Preposition
    - Conjunction
  - Usage
    - Subject-verb agreement
    - Verb tenses: present, past, present perfect, past perfect, future, and future perfect
    - Voice of verb: active or passive
    - Pronoun-antecedent agreement and weak reference
    - Correct use of infinitive and participle
  - Mechanics
    - Punctuation
      - Comma
      - Semicolon
    - Capitalization

★ What are the most common errors that middle school students make in agreement and punctuation? What are some strategies for helping them to address these difficulties?

- Some questions may ask you to identify the grammatical elements in a given sentence or excerpt. Other questions may ask you to recognize definitions of various grammatical elements. For example,
  - "The underlined word in the sentence above is functioning as which of the following parts of speech?"
  - "The sentence above is a definition of what grammatical element?"

- Other questions may present sentences with grammatical errors and ask you to choose the appropriate corrections or identify the kind of error. For example,
  - "The sentence above could be improved by..."
  - "Which of the following sentences is grammatically correct?"

Syntax and semantics

- Some questions will test your knowledge of specific terms, which may include, but are not limited to,
  - Euphemisms
  - Idioms
  - Diction
  - Phrases
    - Participial phrase
    - Prepositional phrase
    - Appositive phrase
  - Clauses
    - Independent clause
    - Dependent clause
  - Sentence types
    - Declarative
    - Interrogative
    - Exclamatory
    - Imperative

- ▶ Sentence structure
  - ◆ Simple
  - ◆ Compound
  - ◆ Complex
  - ◆ Compound-complex
  - ◆ Fragment
  - ◆ Run-on

- Some questions will ask you to recognize how words can connote different things based on context. For example,

  - ▶ "In which of the following sentences is the word *triumph* used correctly?"

  - ▶ "Which of the following lists contains words that are pronounced differently depending on whether they are used as nouns or verbs?"

- Some questions will ask you to recognize how euphemism and other semantic strategies are used to obscure or alter meaning. For example,

  - ▶ "How would you interpret the meaning of the sentence above?"

  - ▶ "All of the following are pairs of homophones EXCEPT..."

- Some questions will ask you to recognize sentence types and structures. For example,

  - ▶ "The sentence above is an example of what sentence type?"

  - ▶ "The structure of the sentence above can be best described as..."

★ How can meaning be affected by word order in a sentence?

★ What is jargon? What are examples of jargon used in everyday language?

★ What are some examples of ambiguity? What causes a sentence to be ambiguous?

Language acquisition and development

- Some questions will address basic knowledge of how language skills develop, and influences on individuals' use of language. Topics that may be addressed include

  - ▶ Linguistic terms, such as etymology, cognates, affixes, functional shift, slang, morphemes, orthography

  - ▶ Relationships between pronunciation and spelling

  - ▶ The use of dialect, including its historical origins in different parts of the United States

  - ▶ Strategies for building English proficiency for students with limited English proficiency

---

★ What are the phases of language development, especially for middle school students learning English?

★ What are the characteristics of a middle school student new to the United States who is learning English and who is said to have "beginning proficiency" in English? "Intermediate proficiency"? "Advanced proficiency"?

Composition and Rhetoric

These questions focus on knowledge of strategies for teaching writing for multiple contexts and audiences. You will need some factual knowledge about common rhetorical features and organizational techniques. You will also need to draw upon your knowledge of techniques for assessing and evaluating student writing. In addition, you will need to be familiar with a range of audiences, purposes, and discourses for writing.

Teaching writing

- Some questions will test your ability to recognize and employ individual and collaborative approaches to teaching the writing process, including prewriting, drafting, revision, and peer review. Some questions may ask you to associate particular activities and strategies with each stage of the writing process or with a specific teaching objective. For example,

▶ "Which of the following is a basic principle of process writing?"

▶ "Which of the following activities is part of the revision stage of the writing process?"

▶ "Which of the choices above are appropriate purposes for student journals?"

★ What are some central strategies for building students' writing skills and processes?

■ Some questions also may ask you to apply knowledge of writing conventions and mechanics in helping students to revise and edit their own work. For example,

▶ "Based on the student responses above, which student does the best job of focusing his or her response using a topic sentence?"

▶ "Which student response best reflects an effective use of specific examples to support an argument?"

▶ "The exercise above would be most useful in helping students write which of the following kinds of essays?"

■ Other questions will require you to demonstrate your ability to evaluate and assess student writing. These questions will draw upon your knowledge of various assessment tools and response strategies. Some relevant assessment tools and response strategies covered include

▶ Peer review
▶ Portfolios
▶ Holistic scoring
▶ Scoring rubrics
▶ Self-assessment

★ How can you assess students' writing in order to determine the classroom activities and writing assignments that will help them improve?

■ Some questions will ask you to apply a specific assessment strategy to a particular piece of student writing or type of writing assignment. For example,

▶ "Which of the following might be an effective strategy for assessing student essays written in class?"

▶ "Which student has most directly responded to the task outlined in the assignment?"

Thesis statements and supporting evidence

■ These questions ask you to identify an author's thesis statement and analyze how an author creates an argument and supports it with evidence and examples. You should be familiar with the conventions used in written materials to present an argument, including the following:

▶ Appropriate generalizations
▶ Arguments
▶ Direct quotations
▶ Examples
▶ Indirect quotations
▶ Paraphrasing
▶ Organization
▶ Summarizing
▶ Supporting details
▶ Thesis statements
▶ Topic sentences
▶ Transitions

★ Select essays from books or journals and identify the author's main idea. Think about the ways in which authors support their arguments.

Audience and purpose

- Some questions will ask you to make connections between writing conventions and the audiences or purposes for a passage. Types of audience and purpose questions may include

  ► "The desired audience indicated by the passage is..."

  ► "The passage is primarily concerned with..."

  ► "The passage shows the writer's primary purpose to be..."

  ► "The author gains the reader's attention by..."

★ How does the purpose or intended audience for a piece of writing shape its form?

Types of discourse and strategies for development

- Some questions will ask you to identify the type of discourse used in a given passage. For example,

  ► "Which of the following narrative strategies is most prevalent in the passage?"

  ► "Which of the following techniques is found in creative discourse more frequently than in expository discourse?"

★ How does the discourse of the circumstances one writes for (professional, personal, creative) affect the form and tone of the writing?

Coherence and organization

- Some questions will test your ability to recognize and deploy strategies for organization and the preservation of coherence. Such strategies may include, but are not limited to,

  ► Compare and contrast

  ► Chronological sequence

  ► Spatial sequence

  ► Cause and effect

  ► Problem and solution

★ How is organization linked to an essay's purpose? For example, how could a cause-and-effect organizational pattern be effective in a persuasive essay?

- Types of coherence and organization questions may include

  ► "Which of the following best describes the organization of the paragraph?"

  ► "Which of the following sentences, if added to the passage above, best preserves the passage's coherence?"

  ► "The passage above could be improved by introducing the student to which organizational strategy?"

  ► "Which of the following would make the best introductory sentence for the paragraph above?"

  ► "The author of the passage cites an expert for which of the following reasons?"

Critical reasoning

- Some questions will ask you to recognize bias, stereotypes, inferences, and assumptions, or will ask you to distinguish between fact and opinion. For example,

  ► "The phrase in quotation marks in the passage works persuasively because it refers to..."

  ► "Which of the following student responses is based on a stereotype?"

  ► "All of the following statements represent opinions EXCEPT..."

  ► "Which of the following student responses to the passage above relies upon assumptions not supported by the passage?"

★ How do stereotypes and biases interfere with constructing persuasive points of view?

Part Two: Constructed-Response Questions

This section of the chapter is intended to provide you with strategies for reading, analyzing, and understanding the constructed-response questions on the *Middle School English Language Art*s test and for writing successful responses.

The test contains two equally weighted constructed-response questions that constitute approximately 25 percent of the test taker's total test score and emphasize the use of critical-thinking skills. It is expected that about 15 minutes will be spent on each essay question, for an approximate total of 30 minutes of the 2-hour test.

This test contains two different types of constructed-response questions.

The first type of question assesses your understanding of how the formal literary devices used in a poem or prose excerpt contribute to the development of meaning in the excerpt. The question will ask you to interpret a piece of literary or nonfiction text and/or to discuss an approach to interpreting text.

The second type of question assesses your understanding of how the rhetorical features of a fiction or nonfiction passage contribute to the development of the author's intent. The question will ask you to discuss an approach to the writing process and/or a strategy for rhetorical development.

In the sections that follow, you will find detailed descriptions of these question types.

What to Study

Success on this section of the test is not simply a matter of learning more about the structure of constructed-response questions. Cogent organization is important, but success on the test also requires real knowledge of the field. The constructed-response questions evaluate your ability to convey an understanding of some of the significant themes in textual interpretation and rhetoric and composition. You have probably already encountered and used most of the concepts in the college-level English courses you have taken as part of your career preparation.

The following books, articles, and Web sites are particularly relevant to the types of knowledge, topics, and skills covered on the test. *Note:* The test is not based on these resources, nor do they necessarily cover every topic that may be included in the test. Instead, these works are intended to help you revisit topics you have already covered in your education and English courses.

> *Guides to literary terms and methods of interpretation:* The following texts can help you review the literary terms and critical approaches highlighted in this study guide. Each text is organized by central literary terms and their definitions. You can use these texts to look up specific literary concepts; each concept is usually illustrated through references to classic literary works with which you are likely to be familiar already.
>
> Abrams, M. H. A. 1998. *Glossary of Literary Terms*. 7th ed. Fort Worth: Harcourt Brace College Publishers.
>
> *Gale Glossary of Literary Terms:* http://www.galegroup.com/free_resources/glossary/index.htm
>
> Harmon, William, et al. 2002. *A Handbook to Literature*. 9th ed. New York: Prentice Hall.

Guides to rhetorical terms and methods of interpretation: While many common rhetorical terms are covered in the guides listed above, the guides listed below concentrate more specifically on the kinds of rhetorical techniques used in nonfiction essays. You might use them for more detailed explanations of the rhetorical concepts listed in this study guide, and for brief examples of how those terms are used in relation to literary texts.

Trail, George Y. 2000. *Rhetorical Terms and Concepts: A Contemporary Glossary.* Fort Worth: Harcourt Brace College Publishers.

The UVic Writer's Guide: Literary and Rhetorical Terms (University of Victoria, Canada): http://web.uvic.ca/wguide/Pages/LiteraryTermsTOC.html

Textual Interpretation

Literary interpretation

The literary interpretation constructed-response question asks you to connect the use of literary devices and techniques to the development of a passage's meaning. You should be prepared to demonstrate your ability to interpret literary texts fully and accurately. Although you have most likely developed this skill over time through your training in your English courses, you may wish to practice and review this skill in preparation for this exam.

Literary devices

Be familiar with literary devices that are used to create meaning and effect in literature. These devices are the same as those you will have encountered in the multiple-choice portion of the test (see the first part of this chapter). The devices include, but are not limited to,

- Allusion
- Ambiguity
- Dialogue
- Diction
- Figurative language (such as metaphor, simile, and personification)
- Imagery
- Narrative techniques (such as stream of consciousness)
- Parody
- Point of view
- Rhyme and rhythm
- Specific details (such as details of the setting)
- Symbolism
- Tone

Suggested strategies for studying literary devices

- Using a literary anthology (for example, *The Norton Anthology of American Literature*), select short poems or brief excerpts from prose works. Practice identifying the literary devices used in these texts and connecting those devices to the development of meaning in the work.

- Look up those literary terms with which you are less familiar. Put the definition of each term in your own words. Try finding examples of each term in literature with which you are already familiar, or try to develop your own creative examples.

Composition and Rhetoric

The composition and rhetoric constructed-response question covers understanding of the structure and organization of fiction and nonfiction prose selections. You will need to be able to identify rhetorical techniques commonly used in prose and to explain how those techniques contribute to the development of a passage's meaning. As with your literary interpretation skills, you have most likely developed these skills over time through your training in English. Below are some suggestions of rhetorical techniques you may want to review and study strategies you may want to use in preparation for this exam.

Rhetorical techniques

Be familiar with rhetorical techniques that are used to create meaning and effect in essays, such as the following:

- Allusion

- Analogy

- Antithesis

- Cliché

- Direct address

- Emotional appeal

- Euphemism

- Hyperbole

- Irony

- Paradox

- Parallelism

- Persuasive language

- Understatement

Suggested strategies for studying rhetorical techniques

- Look up descriptions of the rhetorical techniques with which you are less familiar in a rhetoric handbook (such as one suggested in the brief bibliography above). Put the definition of each term in your own words. Try finding examples of each term in prose texts with which you are already familiar, or try to develop your own creative examples.

- Using essays in magazines or literary anthologies, practice identifying the rhetorical techniques that appear as you read. Consider how these techniques contribute to your understanding of the work as a whole.

What the Test Scorers Are Looking For

Even if you feel confident about your knowledge of the content to be tested, you still may wonder how you will be able to tell what the test scorers want.

In fact, you can find out what the test scorers want by looking at the questions themselves. The constructed-response test questions are crafted to be as clear as possible regarding what tasks you are expected to do. No expectations are hidden in the question or expressed in code words. The English Language Arts educators who score your responses base your score on two considerations:

- Whether you do the tasks that the question asks for

- How well you do those tasks

So, to answer more specifically the question "What do the scorers want?" we should look at test questions, much like the ones on the test.

Understanding What the Questions Are Asking

It is impossible to write a successful response to a question unless you thoroughly understand the question. Often test takers jump into their written response without taking enough time to analyze exactly what the question is asking, how many different parts of the question need to be addressed, and how <u>the information provided in the excerpt can be used to support the answer</u>. The time you invest in making sure you understand what the question is asking will very likely pay off in a better performance, as long as you budget your time and do not spend a large proportion of the available time just reading the question.

To illustrate the importance of understanding the question before you begin writing, let's look at a sample question.

Sample Question: Composition and Rhetoric

> *"Why, thank you so much. I'd adore to."*
>
> **I don't want to dance with him. I don't want to dance with anybody. And even if I did, it wouldn't be him. He'd be well down among the last ten. I've seen the way he dances. . . . Just think, not a quarter of an hour ago, here I was sitting, feeling sorry for the poor girl he was dancing with. And now I'm going to be the poor girl.**

"The Waltz," a short story by humorist Dorothy Parker, opens with the lines above. Explain how Parker establishes tone and uses perspective in the excerpt.

Identifying the Key Components of the Question

- How does Parker establish tone?

- How does Parker use perspective?

Organizing Your Response

Successful responses start with successful planning, either in the form of an outline or another form of notes. By planning your response, you greatly decrease the chances that you will forget to answer any part of the question. You also increase the chances of creating a well-organized response. Your note-taking space in the test book also gives you a place to jot down thoughts whenever you think of them—for example, when you have an idea about one part of the question when you are writing your response to another part. Planning your response is time well invested, although you must keep your eye on the clock so that you have sufficient time to write your response.

To illustrate a possible strategy for planning a response, let us focus again on the sample question introduced above. We analyzed the question and found that it necessitated a two-part response. You might begin by jotting down those parts on your notes page, leaving space under each. This will ensure that you address each part when you begin writing. In addition, you should underline key parts of the passage that can serve as examples in your response.

Sample Notes—Main Parts to Be Answered

Here you start by identifying each part of the question:

- *How does Parker establish tone?*

- *How does Parker use perspective?*

You then might quickly fill out the main ideas you want to address in each part, like this:

Sample Notes—Ideas Under Each Main Part

How does Parker establish tone?

— Use of contrast

— Exaggeration

How does Parker use perspective?

— First-person point of view

— Use of dialogue and internal monologue

Writing Your Response

Now the important step of writing your response begins. The scorers will not consider the notes that you wrote in your test book when they score your paper, so it is crucial that you integrate all the important ideas from your notes into your actual written response.

Sample Response That Received a Score of 3

Dorothy Parker tells the story in the first person with two contrasting perspectives: what her character says and what she is really thinking. This sets an amusing and intimate tone throughout the excerpt.

Contributing to the sense of intimacy with her character is the conversational tone of her thoughts. Immediately the reader identifies with the character. Also, the use of present tense, so we are overhearing the character's thoughts as she is having them, contributes to the intimacy of the internal dialogue. When she says that she didn't want to dance with anyone, and even if she did "it wouldn't be him," it feels like the character is having a private conversation with the reader.

Finally, the reader is left with a feeling of ironic amusement. The character who so politely agrees to dance has just been feeling sorry for her partner's previous victim: "Just think, not a quarter of an hour ago, here I was sitting, feeling sorry for the poor girl he was dancing with. And now I'm going to be the poor girl." Again, the reader identifies with the intimate tone the character uses since at one time or another most of us have also agreed to do something we would have preferred not to, just to be polite.

Commentary on Sample Response That Earned a Score of 3

This is an example of a strong response because it identifies the elements of the passage that contribute to the construction of tone and perspective, as requested by the prompt. It also explains *how* and *why* those elements produce specific effects by referring directly to features and phrases from the passage. In supporting the claim that the passage produces an intimate perspective, the writer highlights specific features: the first-person point of view, internal dialogue, and use of the present tense. These observations show the writer's knowledge of narrative techniques and the ability to use that knowledge to interpret a passage accurately. The writer also gives a very specific example, showing how a specific phrase in the passage is evidence of the creation of that intimate perspective: "she says that she didn't want to dance with anyone, and even if she did 'it wouldn't be him.'" The writer also specifically identifies the tone as one of "ironic amusement" and once again refers to a specific moment in the text where that irony is evident: the contrast between her sympathy for the young man's previous partner, and her fate of being his next partner.

Sample Response That Received a Score of 1

> In the above passage, Parker establishes tone with short, precise sentences, gradually getting longer. She used perspective in dealing with the fact that she does not want to dance and especially with him. She also was putting herself in the other girl's position.

Commentary on Sample Response That Earned a Score of 1

This response is not strong because it relies on description and summary of the passage rather than upon analysis of its literary elements. It also does not fully respond to the prompt. While the writer mentions a method for constructing tone (the use of short, precise sentences), the writer does not identify the *effect* of that method. Based on this response, a reader cannot tell if the tone of Parker's story is grief stricken, ebullient, or ironic. The writer also fails to adequately address the literary use of "perspective," which refers to *how* characters' attitudes toward a given situation are revealed. Although the writer correctly identifies that the young woman does not want to dance with her partner, the writer does not identify any literary devices (such as point of view) that show *how* that feeling is conveyed. The response is also severely underdeveloped; the writer does not provide direct references back to the text to support his or her claims.

In Conclusion

Whatever format you select, the important thing is that your answer be thorough, complete, and detailed. You need to be certain that you do the following:

- Answer all parts of the question.

- Give reasons for your answers.

- Demonstrate subject-specific knowledge in your answer.

- Refer to the examples in the passage provided.

It is a good idea to use the practice test in the next chapter to help you develop a plan for how you will take the test on the actual testing day, especially if you tend to get nervous or freeze up in a testing situation. Remember to consider your time so that you may give appropriate consideration to both essay questions. Stay within the framework of the question.

Chapter 6

Practice Questions for the *Middle School English Language Arts* Test

▶ ▶ ▶ ▶ ▶ ▶ ▶ ▶ ▶ ▶ ▶ ▶

Now that you have studied the content topics and have worked through strategies relating to multiple-choice and constructed-response questions, you should take the following practice test. You will probably find it helpful to simulate actual testing conditions, giving yourself a set amount of time to work on the questions. If you wish, you can cut out and use the answer sheet provided to answer the multiple-choice questions and write your responses to the constructed-response questions on the lined answer pages.

Keep in mind that the test you take at an actual administration will have different questions, although the proportion of questions in each area and major subarea will be approximately the same. You should not expect the percentage of questions you answer correctly in these practice questions to be exactly the same as when you take the test at an actual administration, since numerous factors affect a person's performance in any given testing situation.

When you have finished the practice questions, you can score your answers to the multiple-choice questions, see sample scored responses to the constructed-response questions, and read explanations of the answers and responses in Chapter 7.

Note: If you are taking these practice questions to help you prepare for the *Middle School: Content Knowledge* test, you should keep in mind that the test you take at the actual administration will have 120 multiple-choice questions, with 30 questions in each of the four content areas. You will be allowed 120 minutes to complete the test. The test does not contain any constructed-response questions.

THE PRAXIS SERIES

Professional Assessments for Beginning Teachers ®

TEST NAME:

Middle School English Language Arts

67 Practice Questions

Approximate time for the whole practice test—95 minutes

Suggested time for Part A (multiple choice)—65 minutes

Suggested time for Part B (constructed response)—30 minutes

(**Note:** At the official administration of this test, there will be 90 multiple-choice questions and 2 constructed-response questions. You will be allowed 120 minutes total to complete the test. The sections of the test will not be timed separately, though it is recommended that you spend 90 minutes on the multiple-choice questions and 30 minutes on the constructed-response questions.)

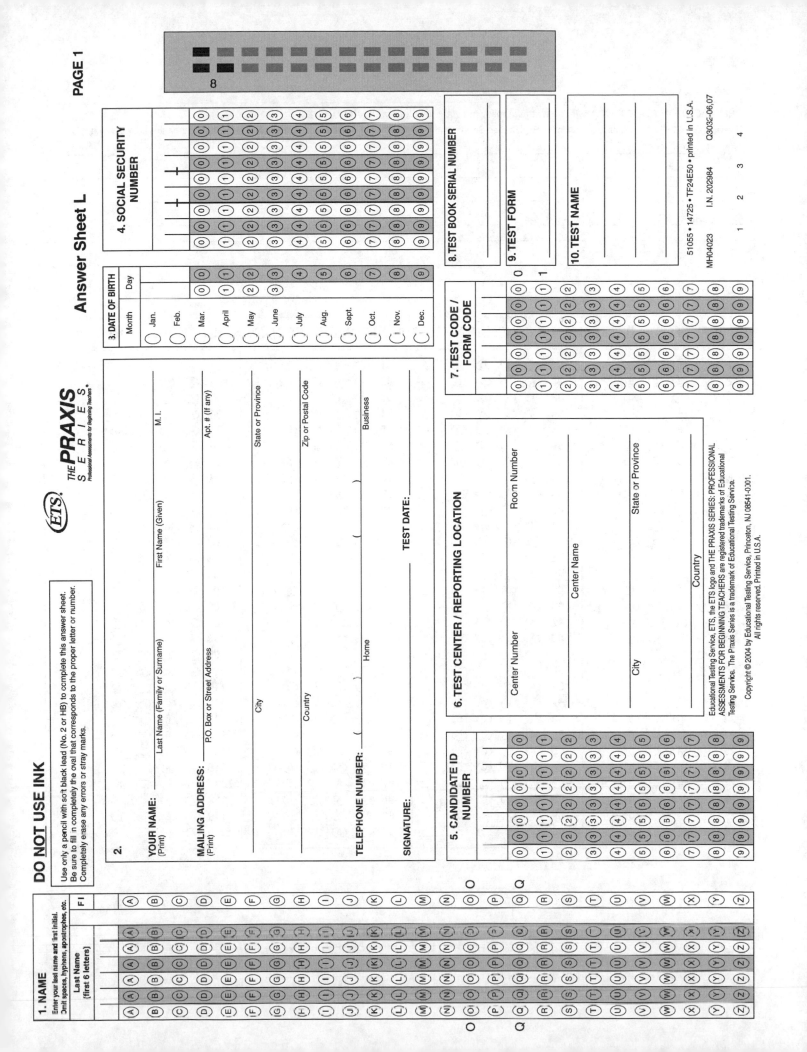

DO NOT USE INK

Use only a pencil with soft black lead (No. 2 or HB) to complete this answer sheet.
Be sure to fill in completely the oval that corresponds to the proper letter or number.
Completely erase any errors or stray marks.

PAGE 1

(ETS.)

THE PRAXIS SERIES®
Professional Assessments for Beginning Teachers®

Answer Sheet L

1. NAME

Enter your last name and first initial.
Omit spaces, hyphens, apostrophes, etc.

Last Name (first 6 letters) | FI

(A) through (Z) ovals

2.

YOUR NAME: (Print)
Last Name (Family or Surname) — First Name (Given) — M.I.

MAILING ADDRESS: (Print)
P.O. Box or Street Address — Apt. # (If any)
City — State or Province
Country — Zip or Postal Code

TELEPHONE NUMBER: ( ) Home — ( ) Business

SIGNATURE:

TEST DATE:

3. DATE OF BIRTH

Month	Day
Jan.	
Feb.	
Mar.	
April	
May	
June	
July	
Aug.	
Sept.	
Oct.	
Nov.	
Dec.	

4. SOCIAL SECURITY NUMBER

(0)(1)(2)(3)(4)(5)(6)(7)(8)(9)

5. CANDIDATE ID NUMBER

(0)(1)(2)(3)(4)(5)(6)(7)(8)(9)

6. TEST CENTER / REPORTING LOCATION

Center Number — Room Number
Center Name
City — State or Province
Country

7. TEST CODE / FORM CODE

(0)(1)(2)(3)(4)(5)(6)(7)(8)(9)

8. TEST BOOK SERIAL NUMBER

9. TEST FORM

10. TEST NAME

Educational Testing Service, ETS, the ETS logo and THE PRAXIS SERIES: PROFESSIONAL ASSESSMENTS FOR BEGINNING TEACHERS are registered trademarks of Educational Testing Service. The Praxis Series is a trademark of Educational Testing Service.

Copyright © 2004 by Educational Testing Service, Princeton, NJ 08541-0001. All rights reserved. Printed in U.S.A.

51055 • 14725 • TF24E50 • printed in U.S.A.
MH04023   I.N. 202984   Q303z-06,07

1 2 3 4

PAGE 2

CERTIFICATION STATEMENT: (Please write the following statement below. DO NOT PRINT.)

"I hereby agree to the conditions set forth in the Registration Bulletin and certify that I am the person whose name and address appear on this answer sheet."

_____

_____

_____

SIGNATURE: _____ DATE: _____ / _____ / _____

Month   Day   Year

BE SURE EACH MARK IS DARK AND COMPLETELY FILLS THE INTENDED SPACE AS ILLUSTRATED HERE: ● .

#	A B C D	#	A B C D	#	A B C D	#	A B C D
1	Ⓐ Ⓑ Ⓒ Ⓓ	31	Ⓐ Ⓑ Ⓒ Ⓓ	61	Ⓐ Ⓑ Ⓒ Ⓓ	91	Ⓐ Ⓑ Ⓒ Ⓓ
2	Ⓐ Ⓑ Ⓒ Ⓓ	32	Ⓐ Ⓑ Ⓒ Ⓓ	62	Ⓐ Ⓑ Ⓒ Ⓓ	92	Ⓐ Ⓑ Ⓒ Ⓓ
3	Ⓐ Ⓑ Ⓒ Ⓓ	33	Ⓐ Ⓑ Ⓒ Ⓓ	63	Ⓐ Ⓑ Ⓒ Ⓓ	93	Ⓐ Ⓑ Ⓒ Ⓓ
4	Ⓐ Ⓑ Ⓒ Ⓓ	34	Ⓐ Ⓑ Ⓒ Ⓓ	64	Ⓐ Ⓑ Ⓒ Ⓓ	94	Ⓐ Ⓑ Ⓒ Ⓓ
5	Ⓐ Ⓑ Ⓒ Ⓓ	35	Ⓐ Ⓑ Ⓒ Ⓓ	65	Ⓐ Ⓑ Ⓒ Ⓓ	95	Ⓐ Ⓑ Ⓒ Ⓓ
6	Ⓐ Ⓑ Ⓒ Ⓓ	36	Ⓐ Ⓑ Ⓒ Ⓓ	66	Ⓐ Ⓑ Ⓒ Ⓓ	96	Ⓐ Ⓑ Ⓒ Ⓓ
7	Ⓐ Ⓑ Ⓒ Ⓓ	37	Ⓐ Ⓑ Ⓒ Ⓓ	67	Ⓐ Ⓑ Ⓒ Ⓓ	97	Ⓐ Ⓑ Ⓒ Ⓓ
8	Ⓐ Ⓑ Ⓒ Ⓓ	38	Ⓐ Ⓑ Ⓒ Ⓓ	68	Ⓐ Ⓑ Ⓒ Ⓓ	98	Ⓐ Ⓑ Ⓒ Ⓓ
9	Ⓐ Ⓑ Ⓒ Ⓓ	39	Ⓐ Ⓑ Ⓒ Ⓓ	69	Ⓐ Ⓑ Ⓒ Ⓓ	99	Ⓐ Ⓑ Ⓒ Ⓓ
10	Ⓐ Ⓑ Ⓒ Ⓓ	40	Ⓐ Ⓑ Ⓒ Ⓓ	70	Ⓐ Ⓑ Ⓒ Ⓓ	100	Ⓐ Ⓑ Ⓒ Ⓓ
11	Ⓐ Ⓑ Ⓒ Ⓓ	41	Ⓐ Ⓑ Ⓒ Ⓓ	71	Ⓐ Ⓑ Ⓒ Ⓓ	101	Ⓐ Ⓑ Ⓒ Ⓓ
12	Ⓐ Ⓑ Ⓒ Ⓓ	42	Ⓐ Ⓑ Ⓒ Ⓓ	72	Ⓐ Ⓑ Ⓒ Ⓓ	102	Ⓐ Ⓑ Ⓒ Ⓓ
13	Ⓐ Ⓑ Ⓒ Ⓓ	43	Ⓐ Ⓑ Ⓒ Ⓓ	73	Ⓐ Ⓑ Ⓒ Ⓓ	103	Ⓐ Ⓑ Ⓒ Ⓓ
14	Ⓐ Ⓑ Ⓒ Ⓓ	44	Ⓐ Ⓑ Ⓒ Ⓓ	74	Ⓐ Ⓑ Ⓒ Ⓓ	104	Ⓐ Ⓑ Ⓒ Ⓓ
15	Ⓐ Ⓑ Ⓒ Ⓓ	45	Ⓐ Ⓑ Ⓒ Ⓓ	75	Ⓐ Ⓑ Ⓒ Ⓓ	105	Ⓐ Ⓑ Ⓒ Ⓓ
16	Ⓐ Ⓑ Ⓒ Ⓓ	46	Ⓐ Ⓑ Ⓒ Ⓓ	76	Ⓐ Ⓑ Ⓒ Ⓓ	106	Ⓐ Ⓑ Ⓒ Ⓓ
17	Ⓐ Ⓑ Ⓒ Ⓓ	47	Ⓐ Ⓑ Ⓒ Ⓓ	77	Ⓐ Ⓑ Ⓒ Ⓓ	107	Ⓐ Ⓑ Ⓒ Ⓓ
18	Ⓐ Ⓑ Ⓒ Ⓓ	48	Ⓐ Ⓑ Ⓒ Ⓓ	78	Ⓐ Ⓑ Ⓒ Ⓓ	108	Ⓐ Ⓑ Ⓒ Ⓓ
19	Ⓐ Ⓑ Ⓒ Ⓓ	49	Ⓐ Ⓑ Ⓒ Ⓓ	79	Ⓐ Ⓑ Ⓒ Ⓓ	109	Ⓐ Ⓑ Ⓒ Ⓓ
20	Ⓐ Ⓑ Ⓒ Ⓓ	50	Ⓐ Ⓑ Ⓒ Ⓓ	80	Ⓐ Ⓑ Ⓒ Ⓓ	110	Ⓐ Ⓑ Ⓒ Ⓓ
21	Ⓐ Ⓑ Ⓒ Ⓓ	51	Ⓐ Ⓑ Ⓒ Ⓓ	81	Ⓐ Ⓑ Ⓒ Ⓓ	111	Ⓐ Ⓑ Ⓒ Ⓓ
22	Ⓐ Ⓑ Ⓒ Ⓓ	52	Ⓐ Ⓑ Ⓒ Ⓓ	82	Ⓐ Ⓑ Ⓒ Ⓓ	112	Ⓐ Ⓑ Ⓒ Ⓓ
23	Ⓐ Ⓑ Ⓒ Ⓓ	53	Ⓐ Ⓑ Ⓒ Ⓓ	83	Ⓐ Ⓑ Ⓒ Ⓓ	113	Ⓐ Ⓑ Ⓒ Ⓓ
24	Ⓐ Ⓑ Ⓒ Ⓓ	54	Ⓐ Ⓑ Ⓒ Ⓓ	84	Ⓐ Ⓑ Ⓒ Ⓓ	114	Ⓐ Ⓑ Ⓒ Ⓓ
25	Ⓐ Ⓑ Ⓒ Ⓓ	55	Ⓐ Ⓑ Ⓒ Ⓓ	85	Ⓐ Ⓑ Ⓒ Ⓓ	115	Ⓐ Ⓑ Ⓒ Ⓓ
26	Ⓐ Ⓑ Ⓒ Ⓓ	56	Ⓐ Ⓑ Ⓒ Ⓓ	86	Ⓐ Ⓑ Ⓒ Ⓓ	116	Ⓐ Ⓑ Ⓒ Ⓓ
27	Ⓐ Ⓑ Ⓒ Ⓓ	57	Ⓐ Ⓑ Ⓒ Ⓓ	87	Ⓐ Ⓑ Ⓒ Ⓓ	117	Ⓐ Ⓑ Ⓒ Ⓓ
28	Ⓐ Ⓑ Ⓒ Ⓓ	58	Ⓐ Ⓑ Ⓒ Ⓓ	88	Ⓐ Ⓑ Ⓒ Ⓓ	118	Ⓐ Ⓑ Ⓒ Ⓓ
29	Ⓐ Ⓑ Ⓒ Ⓓ	59	Ⓐ Ⓑ Ⓒ Ⓓ	89	Ⓐ Ⓑ Ⓒ Ⓓ	119	Ⓐ Ⓑ Ⓒ Ⓓ
30	Ⓐ Ⓑ Ⓒ Ⓓ	60	Ⓐ Ⓑ Ⓒ Ⓓ	90	Ⓐ Ⓑ Ⓒ Ⓓ	120	Ⓐ Ⓑ Ⓒ Ⓓ

PRAXIS MIDDLE SCHOOL ENGLISH LANGUAGE ARTS

Part A

65 Multiple-choice Questions
(Suggested time—65 minutes)

Directions: Each of the questions or incomplete statements below is followed by four choices (A, B, C, and D). Choose the best response to each question and fill in the appropriate space for that question on your answer sheet.

1. Buck did not read the newspapers, or he would have known that trouble was brewing, not alone for himself, but for every tidewater dog, strong of muscle and with warm, long hair, from Puget Sound to San Diego. Because men, groping in the Arctic darkness, had found a yellow metal, and because steamship and transportation companies were booming the find, thousands of men were rushing into the Northland. These men wanted dogs…

   The excerpt above is from

   (A) Marjorie Kinnan Rawlings' *The Yearling*
   (B) Scott O'Dell's *Island of Blue Dolphins*
   (C) Jean Craighead George's *Julie of the Wolves*
   (D) Jack London's *The Call of the Wild*

2. *A Swiftly Tilting Planet, A Wind in the Door,* and *A Wrinkle in Time* were all written by

   (A) Daphne du Maurier
   (B) Madeleine L'Engle
   (C) Joan Aiken
   (D) Ursula Le Guin

3. Which of the following authors is associated with the Colonial, or Puritan, period of American literature?

   (A) Anne Bradstreet
   (B) Washington Irving
   (C) Nathaniel Hawthorne
   (D) Louisa May Alcott

Questions 4-5 are based on the following passage.

The book, though published in a radical period (1972) and an expanding economy, has a conservative ecological message. It relates the adventures of a tribe of British rabbits who must flee their warren in the Berkshires when it is bulldozed flat for a construction site. The author was for many years an air-pollution expert with the British Department of the Environment; he saw what was happening to the British landscape long before many of his contemporaries did, and his portrait of the process is devastating. He was also a gifted naturalist, able to portray the daily life of his characters in accurate and fascinating detail.

4. The novel described above is

   (A) *Animal Farm* by George Orwell
   (B) *The Hobbit* by J. R. R. Tolkien
   (C) *Watership Down* by Richard Adams
   (D) *The Lion, the Witch, and the Wardrobe* by C. S. Lewis

5. The author of the passage characterizes the book she describes as a

   (A) documentary novel intended to reveal political secrets
   (B) fictional portrayal based on the author's contemporaries
   (C) fable with animal characters intended primarily for children
   (D) fantasy intended to comment on a contemporary phenomenon

6. No more be grieved at that which thou hast
done.
Roses have thorns, and silver fountains mud,
Clouds and eclipses stain both moon and sun,
And loathsome canker lives in sweetest bud.

   —William Shakespeare, Sonnet 35

   Which of the following statements best
   expresses the main idea of the excerpt?

   (A) People are evil by nature.
   (B) Nothing in this world is perfect.
   (C) Good deeds mean more than good
   intentions.
   (D) Evil, like beauty, is in the eye of the
   beholder.

**Questions 7-8 are based on the following excerpt
from Daniel Defoe's _Robinson Crusoe_.**

Being the third son of the family, and not bred to
any trade, my head began to be filled very early
with rambling thoughts. My father, who was
very ancient, had given me a competent share of
learning, as far as house education and a country
free school generally goes, and designed me for
the law; but I would be satisfied with nothing
but going to sea; and my inclination to this led
me so strongly against the will, nay the
commands, of my father, and against all the
entreaties and persuasions of my mother and
other friends that there seemed to be something
fatal in that propension of nature tending
directly to the life of misery which was to
befall me.

7. In the passage, the narrator is primarily
concerned with

   (A) defending an impulsive but ultimately
   beneficial decision he has made
   (B) assessing the reasons for his lack of
   success
   (C) discussing a fateful decision he made in
   spite of opposition
   (D) criticizing his family for their lack of
   concern for his well-being

8. The passage ends with which of the
following?

   (A) An attempt to account for past events
   (B) A foreshadowing of events to come
   (C) A remembrance of disappointing events
   (D) An explanation of unexpected events

9. The following excerpt is from Toni Morrison's
Sula.

   Helene Wright was an impressive woman, at
   least in Medallion she was. Heavy hair in a
   bun, dark eyes arched in perpetual query about
   other people's manners. A woman who won all
   social battles with presence and a conviction of
   the legitimacy of her authority.

   This passage portrays Helene Wright as

   (A) joyful
   (B) intimidating
   (C) informal
   (D) melancholy

10. The following passage is from J. R. R.
Tolkien's _The Lord of the Rings: The Two
Towers_.

   The dale ran like a stony trough between the
   ridged hills, and a trickling stream flowed
   among the boulders at the bottom. A cliff
   frowned upon their right; to the left rose gray
   slopes, dim and shadowy in the late night.

   Which of the following literary devices is used
   in the first sentence of the passage?

   (A) Onomatopoeia
   (B) Inverted syntax
   (C) Irony
   (D) Simile

Questions 11-12 are based on the following excerpt from Leslie Marmon Silko's "Lullaby."

The storm passed swiftly. The clouds moved east. They were massive and full, crowding together across the sky. She watched them with the feeling of horses—steely blue-gray horses startled across the sky. The powerful haunches pushed into the distances and the tail hairs streamed white mist behind them. The sky cleared. Ayah saw that there was nothing between her and the stars.

11. In this passage, the "powerful haunches" and "tail hairs" refer to

    (A) animals taking shelter in a nearby field
    (B) the stars shining above Ayah's head
    (C) storm clouds moving across the sky
    (D) the horse Ayah is riding

12. The passage represents the storm through

    (A) metaphor
    (B) onomatopoeia
    (C) personification
    (D) apostrophe

Questions 13-15 are based on the following poem by William Blake.

Can I see another's woe,
And not be in sorrow too?
Can I see another's grief,
And not seek for kind relief?

Can I see a falling tear,
And not feel my sorrow's share?
Can a father see his child
Weep, nor be with sorrow fill'd?

Can a mother sit and hear
An infant groan an infant fear?
No, no! never can it be!
Never, never can it be!

13. The structure of the poem is best described as

    (A) quatrains
    (B) blank verse
    (C) a sonnet
    (D) ballad stanzas

14. What is the theme of the poem?

    (A) It is important to take parenting seriously.
    (B) People cannot help feeling the unhappiness of others.
    (C) Children's tears will not last long.
    (D) The world is difficult and can never be a happy place.

15. The dominant grammatical construction the poet uses is the

    (A) accusative interrogative
    (B) direct statement
    (C) rhetorical question
    (D) general imperative

Questions 16-17 are based on the following excerpt from Amy Tan's *The Bonesetter's Daughter*.

They were pages written in Chinese, her mother's writing. LuLing had given them to her five or six years before. "Just some old things about my family," she had said, with the kind of awkward nonchalance that meant the pages were important. "My story, begin little-girl time. I write for myself, but maybe you read, then you see how I grow up, come to this country." Ruth had heard bits of her mother's life over the years, but she was touched by her shyness in asking Ruth to read what she had obviously labored over. The pages contained precise vertical rows, without crossouts, leaving Ruth to surmise that her mother had copied over her earlier attempts.

16. The narration in this passage is best described as

    (A) first person, from LuLing's point of view
    (B) first person, from Ruth's point of view
    (C) second person
    (D) third person

17. Ruth's attitude towards her mother's writing is best described as one of

    (A) concealed disdain
    (B) tender respect
    (C) pretended indifference
    (D) apologetic skepticism

Questions 18-19 are based on the following excerpt from Lois Lowry's *The Giver*.

Jonas reached the opposite side of the river, stopped briefly, and looked back. The community where his entire life had been lived lay behind him now, sleeping. At dawn, the orderly, disciplined life he had always known would continue again, without him. The life where nothing was ever unexpected. Or inconvenient. Or unusual. The life without color, pain, or past.

18. In the passage, the community is described using which of the following literary devices?

    (A) Analogy
    (B) Personification
    (C) Hyperbole
    (D) Allusion

19. Which of the following best describes the last four sentences of the passage?

    (A) Negative statements used to describe what Jonas will be sorry to leave behind when he leaves the community
    (B) Exclamations used to reflect the disordered nature of Jonas' thinking
    (C) Simple sentences used to describe a community that has little emotional complexity
    (D) Sentence fragments used to emphasize the characteristics of the community Jonas is leaving

Questions 20-21 are based on an excerpt from Tillie Olsen's "These Things Shall Be."

Line   For forty-seven years they had been married.
       How deep back the stubborn, gnarled roots
       of the quarrel reached, no one could say—
       but only now, when tending to the needs of
   5   others no longer shackled them together,
       the roots swelled up visible, split the earth
       between them, and the tearing shook even to
       the children, long since grown.

20. The narrator suggests that the timing of the "tearing" mentioned in line 7 was brought about by which of the following factors?

    (A)   A refusal to face the past
    (B)   The memories of the children
    (C)   The loss of a shared focus
    (D)   Changes in society's values

21. Each of the following phrases from the passage serves to develop the main metaphor presented in the passage EXCEPT

    (A)   "swelled up visible" (line 6)
    (B)   "split the earth between them" (lines 6-7)
    (C)   "shook even to the children" (lines 7-8)
    (D)   "long since grown" (line 8)

Questions 22-24 are based on the following poems.

(A)   With every gust of wind,
      the butterfly changes its place
      on the willow.

(B)   Know then thyself, presume not God to scan;
      The proper study of Mankind is Man.
      Placed on this isthmus of a middle state,
      A being darkly wise, and rudely great:

(C)   All in a hot and copper sky
      The bloody Sun, at noon,
      Right up above the mast did stand,
      No bigger than the Moon.

(D)   I loafe and invite my soul;
      I lean and loafe at my ease observing a
      spear of summer grass.
      My tongue, every atom of my blood,
      form'd from this soil, this air.

22. Which is an example of a ballad stanza?

23. Which is an example of free verse?

24. Which is an example of haiku?

25. Ralph Waldo Emerson, Henry David Thoreau, and Margaret Fuller are all associated with which of the following schools of thought?

    (A)   Transcendentalism
    (B)   Realism
    (C)   Naturalism
    (D)   Classicism

26. Among the most obvious general features of
_____ poetry are persistent references to
nature and natural objects, intimate self-
revelation of the poet, and direct expression of
strong, personal emotion.

Which of the following would best fill in the
blank in line 2?

(A) Neoclassical
(B) Romantic
(C) Modern
(D) Postmodern

27. Aristotle moved from place to place in the
Lyceum while he taught. He was the prototype
of peripatetic teachers. So say those who enjoyed
not only hours, but days, walking with C. S.
Lewis or Francis Schaeffer.

To determine the meaning of the underlined
word in the passage above, a student would find
which of the following most helpful?

(A) The use of structural cues
(B) The use of context cues
(C) Understanding of figurative language
(D) Understanding of euphemisms

28. A high school teacher wants to meet the needs of
reluctant readers who are required to read Emily
Brontë's *Wuthering Heights*. Which of the
following is most likely to motivate students to
become engaged in the book?

(A) A book about customs and traditions in
Brontë's country
(B) Photographs of Brontë and her family
(C) Copies of the novel that are printed in
large, easy-to-read print
(D) Software allowing students to interact with
the setting of the novel

29. Traveling at a speed of 80 miles per hour, he
saw the car go by in a blur.
Swimming swiftly through the aquarium, the
children were delighted by the fish.

Which of the following correctly describes the
cause of confusion in the sentences above?

(A) The participial phrases at the beginning
of the sentences do not refer to the
grammatical subjects.
(B) Commas rather than semicolons are
used to separate two independent
clauses.
(C) The number of the subject does not
determine the number of the verb.
(D) Commas should not have been used to
set off the introductory phrases from the
rest of the sentences.

30. Which of the following sentences contains a
split infinitive?

(A) Although Anne was looking forward to
the vacation, she was worried about
leaving her job for such a long period.
(B) One of the best parts of getting ready for
the trip was going to the store to buy all
of the gear needed for skin diving.
(C) For your safety, we ask you to kindly
stay in your seats until the "fasten your
seatbelts" sign has been turned off.
(D) To be fully prepared, the campers made
sure that they had checked all of the
batteries in their equipment.

Questions 31-33 are based on the following sentences from Charles Dickens' *Great Expectations*.

I. I had seen the damp lying on the outside of my little window, as if some goblin had been crying there all night, and using the window for a pocket-handkerchief.

II. Sometimes, she would coldly tolerate me; sometimes, she would condescend to me; sometimes, she would be quite familiar with me; sometimes, she would tell me energetically that she hated me.

III. As soon as I could recover myself sufficiently, I hurried out after him and looked for him in the neighboring streets; but he was gone.

IV. We ate the whole of the toast, and drank tea in proportion, and it was delightful to see how warm and greasy we all got after it.

V. It was then that I began to understand that everything in the room, like the watch and the clock, had stopped a long time ago.

31. Which sentence contains a series of independent clauses?

(A) Sentence I
(B) Sentence II
(C) Sentence III
(D) Sentence V

32. Which sentence opens with a subordinate clause?

(A) Sentence I
(B) Sentence II
(C) Sentence III
(D) Sentence IV

33. Which sentence contains an appositive?

(A) Sentence II
(B) Sentence III
(C) Sentence IV
(D) Sentence V

34. Each of the following sentences contains an ambiguity EXCEPT:

(A) I like to listen to the radio doing my homework.
(B) Students who like to read often can improve their grades.
(C) Not all the students were present.
(D) You can call your friend and tell her about the new books you bought for sixty cents.

35. Which of the following pairs of words are homophones?

(A) The nouns "flower" and "flour"
(B) The adjectives "polite" and "courteous"
(C) The verb "run" and the adjective "runny"
(D) The adjectives "fast" and "slow"

36. *phone, auto, ad, math*

The words above are all examples of

(A) clipped forms
(B) back-formation
(C) blends
(D) echoic words

37. English has taken words from various ------- languages. A good many words were adopted from Spanish in the nineteenth century: adobe, bonanza, canyon, and mustang. From Italian, English has also acquired many words, including much of our musical terminology. As early as the sixteenth century, duo, fugue, madrigal, and violin appeared in English.

The blank in line 1 can best be completed as

(A) Celtic
(B) Ural-Altaic
(C) Malay-Polynesian
(D) Romance

38. In his much praised book *Albion's Seed,* David Hackett Fischer argues that regional accents were in place in America by the time of the Revolution. He points out that American colonists came in four distinct waves from four different parts of Britain. By assembling in America in enclaves that reflected their geographic origins, the four main waves of immigrants managed to preserve distinctive regional identities. That is why, for instance, horses in New England *neigh,* while those in the middle states of America *whinny.*

    The passage provides a discussion of which of the following?

    (A) Euphemism
    (B) Slang
    (C) Dialect
    (D) Etymology

39. -------, the process by which a word from one part of speech is changed to another, can also be achieved by adding ------- to words. For example, "fuse" becomes "refuse" or "govern" becomes "governor."

    Which of the following words correctly fill the blanks in the sentence above?

    (A) Functional shift...affixes
    (B) Orthography...roots
    (C) Lexical change...blends
    (D) Usage...gerunds

40. Each of the following is true of the approach known as mapping EXCEPT:

    (A) The central topic of a student's composition is commonly placed in a dominant position in the map.
    (B) Students can use mapping both in prewriting and as a revising activity.
    (C) The most effective shape for maps developed by students is the pinwheel.
    (D) A map helps students distinguish between primary, secondary, and tertiary ideas.

41. A middle school writing teacher asks students to look through magazines for examples of advertisements and to analyze the techniques the advertisements use to influence readers to buy certain products or to change their behavior. Students are then instructed to write an essay in which they use the techniques used in advertising. This exercise would be most useful in helping students write which of the following kinds of essays?

    (A) Descriptive
    (B) Persuasive
    (C) Argumentative
    (D) Prescriptive

42. He had intended to work for three hours each day, but then he realizes that he wasn't getting the project done on schedule.

    The sentence above could best be revised by

    (A) making the verb tenses consistent
    (B) deleting inappropriately elevated language
    (C) making all pronoun references clear
    (D) eliminating split infinitives

Questions 43-47 are based on the following description of an assignment and four student responses.

After reading Nathaniel Hawthorne's *The Scarlet Letter*, students were asked to argue whether they found Hester Prynne to be a sympathetic character. Read the student responses that follow.

Student A: Hester Prynne must have been very pretty to have two men fall in love with her. I think the novel would have been better if she had married Pearl's father at the end.

Student B: Hester was not a sympathetic character, she betrayed her husband. And then she wouldn't tell anyone who was Pearl's father he was revealed in the end anyway and they were both punished.

Student C: Although she did make mistakes, Hester Prynne was a sympathetic character. She was trapped in an unhappy marriage, so I can understand why she was not faithful to her husband. Throughout the novel, she showed love to her daughter and demonstrated loyalty by protecting the identity of Pearl's father. These positive qualities revealed her good character.

Student D: I did not feel sympathy for Hester Prynne because she was responsible for her situation. On the other hand, it must have been hard for her to wear the scarlet letter all of the time. She knew that everyone was gossiping about her. I don't like it when I know other people are talking about me and Hester probably didn't like it either.

43. This assignment draws primarily on what critical approach?

(A) Formalism
(B) Shared inquiry
(C) Historicism
(D) Reader response

44. Which student is having the most trouble with sentence errors, such as comma splices and run-ons?

(A) Student A
(B) Student B
(C) Student C
(D) Student D

45. Which student does the best job of using specific examples from the text to support a point of view?

(A) Student A
(B) Student B
(C) Student C
(D) Student D

46. Which student has not responded to the task outlined in the assignment?

(A) Student A
(B) Student B
(C) Student C
(D) Student D

47. Which student uses the most-complex sentence structures?

(A) Student A
(B) Student B
(C) Student C
(D) Student D

Questions 48-49 are based on the following passage.

There have now been many studies of elite performers—concert violinists, chess grand masters, professional ice-skaters, mathematicians, and so forth. The biggest difference researchers find between them and lesser performers is the amount of deliberate practice they have accumulated. Indeed, the most important talent may be the talent for practice itself. <u>K. Anders Ericsson, a cognitive psychologist and an expert on performance, notes that the most important role that innate factors play may be in a person's willingness to engage in sustained training.</u> He has found, for example, that top performers dislike practicing just as much as others do. (That is why, for example, athletes and musicians usually quit practicing when they retire.) But, more than others, they have the will to keep at it anyway.

48. The author of the passage uses the underlined sentence to

(A) summarize the thesis of the passage
(B) suggest a refinement of the thesis of the passage
(C) provide supporting evidence
(D) consider an alternative point of view

49. The primary purpose of the passage is to

(A) contrast two different views about the relationship between practice and performance
(B) explain why many athletes and musicians dislike their jobs
(C) refute the argument that willpower is a significant part of success
(D) present an argument about the relationship between practice and performance

Questions 50-52 are based on the following passage.

My people, the Arapaho, are scattered now. There are fewer than one thousand of us who are full-bloods now living in Oklahoma, and many of us who are left do not know our language or our old ways and our old songs and stories. The Cheyenne-Arapaho Agency at Darlington is gone; Fort Reno, across the river from the old agency, is no longer a fort; our white lodges no longer stand in circles on the prairie with their poles pointed toward the blue sky. Mornings and evenings no smoke from hundreds of campfires rises into the air; no coyotes howl at night and no prairie dogs build their towns on the uplands. No ponies graze in herds on the open ranges.

50. Which of the following statements best represents the author's main idea?

(A) Native animals are becoming extinct in Oklahoma.
(B) Military forts should be preserved as historical sites.
(C) The Arapaho people are disappearing and their land is changing.
(D) Industrialization and new settlements should be stopped.

51. The author's argument is supported primarily by

(A) presenting demographic statistics
(B) offering descriptive observations
(C) describing the steps in a process
(D) refuting a number of assertions

52. The approach used by the writer is best described as

(A) poetic and personal
(B) argumentative and aggressive
(C) elliptical and abstract
(D) technical and detailed

53. Michael Ondaatje's first book, *The Collected Works of Billy the Kid,* is a postmodern blend of genres, a puzzling and rewarding collage of poetry, character sketches, songs, newspaper interviews, fiction, quotations from secondary sources, even photographs.

The sentence above is most likely to begin an essay that employs which of the following methods of development?

(A) Contrast
(B) Narration
(C) Argumentation
(D) Description

Questions 54-55 are based on the following passage.

Promoting novels in a sound-bite culture is like selling elephants from a gum-ball machine. Cramped. Put in your nickel and stand back. Interviewers keep asking, "What is your book *about*?" They mean well. They are kindly giving me a chance to pitch my product. But you should sooner say to a hypochondriac "How are you?" than ask an author this question. Shall I grab you by the lapels and really tell you? Have you got all day? No. What they need is a seven-word answer, and the only accurate one I can think of is: "It's *about* three hundred pages long—*read it*!!"

54. The author uses the image of elephants in a gumball machine to suggest that novels are

(A) as inexpensive as gum balls
(B) difficult to summarize in a sound bite
(C) as unusual as an elephant in a gum-ball machine
(D) hard to promote because few people are interested in reading

55. The author is primarily concerned with

(A) explaining her reaction to a particular situation
(B) exaggerating the difficulty of writing a novel
(C) presenting a humorous anecdote about a particular experience
(D) complaining about the critical reaction to her work

Questions 56-58 are based on the following passage.

Make a circle with the fingers on your left hand by touching the tip of your index finger to the tip of your thumb. Now poke your head through that circle.

If you unsuccessfully tried to fit your head through the small digital circle, you (and almost any reader) thought that the phrase "poke your head" meant that your head was the poker. But if you raised your left hand with the circle of fingers up close to your forehead and poked your right index finger through that circle until it touched your forehead, you realized that the phrase "poke your head" has a second, and opposite, meaning. Such words or phrases are called *contronyms*.

56. Which of the following pairs of sentences provides the best example of a contronym?

(A) To be safe, you should *think better* of your plan to vacation alone. Most people *think better* in a quiet environment than in a noisy one.
(B) It is important to *find out* what your adversary's plans are. What did the farmer *find out* in the field?
(C) The company gives a test to *screen* job applicants. The television's *screen* is larger than most.
(D) Airplanes are not the only vehicles used to *dust* crops. In a luxury hotel, staff members *dust* the furniture daily.

57. The primary purpose of the passage is to

(A) defend an assertion
(B) define a term
(C) compare two points of view
(D) provide detailed instructions

58. The author gains the reader's attention by

(A) flattering the reader
(B) involving the reader directly
(C) attacking the reader's beliefs
(D) pointing out the reader's weaknesses

Questions 59-60 are based on the following passage.

Where written literature provides us with a tradition of texts, oral literature offers a tradition of performances. Traditional folkloric studies of Native American oral literature worked with transcriptions of the verbal component of the performance, as if those "texts" represented the reality. But transcribing an oral performance produces an anomaly that is neither a part of a living folkloric tradition nor of a truly literary one. Consequently, literary criticism of Native American oral literatures founded on a conventional notion of text and evolved from analogies to Western genres, styles, and aesthetic values soon proves of little value.

59. The passage suggests that the literary criticism described in the last sentence "proves of little value" for which of the following reasons?

   (A) The criticisms are based on verbal transcriptions that are difficult to read.

   (B) The critics ignore an important element in the presentation of the literature.

   (C) The critics are attempting to understand an unfamiliar folkloric tradition.

   (D) The criticisms are based on misreadings of the verbal transcriptions.

60. The passage is primarily concerned with

   (A) evaluating a particular approach to studying Native American oral literature

   (B) providing an explanation for the lack of critical interest in Native American oral literature

   (C) emphasizing the effect that literary critics have had on the development of Native American oral literature

   (D) suggesting a way in which critics can improve their understanding of transcriptions of Native American oral literature

61. Maya Angelou's "On the Pulse of Morning" is a poem rich in references to toxic waste and pollution—issues that were the subjects of the 1992 United Nations Conference on Environment and Development. The poem's references to mastodons and dinosaurs suggest the prehistoric beasts of Steven Spielberg's 1993 film *Jurassic Park*. In these and other instances Angelou writes with passion about contemporary concerns.

Which of the following best describes the organization of the paragraph?

   (A) A topic is introduced and then examples are supplied.

   (B) A poem is described and then other works on the same topic are mentioned.

   (C) Opinions are expressed and then the reasoning that supports them is discussed.

   (D) Examples are provided and then a summary statement is made.

62. Literary critic Edmund Wilson regarded detective novels as terminally subliterary, either an addiction or a harmless vice on a par with crossword puzzles. But the truth is that for every Edmund Wilson who resists the genre, there are dozens of intellectuals who have embraced it wholeheartedly. The proliferation of the detective novel—and its close cousin, the spy thriller—is one of the literary highlights of our time.

The opinion of the author of the passage about the literary value of the detective novel is expressed in which of the following words found in the passage?

   (A) Subliterary
   (B) Addiction
   (C) Proliferation
   (D) Highlights

Questions 63-65 are based on the following passage.

Line   One of the fundamental barriers to understanding and appreciating Asian American literary self-expression has been the existence of race stereotypes about
5   Asians in American popular culture. During the mid-twentieth century, more non-Asian Americans probably knew fictional characters like Fu Manchu and Charlie Chan than knew Asian or Asian American people.
10   Even the elite culture shared the popular stereotypes. Chinese American playwright Frank Chin notes that critics of his play *Chickencoop Chinaman* complained in the early 1970's that his characters did not
15   speak, dress, or act like Asians.

63. The author's primary purpose is to

    (A)   pose a question
    (B)   explain the reasons for a disagreement
    (C)   suggest a solution to a persistent problem
    (D)   provide support for an assertion

64. The passage suggests that the complaint about *Chickencoop Chinaman* made by the "critics" mentioned in line 12 can best be described as

    (A)   an observation based on the critics' experience with real people
    (B)   an opinion of the critics that was based on cultural stereotypes
    (C)   an opinion of the critics with which the author of the play agreed
    (D)   a statement of fact for which the author of the passage presents supporting evidence

65. The passage suggests that which of the following was one reason for the existence of race stereotypes about Asian Americans in the mid-twentieth century?

    (A)   Few plays had been written about Asian Americans.
    (B)   Literary works by Asian Americans were rarely published.
    (C)   Most non-Asian Americans learned about Asian Americans through fictional portrayals.
    (D)   An elite culture undermined Asian Americans' efforts to prevent stereotyping.

Part B

2 Constructed-Response Questions
(Suggested time-30 minutes)

General Directions for Questions 66-67: There are two constructed-response questions below. Write your answers to these questions in the space provided on the lined pages following the questions. If a question has more than one part, be sure to answer each part of the question.

Question 66

The following excerpt comes from the opening of Edgar Allan Poe's short story "The Tell-Tale Heart."

> True!—nervous—very, very dreadfully nervous I had been and am; but why *will* you say that I am mad? The disease had sharpened my senses—not destroyed—not dulled them. Above all was the sense of hearing acute. I heard all things in the heaven and in the earth. I heard many things in hell. How, then, am I mad? Hearken! and observe how healthily—how calmly I can tell you the whole story.

Write a brief response to each of the following.

- Identify the point of view in this excerpt.

- Using specific references to the excerpt, describe how the point of view develops the characterization of the protagonist as an unreliable narrator.

- Analyze how this characterization will most likely affect the reader.

Notes
(use this space for note-taking)

Question 67

The following is an excerpt from Martin Luther King Jr.'s "I Have a Dream" speech, delivered in Washington, D.C., on August 28, 1963.

I say to you today, my friends, that in spite of the difficulties and frustrations of the moment, I still have a dream. It is a dream deeply rooted in the American dream.

I have a dream that one day this nation will rise up and live out the true meaning of its creed: "We hold these truths to be self-evident: that all men are created equal."

I have a dream that one day on the red hills of Georgia the sons of former slaves and the sons of former slave owners will be able to sit down together at a table of brotherhood.

I have a dream that one day even the state of Mississippi, a desert state, sweltering with the heat of injustice and oppression, will be transformed into an oasis of freedom and justice.

I have a dream that my four children will one day live in a nation where they will not be judged by the color of their skin but by the content of their character.

I have a dream today....

Describe three techniques King uses in this speech to communicate his message to the audience <u>and</u> analyze the effectiveness in the speech of each of these three techniques.

Notes
(use this space for note-taking)

Begin your response to Question 66 here.

_____

_____

_____

_____

_____

_____

_____

_____

_____

_____

_____

_____

_____

_____

_____

_____

_____

_____

_____

_____

_____

_____

_____

(Question 66 continued)

_____

_____

_____

_____

_____

_____

_____

_____

_____

_____

_____

_____

_____

_____

_____

_____

_____

_____

_____

_____

_____

_____

_____

(Question 66 continued)

_____

_____

_____

_____

_____

_____

_____

_____

_____

_____

_____

_____

_____

_____

_____

_____

_____

_____

_____

_____

(Question 66 continued)

_____

_____

_____

_____

_____

_____

_____

_____

_____

_____

_____

_____

_____

_____

_____

_____

_____

_____

_____

_____

_____

_____

_____

_____

Begin your response to Question 67 here.

(Question 67 continued)

_____

_____

_____

_____

_____

_____

_____

_____

_____

_____

_____

_____

_____

_____

_____

_____

_____

_____

_____

_____

_____

_____

(Question 67 continued)

_____

_____

_____

_____

_____

_____

_____

_____

_____

_____

_____

_____

_____

_____

_____

_____

_____

_____

_____

_____

_____

_____

(Question 67 continued)

_____

_____

_____

_____

_____

_____

_____

_____

_____

_____

_____

_____

_____

_____

_____

_____

_____

_____

_____

_____

_____

_____

_____

_____

Chapter 7

Right Answers and Sample Responses for the *Middle School English Language Arts* Practice Questions

▶   ▶   ▶   ▶   ▶   ▶   ▶   ▶   ▶   ▶   ▶   ▶

The first part of this chapter contains right answers and sample responses to the multiple-choice practice questions for the *Middle School English Language Arts* test. The second part of this chapter contains scored sample responses to the constructed-response practice questions, along with explanations for why the responses received the scores they did.

Part One: Right Answers and Explanations for the Multiple-Choice Questions

Now that you have answered all of the practice questions, you can check your work. Compare your answers with the correct answers in the table below.

Question Number	Correct Answer	Content Category	Question Number	Correct Answer	Content Category
1	D	Major works and authors	33	D	Grammar
2	B	Major works and authors	34	C	Syntax and semantics
3	A	Major works and authors	35	A	Syntax and semantics
4	C	Major works and authors	36	A	Language acquisition and development
5	D	Types of discourse	37	D	Language acquisition and development
6	B	Interpreting and paraphrasing	38	C	Language acquisition and development
7	C	Interpreting and paraphrasing	39	A	Language acquisition and development
8	B	Figurative language	40	C	Writing process
9	B	Interpreting and paraphrasing	41	B	Writing process
10	D	Figurative language	42	A	Writing conventions and mechanics
11	C	Figurative language	43	D	Critical approaches to interpreting text
12	A	Figurative language	44	B	Writing conventions and mechanics
13	A	Forms and structures	45	C	Evaluation and assessment
14	B	Interpreting and paraphrasing	46	A	Evaluation and assessment
15	C	Syntax and semantics	47	C	Writing conventions and mechanics
16	D	Figurative language	48	C	Thesis statements and supporting evidence
17	B	Interpreting and paraphrasing	49	D	Audience and purpose
18	B	Figurative language	50	C	Thesis statements and supporting evidence
19	D	Interpreting and paraphrasing	51	B	Thesis statements and supporting evidence
20	C	Interpreting and paraphrasing	52	A	Types of discourse
21	D	Figurative language	53	D	Types of discourse
22	C	Forms and structures	54	B	Coherence and organization
23	D	Forms and structures	55	A	Audience and purpose
24	A	Forms and structures	56	D	Thesis statements and supporting evidence
25	A	Historical and cultural contexts	57	B	Audience and purpose
26	B	Historical and cultural contexts	58	B	Audience and purpose
27	B	Teaching reading	59	B	Critical reasoning
28	D	Teaching reading	60	A	Audience and purpose
29	A	Grammar	61	D	Coherence and organization
30	C	Grammar	62	D	Critical reasoning
31	B	Grammar	63	D	Audience and purpose
32	C	Grammar	64	B	Critical reasoning
			65	C	Critical reasoning

Explanations of Right Answers

1. This question presents you with an excerpt from a work and asks you to identify the title and author. The excerpt is the first paragraph from Jack London's *The Call of the Wild*. Therefore, the correct answer is (D).

2. This question tests your knowledge of works of literature for middle school students. The question lists three works and asks you to identify the author. The three works were written by Madeleine L'Engle. Therefore, the correct answer is (B).

3. This question asks you to place an author within a particular period of American history. Washington Irving, Nathaniel Hawthorne, and Louisa May Alcott all wrote in the nineteenth century. Only Anne Bradstreet published poetry during the Colonial period in America. Thus, the correct answer is (A).

4. This question tests your ability to recognize a description of a well-known novel, *Watership Down*, by Richard Adams. The best answer is (C).

5. This question tests your ability to use a description of a work to identify its genre. There is no indication in the passage that the book is intended to reveal political secrets or that the characters are based on the author's contemporaries; that the portrayal of environmental degradation in the story is "devastating" suggests that the story is not primarily for children. Therefore, (D), which refers to the phenomenon of air pollution in the mid-twentieth century, is the best answer.

6. This question tests your ability to understand a poet's use of analogy to make a point. In the first line, the author advises the reader to stop regretting his or her actions. The rest of the poem presents situations in nature in which something beautiful exhibits a less beautiful side, just as each person has some faults. Therefore, (B) is the best answer.

7. This question tests your ability to determine what the narrator relates in the passage. The narrator discusses his longstanding desire and ultimate decision to go to sea in spite of his

family's wishes. Therefore, the best answer is (C).

8. This question requires you to interpret the significance of the phrase "the life of misery that was to befall me." This phrase refers to events that will happen in the future as a result of the narrator's decision. Therefore, (B) is the best answer.

9. This question tests your ability to interpret a literary text. The details the passage provides about Helene Wright—her "impressive" nature, her "heavy hair" and "arched" expression, and her triumphs in "social battles"—suggest that she is an intimidating figure. The best answer is (B).

10. This question tests your ability to identify figurative language. A comparison between two things that uses the words "like" or "as" is a simile. Therefore, (D) is the best answer.

11. This question asks you to interpret figurative language. The passage uses the image of horses to describe the storm clouds as they move across the sky; the large clouds are like "powerful haunches" and are trailed by wispy, white clouds that resemble "tail hairs." Therefore, the correct answer is (C).

12. This question tests your ability to identify a metaphor. A metaphor is a figure of speech that makes an implied comparison of two things by directly identifying one with the other. Thus, the best answer is (A).

13. This question asks you to recognize a specific literary form. A quatrain is a stanza of four lines, usually with an AABB, ABAB, or ABCB rhyme pattern. A ballad stanza, option (D), is also four lines, but alternates tetrameter and trimeter lines. Therefore, the best answer is (A).

14. This question tests your ability to interpret a poem. This poem poses a series of questions that suggest that one person's sorrow must elicit another's sympathy. The last two lines reiterate the inability to ignore another person's pain. Therefore, the best answer is (B).

15. This question asks you to recognize syntactical structures. Rhetorical questions are questions that do not require an answer or that have only one possible answer. Because the poet clearly intends the answer to each question he poses to be answered "No," the correct answer is (C).

16. This question asks you to identify the narrative point of view in the passage. Because the narrator speaks of both Ruth and LuLing in the third person (using "she" and "her") and does not use the personal pronoun "I," this passage is narrated from the third-person point of view. The best answer is (D).

17. This question tests your ability to interpret a literary text. Ruth recognizes that her mother's writing is "important" and is "touched" by the way in which her mother shares the pages. The best description of Ruth's attitude, then, is one of tender respect; (B) is the best answer.

18. In the excerpt, the community is described as "sleeping." This is an example of personification, a literary device in which human characteristics are attributed to an animal, object, or idea. Therefore, the correct answer is (B).

19. The last four sentences of the passage are incomplete sentences (sentence fragments) because they lack an independent subject + verb combination. Each fragment is used to describe a feature of life in the community Jonas is leaving. The author of the passage isolates the features in individual sentence fragments in order to emphasize each feature. Therefore, the correct answer is (D).

20. In the passage, the narrator describes the long-standing quarrel of a married couple as a group of "gnarled roots." In developing this metaphor, the narrator indicates that as soon as "tending to the needs of others" was no longer a necessity, the roots of this old, buried quarrel broke through the ground and "split the earth between" the two spouses. In other words, as soon as the couple lost the shared focus of taking care of others, the "tearing," or breaking through of the old quarrel, began. Thus, choice (C) is best.

21. In the passage, the narrator describes the long-standing quarrel of the married couple as having "gnarled roots." This description serves as the main metaphor of the passage and is expressed by the statements that the "stubborn, gnarled roots" "swelled up visible," (A), and "split the earth between them," (B), as well as by the statement that the roots' tearing of the ground "shook even to the children," (C). Unlike these phrases, the statement that the children were "long since grown" is meant simply to express the fact that children had reached adulthood. Thus, (D), the correct answer, is the only choice that does NOT develop the main metaphor of the passage.

22. A ballad stanza has four lines that rhyme in the second and fourth lines. It has four metrical feet in the first and third lines and three in the second and fourth. Therefore, the correct answer is (C).

23. Free verse is poetry based on irregular rhythmic cadence rather than the conventional use of meter. Rhyme may or may not be present in free verse. Therefore, the correct answer is (D).

24. Haiku have three lines and seventeen syllables, distributed 5, 7, and 5. It usually renders a moment or sensation and is often concerned with nature. Therefore, (A) is the correct answer.

25. This question tests your ability to place certain authors in their historical and literary context. The question mentions three literary figures and asks you to identify what school of thought they are identified with. Emerson, Thoreau, and Fuller are all associated with Transcendentalism. Therefore, the correct answer is (A).

26. This question presents a description of a type of poetry associated with a particular literary/historical period. The features mentioned in the description—persistent references to nature, self-revelation, and expression of personal emotion—are all features associated with literature produced in the Romantic period. Therefore, the correct answer is (B).

27. This question tests your knowledge of strategies for building students' vocabulary. The passage does not include either figurative language or euphemisms. The word *peripatetic* does not come from a common Latin or Greek root. It does not have a structural cue, such as a common prefix or suffix, that would help a student determine its meaning. The context around the word ("moved from place to place," "walking with C. S. Lewis or Francis Schaeffer") gives enough clues to help a student figure out that the word must mean "walking about." Therefore, the correct answer is (B).

28. This question asks you to identify a frequently effective way to foster appreciation of reading among middle school students. Choices (A) and (B), historical and biographical in nature, and noninteractive, would probably not stimulate many students to make the transition from reluctant to interested. A change in format, reflected in (C), would be unlikely to change students' attitudes. Students often become interested in reading a book if they can interact with aspects of the setting of the book—in the case of Brontë, the countryside of nineteenth-century England. Therefore, the correct answer is (D).

29. The phrases at the beginning of both sentences are participial phrases: they begin with verbals ending in "ing" and act as adjectives. The phrases should be right next to the nouns they are modifying. However, in these two sentences the participial phrases are misplaced; in both cases, they erroneously appear to be modifying the subjects of the sentences rather than the objects. For example, in the first sentence it is not "he" (the subject) who is "traveling at a speed of 80 miles per hour" but rather the "car" (the object). Therefore, the correct answer is (A).

30. A split infinitive is an infinitive verb form with an element, usually an adverb, interposed between *to* and the verb form. Choices (A) and (B) do not contain infinitives, but rather prepositional phrases—"to the vacation" and "to the store." Choice (D) does not contain an infinitive verb form: in (D), the verb is "to be."

Only choice (C) contains a split infinitive "to kindly stay," where the adverb "kindly" comes between "to" and "stay." Therefore, the correct answer is (C).

31. A clause is a group of related words containing a subject and a verb. An independent clause can stand by itself as a separate sentence. The clauses in sentence II are connected by semi-colons. Each has a subject and a verb and could stand on its own as a complete sentence. Therefore, the correct answer is (B).

32. A subordinate clause depends on the rest of the sentence for its meaning. It does not express a complete thought, so it does not stand alone. It must always be attached to a main clause that completes the meaning. Sentence III opens with a subordinate clause, "As soon as I could recover myself sufficiently." Therefore, (C) is the best answer.

33. An appositive is a noun, noun phrase, or noun clause that follows a noun or pronoun and renames or describes the noun or pronoun. Appositives are often set off by commas. Sentence V contains an appositive, "like the watch and the clock," that provides additional information about the noun "everything." Therefore, the correct answer is (D).

34. A word or phrase is considered ambiguous if it can reasonably be interpreted in more than one way. (A) contains an ambiguity: it is not clear whether the "I" is doing the homework or the radio is doing the homework. In (B), "often" is ambiguous: it's not clear whether students who like to read a lot can improve their grades or whether students who like to read can frequently improve their grades. (D) also contains an ambiguity: the phrase "for sixty cents" could be modifying "You can call your friend" or it could be modifying "the new books you bought." Only (C), the best answer, does not contain an ambiguity.

35. This question tests your knowledge of semantics. Homophones are words that sound the same when pronounced but are spelled differently and have different meanings. Only the words "flower" and "flour" meet this

definition. Therefore, (A) is the correct answer.

36. A clipped word is a shortened form of a longer word. The words listed all fall into that category; that is, "phone" is from telephone and "ad" is from advertisement. Therefore, the correct answer is (A).

37. The passage concerns English words that have been taken from other languages; the languages mentioned are Spanish and Italian. Both of these languages are classified as Romance languages. Therefore, the best answer is (D).

38. The passage describes an argument for the origin of regional variations in word usage in the United States. Euphemism is defined as an inoffensive expression substituted for one that is offensive. Slang is defined as informal language that is not appropriate for formal occasions. Etymology is the study of the linguistic sources or history of a word; however, the passage is concerned not with the linguistic sources of the words *neigh* and *whinny,* but with the reason for their occurrence in different parts of the United States. Dialect is defined as vocabulary that is characteristic of a specific group of people; the passage discusses the use of different words for the same thing by groups who settled in different parts of the United States. Therefore, the correct answer is (C).

39. The process by which a word from one part of speech is changed to another is called "functional shift." In the examples in the second sentence, "fuse" becomes "refuse" by adding the prefix "re" and "govern" becomes "governor" by adding the suffix "or." Prefixes and suffixes are known collectively as affixes. Therefore, the best answer is (A).

40. Mapping is a graphic representation of the ideas in a written composition. Students can create effective maps in many different configurations, such as interlocking triangles, ladders, or concentric circles. Therefore, (C) is the best answer.

41. Persuasive essays attempt to convince the reader/audience to adopt the point of view being espoused in the essay. Since most advertisements are designed to convince readers to buy products and behave in a certain way, the correct answer is (B).

42. This question tests your ability to use your knowledge of writing conventions and mechanics to help students revise and edit their work. The sentence contains an error in verb tense. The verb in the beginning of the sentence, "had intended to work," is in the past tense, but the verb in the second part of the sentence, "realizes," is in the present tense. Correctly revising this sentence would entail making the verb tenses consistent; in other words, "realizes" should be "realized." Therefore, the correct answer is (A).

43. This question asks you to recognize a specific critical approach. Because reader-response theory focuses on the reader's involvement with and reactions to the text, (D) is the best answer.

44. This question tests your knowledge of grammar. The first sentence in Student B's response contains a comma splice and the second is a run-on; therefore, the best answer is (B).

45. This question tests your ability to evaluate student writing. Student C makes specific references to Hester's unhappy marriage, love for her daughter, and loyalty to her daughter's father. Therefore, the best answer is (C).

46. This question tests your ability to assess student writing. Student A describes reactions to the novel but does not specifically discuss whether Hester Prynne was a sympathetic character. Thus, the best answer is (A).

47. Student C uses the most-complex sentence structures, smoothly incorporating several subordinate clauses. Therefore, the best answer is (C).

48. This question asks you to identify the rhetorical function of a sentence. The underlined sentence describes the observation of a specific psychologist, and this observation supports the claim made in the third sentence of the passage, "Indeed, the most important

talent may be the talent for practice itself."
Therefore, the best answer is (C).

49. This question tests your ability to recognize the purpose of a rhetorical passage. The author begins the passage by describing researchers' findings about the best performers and practice. The rest of the passage goes on to support the researchers' conclusions. Thus, (D) is the best answer.

50. This question asks you to identify the main idea of a passage. Although the passage also mentions animals that are no longer seen, the writer's primary concern is the absence of the Arapaho people. The details about the absent animals from the last two sentences serve primarily to underline the absence of the Arapaho people themselves and the corresponding changes in the land where they used to live. Therefore, the best answer is (C).

51. This question asks you to recognize a strategy of rhetorical development. Rather than using statistics or dry facts, the writer presents descriptive observations of the changes that are connected with the disappearing Arapaho people and culture (e.g., "no smoke from hundreds of campfires rises into the air"). Therefore, the best answer is (B).

52. This question tests your ability to identify the form of rhetorical discourse. Because the writer relies on specific and poetic descriptions rather than on facts and figures or heated rhetoric, (A) is the best answer.

53. This question asks you to identify the method of development used in an essay that begins with a given sentence. Since the sentence does not contain two different entities that are compared or attempt to convince the reader of a point of view, it is unlikely to be the topic sentence for an essay that presents a contrast or an argument. The sentence also does not begin to describe an incident or a series of events, so it is unlikely to begin an essay that presents a narration. Basically, the sentence describes the elements of Ondaatje's first book. The rest of the essay is most likely to elaborate on the description begun in the first sentence. Therefore, the best answer is (D).

54. This question tests your ability to interpret a rhetorical strategy. The passage compares "selling elephants from a gum-ball machine" to "Promoting novels in a sound-bite culture." This image suggests that it is as difficult to fit a novel into a sound bite as it is to fit an elephant into a gum-ball machine. Therefore, the correct answer is (B).

55. In the passage, the author describes the experience of promoting novels in a particular cultural context. She then describes her reaction to the experience: discomfort and frustration at having to describe what her book is about in a brief answer. Therefore, the correct answer is (A).

56. According to the passage, contronyms are words that have two opposite meanings. In (D), to *dust* in the first sentence means to spread a substance over something; in the second sentence, to *dust* means to sweep a substance away. Therefore, (D) is the correct answer.

57. This question tests your ability to recognize an author's reason for writing. Although the passage does include detailed instructions, the true purpose of the passage is to define the term "contronym." Therefore, (B) is the correct answer.

58. This question concerns the author's relationship with the reader, specifically the way in which the author gains the reader's attention. The first paragraph of the passage presents a seemingly frivolous set of instructions that is shown in the second paragraph to illustrate the main point of the passage: the existence of contronyms. The best answer is therefore (B).

59. This question tests your ability to interpret information about literary genres. The critics base their discussions of Native American oral literature on written transcriptions, ignoring the performance aspects of the genre. For this reason, according to the last sentence, they evaluate the literature as if text were its only element, and so their work is incomplete—of little value. Therefore, (B) is the best answer.

60. This question tests your ability to recognize the author's purpose in writing. In this passage, the author describes a particular approach to studying Native American literature—using transcriptions of the verbal components of Native American oral performances. The author then goes on to point out flaws with this approach. The best answer, therefore, is (A).

61. This question tests your ability to describe the way in which material is presented. The paragraph begins with descriptions of two kinds of references to contemporary concerns found in Maya Angelou's poem; then the last sentence ties the examples together, identifying them as instances of Angelou's involvement with the modern world. The best answer is therefore (D).

62. Choice (A), "subliterary," and choice (B), "addiction," are used in the passage to describe Edmund Wilson's opinion of the detective novels. Choice (C), "proliferation," is used to indicate a fact about the detective novel: that many such novels have been published in our time. Only choice (D), "highlights," reflects the author's opinion of the literary value of the detective novel. By using the word "highlights," the author indicates disagreement with Wilson and expresses a positive opinion of detective fiction. Therefore, the correct answer is (D).

63. This question asks you to identify the author's reason for writing, which in this case is to support an assertion. The statement made by the author of the passage in the first sentence is elaborated in the next two sentences and supported by an example in the last sentence of the passage. Therefore, the best answer is (D).

64. This question tests your ability to reason critically about the views expressed by the critics mentioned in line 6. The author of the passage points out the critics' statement to support her view about popular stereotypes. Since Chinese American playwright Frank Chin could be expected to have an understanding of what Asians are like, it is clear that the critics are expressing an opinion based on misinformation—in this case, a stereotype. Therefore, (B) is the best answer.

65. This question tests your ability to draw an inference from the text. According to the passage, "more non-Asian Americans probably knew fictional characters like Fu Manchu and Charlie Chan"—fictional Asian characters— than knew actual Asian Americans. It can be inferred that this situation led to the development of popular stereotypes. Therefore, the correct answer is (C).

Part Two: Sample Responses to the Constructed-Response Questions and How They Were Scored

This section presents actual scored sample responses to the constructed-response questions in the practice test in chapter 6 and explanations for the scores the responses received.

As discussed in chapter 4, each constructed-response question on the *Middle School English Language Arts* test is scored on a scale from 0 to 3. The general scoring guide used to score these questions is reprinted here for your convenience.

Praxis *Middle School English Language Arts* General Scoring Guide

Score	Comment
3	The response is successful in the following ways:
	■ It demonstrates an ability to analyze the stimulus material thoughtfully and in depth.
	■ It demonstrates a strong knowledge of the subject matter relevant to the question.
	■ It responds appropriately to all parts of the question.
	■ It demonstrates facility with conventions of standard written English.
2	The response demonstrates some understanding of the topic, but it is limited in one or more of the following major ways:
	■ It may indicate a misreading of the stimulus material or provide superficial analysis.
	■ It may demonstrate only superficial knowledge of the subject matter relevant to the question.
	■ It may respond to one or more parts of the question inadequately or not at all.
	■ It may contain significant writing errors.
1	The response is seriously flawed in one or more of the following ways:
	■ It may demonstrate weak understanding of the subject matter or of the writing task.
	■ It may fail to respond adequately to most parts of the question.
	■ It may be incoherent or severely underdeveloped.
	■ It may contain severe and persistent writing errors.
0	■ Response is blank, off-topic, totally incorrect, or merely rephrases the question

Constructed-Response Question 1—Sample Responses

We will now look at three scored responses to the first constructed-response question and see comments from the scoring leader about why each response received the score it did.

Sample Response 1: Score of 3

Edgar Allen Poe used his effective style of writing to immerse his audience in his horror story "The Tell-Tale Heart." His use of first person narration helped to place the reader in the story.

By using the first person point of view, Poe brings the reader into his story. The narrator appears to be speaking directly to the reader ("but why WILL you say that I am mad?").

However, because of the first person point of view, the protagonist is perceived as being an unreliable narrator. How can we believe a person who claims to hear "all things in heaven and in the earth" and even more bizarre, he claims he heard "many things in hell." Yet, he again asks the reader, "How, then, am I mad?" The narrator has his own take on his situation, which does not agree with what the reader observes. For example, the narrator says he will tell the story "healthily" and "calmly," but he shouts this assertion at the reader. "Hearken! and observe..."

He is both dreadfully nervous and calm. He can hear all things on earth, heaven and many things in hell. The reader sees a delusional, deranged character—not to be trusted or believed but yet one that is fascinating and demands attention. The effect is to keep reading, as the reader is both horrified and fascinated by this bizarre character and his tale. The horror writer, Poe, is successful in drawing in another reader.

Commentary on Sample Response That Earned a Score of 3

The response successfully presents an in-depth analysis of the excerpt; each part of the prompt is answered thoroughly. The response is also well developed in that it links the topics together into a coherent essay. For example, the response identifies the point of view as first person and then explains how Poe uses first-person narration to create a character whose reliability is questioned by the reader. The response then speaks to how the reader is affected by Poe's use of first-person narration. The response is also effective because all assertions are supported by references, either paraphrased or directly quoted, from the excerpt. For example, the response claims that the narrator is unreliable and then supports that claim by asking "How can we believe a person who claims to hear 'all things in heaven and in the earth.'"

Sample Response 2: Score of 2

Poe in "The Tell-Tale Heart" utilizes the first person point of view. This is indicated by the use of the pronoun "I" throughout the text.

The narrator's character is developed by the contradictions between his claim of calmness and sanity and his actions and reported beliefs. He claims to be calm yet appears to be somewhat rattled. He claims to be rational yet also claims to have been able to do the impossible. This calls his sanity and reliability into question.

The reader's reaction will be distanced—that is, the reader will withhold his or her faith in the narrator as one who can be trusted. The reader will continue to question the narrator's sanity throughout the text.

Commentary on Sample Response That Earned a Score of 2

The response demonstrates an understanding of the excerpt and addresses all three parts of the question. The response identifies the point of view as first person and indicates that the narrator's "sanity and reliability" are called "into question." The response also indicates what the reader's response will be to the narrator: "The reader will continue to question the narrator's sanity throughout the text." However, the response is limited because it does not provide examples to support the textual analysis. The response refers to the narrator's "actions and reported beliefs" but does not provide any examples of those beliefs. The response indicates that the narrator claims "to have been able to do the impossible" but does not indicate specifically what that "impossible" is.

Sample Response 3: Score of 1

Edgar Allen Poe's short story "The Tell-Tale Heart" is written from the writer's point of view. The writer is telling how he feels and how circumstances have effected him.

In the sixth line "I heard all things in the heaven and the earth" the writer clearly shows that he is not operating at a truely functional level. This insight should show the reader that the writer is a unreliable narrator of his story. If the reader sees from the very start that the writer is "mad" the writer's whole characterization of himself is untrustworthy. The reader may read what is written and try to make deductions himself; however the reader will always be influenced by the "madness" of the writer.

Commentary on Sample Response That Earned a Score of 1

The response demonstrates a weak understanding of the excerpt, specifically the use of point of view. The author of the story, Edgar Allan Poe, is *not* the narrator. Poe created a character, a delusional protagonist, who is telling the story from his—the narrator's—point of view. Though an attempt is made to address the other two parts of the question (how the narrator is unreliable and how the reader would respond to this), the response provides only one example from the text and does not analyze that example in detail.

Constructed-Response Question 2—Sample Responses

Sample Response 1: Score of 3

As an extremely gifted orator of the Civil Rights Movement, Martin Luther King, Jr. used many techniques to reach his audience effectively. "I Have A Dream" uses several techniques to clearly communicate King's message. The most outstanding and notable technique King uses is repetition. The phrase, "I have a dream" occurs throughout the speech. King begins each new point with this phrase, which serves to rivet the audience's attention and focuses on the importance of King's dream.

Another technique Dr. King uses in his speech is an appeal to patriotism. He says that his dream is "deeply rooted in the American dream." King also evokes patriotic feelings in his audience by urging the nation to live out the creed set in the Declaration of Independence, "that all men are created equal." By using patriotism, King is able to transcend race, class, and religious barriers and to touch the heart of all patriotic Americans.

Dr. King also uses metaphors to enliven his message. He likens Mississippi to a "desert state" that swelters with the heat of injustice and oppression." Yet his dream is that the state will become "an oasis of freedom and justice." This use of metaphor creates a vivid picture of the contrast between the current state of affairs and Dr. King's dream. The natural preference for an oasis over a desert illustrates that the nature of society should be one of freedom and justice.

Commentary on Sample Response That Earned a Score of 3

This response is successful in several ways. All parts of the question are addressed and elaborated upon. Three techniques (repetition, appeal to patriotism, metaphor) are described with examples from the text. Each technique is analyzed in terms of how effectively it communicates a message to an audience. For example, the repetition of the phrase "I have a dream" is described as riveting the audience's attention and placing emphasis on the hopes contained in King's dream. The response successfully describes how King uses an appeal to patriotism to transcend differences and unite people in the country's creed. Finally, metaphor is recognized as a means to illustrate an idea. In this case, oppression is linked to an image of a desert, a barren place; freedom from oppression is linked to an image of an oasis. The metaphor is aptly described as a way to contrast oppression with freedom, dry and barren with lush and blooming. The response fully demonstrates an understanding of rhetorical techniques and also explains through example and explanation how these techniques are used to convey philosophical ideas.

Sample Response 2: Score of 2

Dr. Martin Luther King, Jr. uses three techniques in this speech to communicate his message to the audience. They are repetition, symbolism, and metaphoric language. In this usage of repetition, the phrase "I have a dream" is repeated throughout the entire speech. The effect of this made it clear that Dr. King's dream was evident and important to the entire purpose and his speech. There was also evidence of symbolism used in the speech to give a visual picture of what Dr. King thought to be justice and how he would label the injustice that he viewed in Mississippi. The statement "...sitting down at the table of brotherhood" addresses the metaphoric language that was used to convey Dr. King's point.

All of these techniques combined create the proper elements of an excellent speech with great feeling and emotion. He used these elements to convey his point and to be a catalyst for change.

Commentary on Sample Response That Earned a Score of 2

The response demonstrates an understanding of how King uses techniques to communicate his message to the audience. However, the analysis of the effectiveness of these techniques is superficial. For example, the discussion of symbolism refers to "a visual picture" but does not cite the metaphor of the "desert" state that "swelters" with injustice and oppression. The metaphor of the "table of brotherhood" is quoted but no explanation is offered of how this metaphor is used to convey King's message.

Sample Response 3: Score of 1

Dr. King uses description, comparison and he also gives references. He describes the state of Mississippi. He tells of the injustice and oppression and how he would like for it to be transformed to an oasis of freedom and justice. He used heat, desert state (as hot), and sweltering to describe this state.

He uses comparison in what he dreams for his children. He wants them to not be judged because of the color of their skin but by their character. Who they are.

His references are the slaves, former slaves and slave owners. He goes back to the ones that got it started and wants them all to be joined together as a brotherhood, as one.

Commentary on Sample Response That Earned a Score of 1

The response is flawed in several ways. First, the response demonstrates a weak understanding of the "techniques" used to communicate the message. Though three techniques are mentioned (description, comparison, references), the explanation and examples do not demonstrate an understanding of these techniques. For example, King describes Mississippi *metaphorically* as a desert, "sweltering with the heat of injustice and oppression." The impression in this response is that Mississippi is a desert and literally is hot. The example used in the discussion on comparison ("He wants them to not be judged because of the color of their skin but by their character") could be effective in showing how a comparison can emphasize an author's intent, but the analysis is underdeveloped. Overall, the response does not elaborate on how techniques in the writing style work to support King's message. Lines from the passage and the prompt are merely rephrased with little to no elaboration that demonstrates an understanding of how rhetoric and composition support the meaning of the work.

Chapter 8
Preparing for the *Middle School Mathematics* Test

▶   ▶   ▶   ▶   ▶   ▶   ▶   ▶   ▶   ▶   ▶   ▶

The *Middle School Mathematics* test is designed to measure the subject-area knowledge and competencies necessary for a beginning teacher of mathematics in a middle school. The test contains both multiple-choice and constructed-response questions.

The first part of this chapter focuses on the multiple-choice section of the test. The second part of the chapter contains information about the constructed-response section of the test.

Part One: Multiple-Choice Questions

This section of the chapter is intended to help you organize your preparation for the multiple-choice portion of the test and to give you a clear indication about the depth and breadth of the knowledge required for success on the multiple-choice questions.

The *Mathematics* test contains 45 multiple-choice questions that constitute approximately 75% of the examinee's total test score. It is expected that about 90 minutes will be spent on the multiple-choice questions.

Using the topic lists that follow

You are not expected to be an expert on all aspects of the topics that follow. You should, though, understand the major concepts of each topic. Virtually all accredited undergraduate mathematics programs address the majority of these topics.

You are likely to find that the topics below are covered by textbooks and related resources for courses on algebra, geometry, probability and statistics, precalculus and discrete mathematics. A single survey textbook will not cover all of the subtopics. Consult materials and resources, including lecture notes, from all your mathematics and mathematics methods coursework. You may also find it useful to review some current middle school and high school mathematics textbooks.

Try not to be overwhelmed by the volume and scope of content knowledge in this guide. An overview such as this that lists mathematics topics does not offer you a great deal of context. Many of the items

on the actual Praxis test will provide you with a context to apply these topics or terms, as you will see when you look at the practice questions in Chapter 9.

You will be allowed to use a four-function, scientific or graphing calculator during the examination; however, calculators with QWERTY keyboards will not be allowed.

Special questions marked with stars

Interspersed throughout the list of topics are statements and questions that are outlined in boxes and preceded by a star (★). These statements and questions are intended to help you review and test your knowledge of fundamental concepts and your ability to apply fundamental concepts to situations in the classroom or the real world. Most of the statements require you to think about several pieces of knowledge in order to formulate an integrated understanding and response. If you spend time thinking about the knowledge, skills, and abilities described and about how to answer the questions presented in these boxes, you will gain increased understanding and facility with the subject matter covered on the test. You might want to discuss these topics and your answers to the questions with a teacher or mentor.

Note that the statements and questions presented in the boxes are not short-answer or multiple-choice questions, and this study guide does not provide the answers. The statements and questions are intended as study topics or questions, not practice questions. Thinking about the answers to them should improve your understanding of fundamental concepts and will probably help you answer a broad range of questions on the test. For example, the following box with stars appears in the list of study topics under "Demonstrate an understanding of concepts associated with counting numbers":

★ Be able to apply the concepts of prime or composite numbers, even or odd numbers, factors, multiples, and divisibility

★ Can you describe, for each of these concepts, a real-word context in which you would use this concept?

If you think about the first starred statement and perhaps jot down some notes on how to represent and apply the concepts of prime or composite numbers, even or odd numbers, factors, multiples, and divisibility, you will review your knowledge of the subject and you will probably be ready to answer multiple-choice questions similar to the one below:

> If there are exactly 5 times as many children as adults at a show, which of the following CANNOT be the total number of people at the show?
>
> $5x + x = 6x$
>
> (A) 102
> (B) 80
> (C) 36
> (D) 30

(The correct answer is B. This question requires you to translate a verbal description of a situation into an algebraic representation, then apply your knowledge of factors, multiples, and divisibility. If a represents the number of adults at the show, then $5a$ represents the number of children at the show and $6a$ represents the total number of people at the show. Since $6a$ represents a whole number that is a multiple of 6, the total number of people at the show must be divisible by 6. Of the choices given, only 80 is not divisible by 6, so there cannot be 80 people at the show.)

Study Topics

Arithmetic and Basic Algebra

  ▶ Perform the operations of addition, subtraction, multiplication, and division
  ▶ Apply correctly the order of operations in problem solving

---

★ Be able to correctly solve problems involving some or all basic operations

★ For example, do you know that
  $1 + (4 \times 6) - 8 = 17$?
  $1 + 24 - 8 = 25 - 8 = 17$

★ Can you describe common mistakes students make in applying the rules of algebraic order of operations?

★ Do you know what order of operations your calculator uses?

★ Do you know what assumptions about the order of operations are included in the spreadsheet application you use?

  ▶ Identify the basic properties of the operations of the real number system

---

★ Be able to identify examples of appropriate uses of the closure, commutativity, associativity, and distributivity properties of the operations of the real number system

★ Be able to identify and determine the additive and multiplicative inverses of a number

★ Can you give examples of when you might use additive or multiplicative inverses?

  ▶ Determine whether the closure, commutative, associative, and distributive properties are true for a newly defined operation
  ▶ Use numbers in a way that is most appropriate in the context of a problem
  ▶ Recognize equivalent forms of real numbers

★ Be able to recognize and use multiple representations of fractions, decimals, percents, and integers

★ Can you give examples of when different representations would be useful in developing deeper understanding of mathematical concepts?

  ▶ Classify a number as rational, irrational, real, and/or complex

---

★ Be able to classify such numbers as:
  $\sqrt{2}$, $\sqrt{4}$, $4i$, 5, $9 + 8i$

★ Can you explain the difference between a rational and an irrational number?

▶ Estimate values of expressions involving decimals, exponents, and radicals

▶ Find powers and roots

★ Be able to simplify expressions of the form $(3^2)(3^4)$, $\dfrac{x^3}{x^5}$, $\dfrac{\sqrt{8}}{2}$

★ Can you describe real-life scenarios that are best modeled using expressions containing powers and roots?

▶ Demonstrate an understanding of concepts associated with counting numbers

---

★ Be able to apply the concepts of prime or composite numbers, even or odd numbers, factors, multiples, and divisibility

★ Can you describe, for each of these concepts, a real-word context in which you would use this concept?

▶ Interpret and apply the concepts of ratio, proportion, and percent as appropriate

---

★ Be able to use ratios, proportions, and percents, as appropriate, to solve real-word problems

★ Can you describe the difference between a ratio and a proportion?

★ Can you describe several real-world applications of proportional reasoning?

★ Can you recognize different representations of fractional percents (less than 1 percent)? Of percents greater than 100 percent?

★ Can you describe the common difficulties middle school students have in learning to calculate and use percents less than 1 percent and percents greater than 100 percent?

★ Can you calculate percent change and percent of percents?

★ Can you describe at least one common mistake middle school students often make when calculating percent change?

▶ Use estimation to test the reasonableness of results

▶ Demonstrate the ability to use algebraic expressions, formulas, and equations appropriately

---

★ Can you translate verbal expressions and relationships into algebraic expressions or equations?

▶ Add, subtract, multiply, and divide polynomials and algebraic fractions

---

★ Can you demonstrate the similarities between arithmetic operations with real numbers and the corresponding operations with algebraic (symbolic) representations?

★ Are you fluent with the basic operations of addition, subtraction, multiplication, and division of algebraic expressions?

★ Can you explain how the "FOIL" method of multiplying two binomials is an example of the distributive property of multiplication over addition?

★ Are you able to add, subtract, multiply, and divide polynomials?

★ Can you add, subtract, multiply, and divide algebraic fractions such as

$$\frac{6-x}{5x-30} \ \text{ or } \ \frac{c^2+5c}{c^2+12c+35} \, ?$$

★ Can you simplify $\dfrac{2b-3ab}{9a^2-4}$?

▶ Perform standard algebraic operations with complex numbers, radicals, and exponents, including fractional and negative exponents

---

★ Can you give other representations of $x^{\frac{2}{3}}$, $x^{\frac{5}{2}}$, and x^{-2} ?

★ Do you recall that $\left(x^3\right)^{-1} = (x)^{-3} = \dfrac{1}{x^3}$?

- ▶ Algebraically solve linear equations and inequalities in one or two variables
- ▶ Graph linear equations and inequalities in one or two variables

---

★ Can you graph the solution to an equation or inequality in one variable on a number line?

★ Can you describe what the graph of the solution of an inequality in two variables (in the *xy*-plane) looks like?

- ▶ Algebraically and graphically solve systems of linear equations in two variables.

★ Can you describe, in words, what it means to be the algebraic solution of a system of linear equations?

★ Can you describe, in words, what it means to be the graphical solution of a system of linear equations?

- ▶ Solve and graph nonlinear (quadratic) equations
- ▶ Solve equations and inequalities involving absolute values

---

★ Can you solve equations such as $|2x + 4| = 12$ and $|2x - 5| = 3x + 4$?

★ Can you solve inequalities such as $-3|x + 4| > 15$?

Geometry and Measurement

- ▶ Solve problems that involve measurement in both the metric and traditional systems

---

★ Be able to solve measurement problems in context by using estimation

★ Use provided conversion factors and/or provided formulas to solve measurement problems

---

★ Be able to convert centimeters to meters, inches to feet, and hours to seconds

---

- ▶ Compute perimeter and area of triangles, quadrilaterals, circles, and regions that are combinations of these figures

---

★ Be able to compute and apply basic formulas for deriving perimeter and area for various figures including finding the area of a square when its perimeter is given

★ Can you describe some real-life applications that involve finding perimeters or areas?

- ▶ Compute the surface area and volume of right prisms, cones, cylinders, spheres, and solids that are combinations of these figures
- ▶ Apply the Pythagorean Theorem to solve problems

★ Be able to find a missing length of a side of a right triangle given the lengths of the other two sides

---

- ▶ Solve problems involving special triangles

★ Be able to find missing lengths of sides or missing angles of equilateral and isosceles triangles

---

- ▶ Estimate actual and relative error in the numerical answer to a problem by analyzing the effects of round off and truncation errors introduced in the course of solving a problem
- ▶ Use relationships such as congruency and similarity to solve problems involving two-dimensional and three-dimensional figures

★ Do you recall that corresponding sides of similar figures are proportional?

> ▶ Solve problems involving parallel and perpendicular lines
> ▶ Solve problems using the relationships among the parts of triangles

★ Do you recall the triangle inequality property that describes the relationship among the sides of a triangle?

★ Can you describe classes of triangles that are determined by the angles, such as right, obtuse, and acute triangles?

★ Can you describe classes of triangles that are determined by the sides, such as scalene, isosceles, and equilateral?

★ Do you know how to define the medians and the altitudes of a triangle?

> ▶ Solve problems using properties of special quadrilaterals and describe relationships among sets of special quadrilaterals

★ Be able to identify the essential characteristics of the square, rectangle, parallelogram, rhombus, and trapezoid and recognize distinctions among these quadrilaterals

> ▶ Solve problems involving angles, diagonals, and vertices of polygons with more than four sides
> ▶ Solve problems that involve using the properties of circles

★ Be able to apply properties of circles including those involving inscribed angles, central angles, chords, radii, tangents, secants, arcs, and sectors

★ Can you identify radii, tangents, secants, arcs, and sectors of a circle?

★ Can you define inscribed and central angles of a circle? Do you recall the relationships between the measures of these angles and of their intercepted arcs?

> ▶ Solve problems involving reflections, rotations, and translations of points, lines, or polygons in the plane
> ▶ Execute geometric constructions using straight-edge and compass; prove that a given geometric construction yields the desired result

★ Can you describe how to bisect an angle or construct a perpendicular?

> ▶ Estimate the area of a region in the xy-plane
> ▶ Demonstrate an intuitive understanding of a limit
> ▶ Demonstrate an intuitive understanding of maximum and minimum

★ Can you identify the maximum or minimum of the graph of a parabola?

★ Can you think of a real-life situation that has a maximum or minimum that could be modeled by a quadratic equation?

Coordinate Geometry, Functions and Their Graphs

> ▶ Understand the algebraic definition of a function and be able to use function notation for functions of one variable

★ Can you give an algebraic definition of a function?

★ Can you decide if a given set of conditions determines a function?

★ Can you explain why
$(1, 2)$, $(2, 0)$, $(-1, -2)$, $(1, 3)$ is not a function,
but $(1, -1)$, $(2, -2)$, $(3, 5)$, $(4, 10)$, $(5, 12)$
is a function?

★ Be able to find the domain (*x*-values) and
range (*y*-values) of a function without
necessarily knowing the definitions

▶ Identify the graph of a function in the
plane

★ Be able to identify the graph of a function by
performing the vertical line test

★ Can you explain why $y = x^2$ is the graph of
a function of *x*, while $x = y^2$ is not the graph
of a function of *x* ?

▶ Demonstrate an understanding of the
relationship between an equation and its
graph for various kinds of functions

★ If given the graph of a line, a parabola, a step
function, an absolute value function, or an
exponential function, be able to select the
equation that best represents the graph

★ If given a linear, quadratic, or exponential
equation, be able to describe some important
characteristics of the graph of the equation

▶ Determine the graphical properties and
sketch a graph of a linear, step, absolute
value, or quadratic function

★ If given a linear equation, can you identify
the slope and the intercepts of the graph of
the line?

★ If given a quadratic equation of the form
$y = ax^2 + bx + c$, can you describe the
shape of the graph of the equation? Can you
explain what characteristic of the graph is
determined by whether the coefficient *a* is
positive or negative?

★ Can you describe the shape of the graph of a
step function?

★ Can you describe and sketch the graph of the
function $y = |x|$?

★ Can you identify the intervals of increase and
decrease of a function?

★ Can you identify the axis of symmetry of the
graph of a quadratic function?

★ Can you identify the roots of a quadratic
equation from its graph?

▶ Demonstrate an understanding of how
to develop a model (such as a chart,
graph, equation, or table) based on a
physical situation or a verbal description
of a physical situation

★ Can you describe a physical situation that is
best modeled by a chart or table? By a linear
equation? By a quadratic equation? By an
exponential equation?

★ Can you give a real-life context in which the
graph of a step function would be helpful?

▶ Determine whether a particular
mathematical model can be used to
describe two seemingly different
situations

▶ Determine whether a particular equation
can represent the relationship between
the variables in two different word
problems

★ Can you explain how certain distance-rate-
time problems are similar to some simple-
interest problems?

▶ Determine the equations of lines, given
sufficient information

★ Can you determine the equation of a line,
given any two points on the line?

★ Can you determine the equation of a line, given the slope of the line and one point on the line?

★ Can you determine the equation of a line if you are given the *x*- and *y*- intercepts?

★ Can you explain the concept of slope using tables, graphs, and linear equations?

▶ Solve problems that can be represented on the *xy*-plane

★ Be able to find the distance between any two points

★ Be able to find the coordinates of the midpoint of a line segment

▶ Translate verbal expressions and relationships into algebraic expressions or equations

▶ Provide and interpret geometric representations of numeric and algebraic concepts

★ Given one representation (algebraic, numeric, geometric, or verbal) of a contextualized situation, be able to provide other representations or models of the situation

▶ Solve problems that involve quadratic equations using a variety of methods

★ Can you identify quadratic equations that can be solved by factoring?

★ Can you use the quadratic formula to solve quadratic equations?

★ Can you graphically solve quadratic equations?

★ Can you use a calculator to solve quadratic equations?

Data, Probability, and Statistical Concepts

▶ Organize data into a presentation that is appropriate for solving a problem

★ Be able to understand and present data in various forms including tables, charts, histograms, line graphs, bar charts, double bar charts, double line graphs, circle graphs, scatterplots, stem-and-leaf plots, line plots, and box plots

★ Be able to decide which form of representation is appropriate for different purposes and explain why it is appropriate

▶ Read and analyze data presented in various forms

★ Be able to use data presented in various forms to draw conclusions from data, to make predictions, and to calculate statistical characteristics such as mean, mode, median, and range

▶ Solve problems involving average

★ Be able to find and interpret common measures of central tendency including arithmetic mean, weighted mean, sample mean, median, and mode

★ Be able to know which measure of central tendency is most meaningful to use in a given situation

▶ Solve problems involving measures of dispersion

★ Be able to find and interpret common measures of dispersion such as range, spread of data, and outliers

▶ Solve probability problems involving finite sample spaces

★ Be able to solve problems by actually counting individual outcomes or by using counting techniques

★ Be able to solve problems involving independent and dependent trials

★ Be able to solve problems involving geometric probability

▶ Work with a probability distribution at an intuitive level

★ Can you identify all possible outcomes from tossing a pair of numbered cubes?

Discrete Mathematics and Computer Science

▶ Use and interpret statements containing logical connectives and quantifiers

★ Be able to use logical connectives such as "and," "or," "if — then," correctly and appropriately

★ Can you use logical quantifiers, such as "all," "some," and "none" correctly?

★ Do you understand the meaning, in the context of logic, of negation, converse, inverse, and contrapositive?

▶ Solve problems involving the union and intersection of sets, subsets, and disjoint sets (limiting the number of sets to 3)

★ Can you create a Venn diagram given a description of the union and intersection of sets?

★ Can you describe some real-life problems that could be readily solved using sets and/or Venn diagrams?

▶ Use basic counting methods to solve problems involving permutations and combinations (without necessarily knowing the formulas)

★ Can you describe two problems that can be solved using counting methods: one in which order is important (permutations) and one in which it is not (combinations)?

★ Can you generate the first few rows of Pascal's triangle?

★ Can you describe how Pascal's triangle is used in the context of counting problems?

▶ Base representation of integers other than 10

★ Be able to convert numbers between base 10 and base 2

★ Can you add numbers expressed using base 2?

★ Can you convert numbers from base 10 to base 16?

★ Can you describe common uses of numbers expressed in base 2 and base 16?

▶ Solve problems that involve simple sequences or number patterns

▶ Find rules for number patterns

★ Be able to recognize and represent triangular or other geometric numbers

▶ Use and interpret simple matrices as a tool for displaying data

▶ Draw conclusions from information contained in simple diagrams, flowcharts, paths, circuits, networks, or algorithms

▶ Demonstrate knowledge and appropriate use of calculator

★ Can you describe an example of how to use a calculator as a tool to explore patterns? To make conjectures? To make predictions? To make generalizations?

▶ Demonstrate understanding of basic computer technology

★ Be able to use spreadsheets as a tool to solve problems

Part Two: Constructed-Response Questions

This section of the chapter is intended to provide you with strategies for reading, analyzing, and understanding the constructed-response questions on the *Middle School Mathematics* test and for writing successful responses.

The test contains 3 equally weighted constructed-response questions that constitute approximately 25% of the examinee's total test score and emphasize the use of critical thinking skills. It is expected that about 10 minutes will be spent on each constructed-response question for an approximate total of 30 minutes of the two-hour test.

The three constructed-response questions typically assess an examinee's ability to use appropriate mathematical language and representations of mathematical concepts, connect mathematical concepts to one another and to real-world situations, and integrate mathematical concepts to solve problems. Each of the three major categories (I. Arithmetic and Basic Algebra; II. Geometry and Measurement, Coordinate Geometry, Functions and Graphs; and III. Data, Probability, Statistical Concepts, Discrete Mathematics, and Computer Science) is the primary focus of one of the three constructed-response questions, but the examinee may also be expected to integrate knowledge from the different areas when responding to the questions.

What to Study

Success on this portion of the test is not simply a matter of learning more about the structure of constructed-response questions. Cogent organization is important, but success on the constructed-response questions also requires real knowledge of the field. These questions evaluate your ability to integrate and to convey an understanding of some of the significant concepts in mathematics.

In addition to the Study Topics suggested for preparing for the multiple-choice questions, review of the following topics might help prepare you for the constructed-response questions.

► Recognize errors in student work and the underlying misconceptions; suggest ways to help a student develop correct concepts.

► Identify the prerequisite knowledge and skills students might need to possess in order to correctly learn a particular topic.

► Develop questions that might be asked orally that will best assess a student's conceptual understanding of a particular topic.

► Given a particular problem, identify several problem-solving strategies that can be used to explore or solve the problem with students (for example, guess and check, reduce to a simpler problem, draw a diagram, work backwards).

► Use representations of mathematical concepts (for example, analogies, drawings, examples, symbols, manipulatives) that have the potential to help students understand and learn mathematical concepts.

► Use a variety of teaching strategies (for example, laboratory work, supervised practice, group work, lecture) appropriate for a particular topic or unit and also for a particular group of students.

► Integrate concepts to show relationships among topics.

► Relate mathematical concepts and ideas to real-world situations.

► Identify, evaluate, and use curricular materials and resources for mathematics instructions in ways appropriate for a particular group of students and a particular topic; know when to use technology, particularly calculators.

► Identify, evaluate, and use appropriate evaluation strategies (for example, observations, interviews, questioning, oral discussions, written tests, portfolios) to assess student progress in mathematics; write questions that test specific mathematical skills; develop a set of questions that can be used to probe for both procedural and conceptual understanding.

► Determine appropriate strategies to solve a given problem. Strategies might include conjectures, counterexamples, inductive reasoning, deductive reasoning, proof by contradiction, direct proof, and other types of proof, using tools (i.e., mental math, pencil and paper, calculator, computer, models, trees and graphs).

► Demonstrate with examples when each of the strategies listed above would be appropriate to use.

► After solving a problem, reflect on the strategies used; consider if there are other appropriate strategies; if there are more appropriate strategies; if the strategies employed can be used to solve other types of problems; if the strategies can be used to solve a more general class of problems.

► Communicate the results of reasoning in an appropriate form (for example, the written word, tables, charts, graphs); explain the processes used in solving a problem.

The following books and Web sites are particularly relevant to the types of topics and skills covered by the test. *Note:* The test is not based on these resources, nor do they necessarily cover every topic that may be included in the test. Instead, these works are intended to help you revisit topics you have already covered in your education and mathematics courses.

■ National Council of Teachers of Mathematics (NCTM) Web site: www.nctm.org

■ National Council of Teachers of Mathematics. 2000. *Principles and Standards for School Mathematics*. Reston, VA: National Council of Teachers of Mathematics, Inc.

■ *Traditional high school mathematics texts.* Most textbooks contain difficult problems along with the more straightforward problems to be practiced. The difficult problems are often labeled "extension" or "C" problems and appear at the end of each section.

■ *Reform-oriented high school mathematics texts.* Several recent curriculum projects have developed texts to embody the mathematical content and processes described by the *Principles and Standards for School Mathematics* from the National Council of Teachers of Mathematics (NCTM). The problems in these texts are often more exploratory than those in traditional texts and are intended to be approached via multiple methods, such as with graphs, tables, and algebraic symbols.

■ *Mathematics contest problem books.* Mathematics contests are excellent sources of challenging problems. In particular, the *Contest Problem Book* series includes problems and solutions from the American High School Mathematics Examinations and the American Invitational Mathematics Examinations. These books are available from the Mathematical Association of America at http://www.maa.org/.

What the Test Scorers Are Looking For

Even if you feel confident about your knowledge of the content to be tested, you still may wonder how you will be able to tell what the test scorers want.

In fact, you can find out what the test scorers want by looking at the questions themselves. The constructed-response test questions are crafted to be as clear as possible regarding what tasks you are expected to do. No expectations are hidden in the question or expressed in code words. The mathematics educators who score your responses base your score on two considerations:

- Whether you do the tasks that the question asks for

- How well you do those tasks

So, to answer more specifically the question "What do the scorers want?" we should look at test questions, much like the ones on the test.

Understanding What the Questions Are Asking

It is impossible to write a successful response to a question unless you thoroughly understand the question. Often test takers jump into their written response without taking enough time to analyze exactly what the question is asking, how many different parts of the question need to be addressed, and how <u>the information in the accompanying charts, tables, or graphs needs to be addressed.</u> The time you invest in making sure you understand what the question is asking will very likely pay off in a better performance, as long as you budget your time and do not spend a large proportion of the available time just reading the question.

Examine the overall question closely and then identify what specific questions are being asked, mentally organize your response, identifying the calculations that need to be performed and the explanations that need to be written. If you think out your response beforehand, it will be stronger.

Sample Question

A. On the *xy*-plane, graph the circle $x^2 + y^2 = 25$ with center at (0, 0).   *(0,5) (0,-5)*
   (5,0) (-5,0)

B. Indicate on the circle you have graphed approximately where the points are that have a *y*-coordinate that is twice their *x*-coordinate. Explain your reasoning, perhaps by demonstrating geometrically why these points would, in fact, satisfy the condition.

C. Find the coordinates of the points you have indicated in B. Explain your process and reasoning.

Identifying the Key Components of the Question

- Graph a circle centered at the origin.

- Identify where on the circle points of the form (*x, 2x*) would be located.

- Explain why these points are of the desired form.

- Find the coordinates of these points.

- Explain how to find the coordinates.

Organizing Your Response

Successful responses start with successful planning, either in the form of an outline or another form of notes. By planning your response you greatly decrease the chances that you will forget to answer any part of the question. You also increase the chances of creating a well-organized response, which is something the scorers look for. Your note-taking space also gives you a place to jot down thoughts whenever you think of them—for example, when you have an idea about one part of the question when you are writing your response to another part. Planning your response is time well invested, although you must keep your eye on the clock so that you have sufficient time to write your response.

To illustrate a possible strategy for planning a response, let us focus again on the sample question introduced above. We analyzed the question and found that it necessitated a three-part response in which two of the parts also require explanations. You might begin by jotting down those parts on your notes page, leaving space under each. This will ensure that you address each part when you begin writing. In addition, you should underline key words in the question that could help focus your response appropriately.

Sample Notes—Main Parts to Be Answered

Here you start by identifying each part of the question:

A. Graph a circle centered at the origin.

B. Identify where on the circle points of the form $(x, 2x)$ would be located.
Explain why these points are of the desired form.

C. Find the coordinates of these points.
Explain how to find the coordinates.

You then might quickly fill out the main ideas you want to address in each part, like this:

Sample Notes—Ideas Under Each Main Part

A. Graph a circle centered at the origin

— Draw an xy-coordinate grid

— Find the radius of the circle

B. Identify where on the circle points of the form $(x, 2x)$ would be located
Explain why these points are of the desired form

— Points would be at the intersection of the line y = 2x and the circle

— Because all points on that line have coordinates (x, 2x)

C. Find the coordinates of these points
   Explain how to find the coordinates

— Solve $x^2 + (2x)^2 = 25$

— This will give points that satisfy both equation of line and are on the circle

To earn the highest number of points from the scorers, you will need to do all of the following:

• Answer all parts of the question.

• Give reasons for your answers.

• Demonstrate subject-specific knowledge in your answer.

Writing Your Response

Now the important step of writing your response begins. The scorers will not consider your notes when they score your paper, so it is crucial that you integrate all the important ideas from your notes into your actual written response.

Sample Response that Received a Score of 2

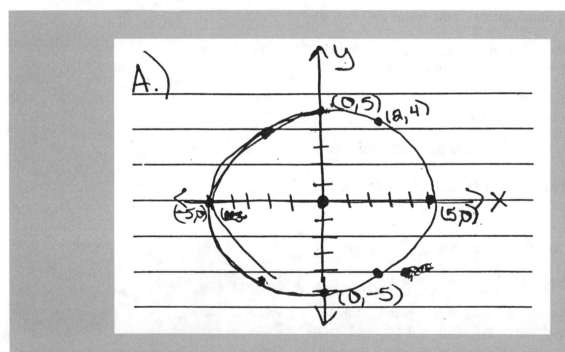

Center (0, 0)   Radius 5

B. I basically looked at points on the circle that would satisfy the condition
   $y = 2x$.

C. $(2,4),(2,-4),(-2,-4),(-2,4)$ The technique I used was find a y-coordinate on the circle and then find an x-coordinate that was half of the y-coordinate. The above coordinates fit the condition, however some coordinates have different signs. The coordinates are all equal distance from the center.

By using algebra,

$$x^2 + (2x)^2 = 25, \ 5x^2 = 25, \ x^2 = 5, \ x = \pm\sqrt{5}, \ y = \pm 2\sqrt{5}.$$

Commentary on Sample Response that Earned a Score of 2

This response received a score of 2 because it demonstrates sufficient, but not strong, knowledge of the subject matter. The graph in Part A is acceptable. It is centered at the origin and has a radius of 5. The axes are labeled and the scales are shown on both axes. The coordinates of the points at which the circle intersects the axes are all shown correctly. (The scorers understand that graphs are drawn "freehand.") The response to Part B contains evidence of some correct thinking. There are 4 points indicated on the graph instead of 2. (In Part C, the response includes an acknowledgement that in some cases the signs of the x- and y-coordinates were different, but did not indicate that they were therefore incorrect.) The points are of the form $(x, 2x)$, but would not lie on the circle. The points $(2, 4)$ and $(-2, -4)$ are close to where the actual points of the form $(x, 2x)$ would be on the circle. Part C includes a correct algebraic solution of the actual x- and y-coordinates of the points on the circle, but does not reconcile why they are different from the coordinates given at the beginning of the Part C response.

Sample Response that Received a Score of 1

A. Center (0, 0)

radius = 5

$$x^2 + y^2 = 25$$

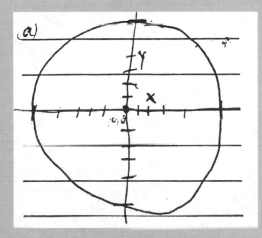

B. If y = 4, then x = 2.

$$x + y = 5$$

Commentary on Sample Response that Earned a Score of 1

This response received a score of 1 because it responds appropriately to part of the question (Part A) and demonstrates a weak knowledge of the subject matter relevant to the question. The graph in Part A is acceptable but not strong. It does show a circle centered at the origin with the radius of 5 correctly identified. The axes are labeled and the scales shown. (If it had been necessary to be able to read points from the graph, the lack of accuracy with which the scales were drawn might have introduced significant error into the result.) Part B identifies a point of the form $(x, 2x)$ but it is not a point that lies on the circle. An incorrect equation is also given. (No penalty is assigned for incorrect or irrelevant information such as this.) No attempt is made to answer Part C of the question.

In Conclusion

Whatever format you select, the important thing is that your answer be thorough, complete, and detailed. You need to be certain that you do the following:

- Answer all parts of the question.

- Give reasons for your answers.

- Demonstrate subject-specific knowledge in your answer.

It is a good idea to use the practice test in the next chapter to help you develop a plan for how you will take the test on the actual testing day, especially if you tend to get nervous or freeze up in a testing situation. Some test takers prefer to start with the question where they feel most comfortable. Remember to consider your time so that you may give appropriate consideration to all three questions. The important thing is that your answers be thorough, complete, and detailed.

Chapter 9

Practice Questions for the *Middle School Mathematics* Test

▶ ▶ ▶ ▶ ▶ ▶ ▶ ▶ ▶ ▶ ▶ ▶

Now that you have studied the content topics and have worked through strategies relating to multiple-choice and constructed-response questions, you should take the following practice test. You will probably find it helpful to simulate actual testing conditions, giving yourself a set amount of time to work on the questions. If you wish, you can cut out and use the answer sheet provided to answer the multiple-choice questions and write your responses to the constructed- response questions on the gridded answer pages.

Keep in mind that the test you take at an actual administration will have different questions, although the proportion of questions in each area and major subarea will be approximately the same. You should not expect the percentage of questions you answer correctly in these practice questions to be exactly the same as when you take the test at an actual administration, since numerous factors affect a person's performance in any given testing situation.

When you have finished the practice questions, you can score your answers to the multiple-choice questions, see sample scored responses to the constructed-response questions, and read explanations of the answers and responses in Chapter 10.

Note: If you are taking these practice questions to help you prepare for the *Middle School: Content Knowledge* test, you should keep in mind that the test you take at the actual administration will have 120 multiple-choice questions, with 30 questions in each of the four content areas. You will be allowed 120 minutes to complete the test. The test does not contain any constructed-response questions.

THE PRAXIS SERIES

Professional Assessments for Beginning Teachers ®

TEST NAME:

Middle School Mathematics

32 Practice Questions

Approximate time for the whole practice test—80 minutes

Suggested time for Part A (multiple choice)—60 minutes

Suggested time for Part B (constructed response)—20 minutes

(**Note:** At the official administration of this test, there will be 45 multiple-choice questions and 3 constructed-response questions. You will be allowed 120 minutes total to complete the test. The sections of the test will not be timed separately, though it is recommended that you spend 90 minutes on the multiple-choice questions and 30 minutes on the constructed-response questions.)

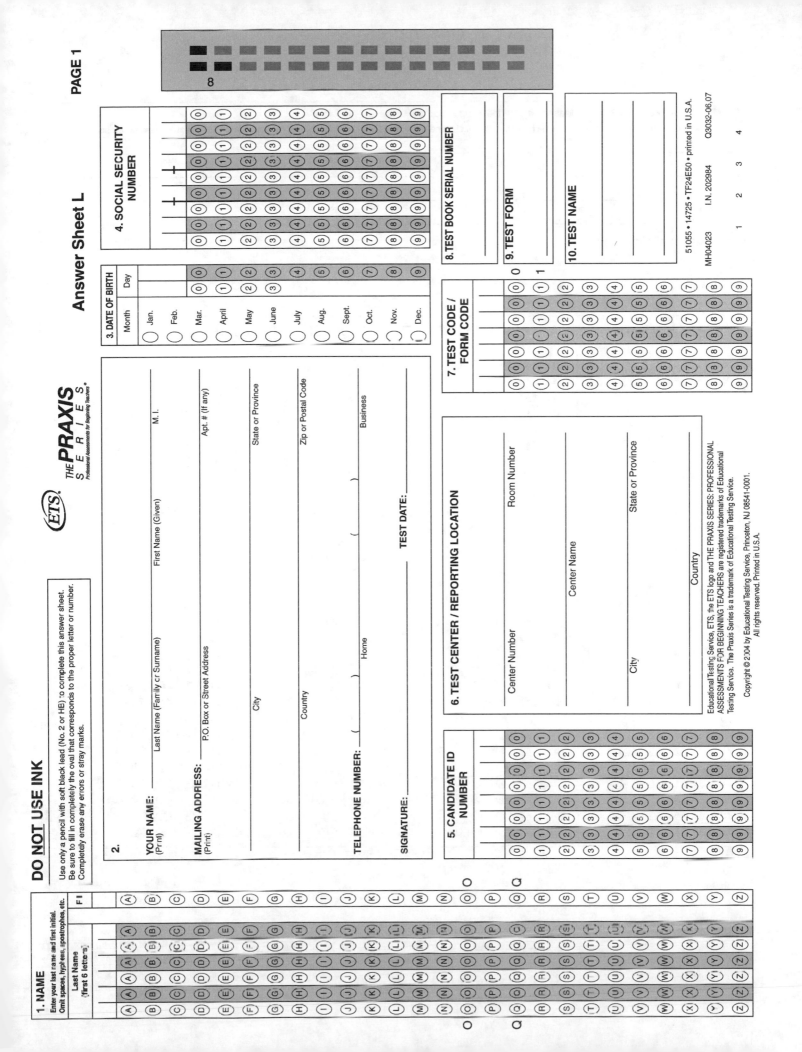

Answer Sheet L

PAGE 1

THE **PRAXIS** SERIES®
Professional Assessments for Beginning Teachers®

DO NOT USE INK

Use only a pencil with soft black lead (No. 2 or HB) to complete this answer sheet.
Be sure to fill in completely the oval that corresponds to the proper letter or number.
Completely erase any errors or stray marks.

1. NAME
Enter your last name and first initial.
Omit spaces, hyphens, apostrophes, etc.

Last Name (first 6 letters)

2.

YOUR NAME: (Print)
Last Name (Family or Surname)   First Name (Given)   M. I.

MAILING ADDRESS: (Print)
P.O. Box or Street Address   Apt. # (If any)

City   State or Province

Country   Zip or Postal Code

TELEPHONE NUMBER: ( )   Home   ( )   Business

SIGNATURE: **TEST DATE:**

3. DATE OF BIRTH
Month   Day
Jan.
Feb.
Mar.
April
May
June
July
Aug.
Sept.
Oct.
Nov.
Dec.

4. SOCIAL SECURITY NUMBER

5. CANDIDATE ID NUMBER

6. TEST CENTER / REPORTING LOCATION
Center Number   Room Number
Center Name
City   State or Province
Country

7. TEST CODE / FORM CODE

8. TEST BOOK SERIAL NUMBER

9. TEST FORM

10. TEST NAME

51055 • 14725 • TF24E50 • printed in U.S.A.

MH04023   I.N. 202984   Q3032-06,07

1   2   3   4

CERTIFICATION STATEMENT: (Please write the following statement below. DO NOT PRINT.)
"I hereby agree to the conditions set forth in the Registration Bulletin and certify that I am the person whose name and address appear on this answer sheet."

_____

_____

_____

SIGNATURE: _____   DATE: _____ / _____ / _____

Month   Day   Year

BE SURE EACH MARK IS DARK AND COMPLETELY FILLS THE INTENDED SPACE AS ILLUSTRATED HERE: ● .

#		#		#		#	
1	Ⓐ Ⓑ Ⓒ Ⓓ	31	Ⓐ Ⓑ Ⓒ Ⓓ	61	Ⓐ Ⓑ Ⓒ Ⓓ	91	Ⓐ Ⓑ Ⓒ Ⓓ
2	Ⓐ Ⓑ Ⓒ Ⓓ	32	Ⓐ Ⓑ Ⓒ Ⓓ	62	Ⓐ Ⓑ Ⓒ Ⓓ	92	Ⓐ Ⓑ Ⓒ Ⓓ
3	Ⓐ Ⓑ Ⓒ Ⓓ	33	Ⓐ Ⓑ Ⓒ Ⓓ	63	Ⓐ Ⓑ Ⓒ Ⓓ	93	Ⓐ Ⓑ Ⓒ Ⓓ
4	Ⓐ Ⓑ Ⓒ Ⓓ	34	Ⓐ Ⓑ Ⓒ Ⓓ	64	Ⓐ Ⓑ Ⓒ Ⓓ	94	Ⓐ Ⓑ Ⓒ Ⓓ
5	Ⓐ Ⓑ Ⓒ Ⓓ	35	Ⓐ Ⓑ Ⓒ Ⓓ	65	Ⓐ Ⓑ Ⓒ Ⓓ	95	Ⓐ Ⓑ Ⓒ Ⓓ
6	Ⓐ Ⓑ Ⓒ Ⓓ	36	Ⓐ Ⓑ Ⓒ Ⓓ	66	Ⓐ Ⓑ Ⓒ Ⓓ	96	Ⓐ Ⓑ Ⓒ Ⓓ
7	Ⓐ Ⓑ Ⓒ Ⓓ	37	Ⓐ Ⓑ Ⓒ Ⓓ	67	Ⓐ Ⓑ Ⓒ Ⓓ	97	Ⓐ Ⓑ Ⓒ Ⓓ
8	Ⓐ Ⓑ Ⓒ Ⓓ	38	Ⓐ Ⓑ Ⓒ Ⓓ	68	Ⓐ Ⓑ Ⓒ Ⓓ	98	Ⓐ Ⓑ Ⓒ Ⓓ
9	Ⓐ Ⓑ Ⓒ Ⓓ	39	Ⓐ Ⓑ Ⓒ Ⓓ	69	Ⓐ Ⓑ Ⓒ Ⓓ	99	Ⓐ Ⓑ Ⓒ Ⓓ
10	Ⓐ Ⓑ Ⓒ Ⓓ	40	Ⓐ Ⓑ Ⓒ Ⓓ	70	Ⓐ Ⓑ Ⓒ Ⓓ	100	Ⓐ Ⓑ Ⓒ Ⓓ
11	Ⓐ Ⓑ Ⓒ Ⓓ	41	Ⓐ Ⓑ Ⓒ Ⓓ	71	Ⓐ Ⓑ Ⓒ Ⓓ	101	Ⓐ Ⓑ Ⓒ Ⓓ
12	Ⓐ Ⓑ Ⓒ Ⓓ	42	Ⓐ Ⓑ Ⓒ Ⓓ	72	Ⓐ Ⓑ Ⓒ Ⓓ	102	Ⓐ Ⓑ Ⓒ Ⓓ
13	Ⓐ Ⓑ Ⓒ Ⓓ	43	Ⓐ Ⓑ Ⓒ Ⓓ	73	Ⓐ Ⓑ Ⓒ Ⓓ	103	Ⓐ Ⓑ Ⓒ Ⓓ
14	Ⓐ Ⓑ Ⓒ Ⓓ	44	Ⓐ Ⓑ Ⓒ Ⓓ	74	Ⓐ Ⓑ Ⓒ Ⓓ	104	Ⓐ Ⓑ Ⓒ Ⓓ
15	Ⓐ Ⓑ Ⓒ Ⓓ	45	Ⓐ Ⓑ Ⓒ Ⓓ	75	Ⓐ Ⓑ Ⓒ Ⓓ	105	Ⓐ Ⓑ Ⓒ Ⓓ
16	Ⓐ Ⓑ Ⓒ Ⓓ	46	Ⓐ Ⓑ Ⓒ Ⓓ	76	Ⓐ Ⓑ Ⓒ Ⓓ	106	Ⓐ Ⓑ Ⓒ Ⓓ
17	Ⓐ Ⓑ Ⓒ Ⓓ	47	Ⓐ Ⓑ Ⓒ Ⓓ	77	Ⓐ Ⓑ Ⓒ Ⓓ	107	Ⓐ Ⓑ Ⓒ Ⓓ
18	Ⓐ Ⓑ Ⓒ Ⓓ	48	Ⓐ Ⓑ Ⓒ Ⓓ	78	Ⓐ Ⓑ Ⓒ Ⓓ	108	Ⓐ Ⓑ Ⓒ Ⓓ
19	Ⓐ Ⓑ Ⓒ Ⓓ	49	Ⓐ Ⓑ Ⓒ Ⓓ	79	Ⓐ Ⓑ Ⓒ Ⓓ	109	Ⓐ Ⓑ Ⓒ Ⓓ
20	Ⓐ Ⓑ Ⓒ Ⓓ	50	Ⓐ Ⓑ Ⓒ Ⓓ	80	Ⓐ Ⓑ Ⓒ Ⓓ	110	Ⓐ Ⓑ Ⓒ Ⓓ
21	Ⓐ Ⓑ Ⓒ Ⓓ	51	Ⓐ Ⓑ Ⓒ Ⓓ	81	Ⓐ Ⓑ Ⓒ Ⓓ	111	Ⓐ Ⓑ Ⓒ Ⓓ
22	Ⓐ Ⓑ Ⓒ Ⓓ	52	Ⓐ Ⓑ Ⓒ Ⓓ	82	Ⓐ Ⓑ Ⓒ Ⓓ	112	Ⓐ Ⓑ Ⓒ Ⓓ
23	Ⓐ Ⓑ Ⓒ Ⓓ	53	Ⓐ Ⓑ Ⓒ Ⓓ	83	Ⓐ Ⓑ Ⓒ Ⓓ	113	Ⓐ Ⓑ Ⓒ Ⓓ
24	Ⓐ Ⓑ Ⓒ Ⓓ	54	Ⓐ Ⓑ Ⓒ Ⓓ	84	Ⓐ Ⓑ Ⓒ Ⓓ	114	Ⓐ Ⓑ Ⓒ Ⓓ
25	Ⓐ Ⓑ Ⓒ Ⓓ	55	Ⓐ Ⓑ Ⓒ Ⓓ	85	Ⓐ Ⓑ Ⓒ Ⓓ	115	Ⓐ Ⓑ Ⓒ Ⓓ
26	Ⓐ Ⓑ Ⓒ Ⓓ	56	Ⓐ Ⓑ Ⓒ Ⓓ	86	Ⓐ Ⓑ Ⓒ Ⓓ	116	Ⓐ Ⓑ Ⓒ Ⓓ
27	Ⓐ Ⓑ Ⓒ Ⓓ	57	Ⓐ Ⓑ Ⓒ Ⓓ	87	Ⓐ Ⓑ Ⓒ Ⓓ	117	Ⓐ Ⓑ Ⓒ Ⓓ
28	Ⓐ Ⓑ Ⓒ Ⓓ	58	Ⓐ Ⓑ Ⓒ Ⓓ	88	Ⓐ Ⓑ Ⓒ Ⓓ	118	Ⓐ Ⓑ Ⓒ Ⓓ
29	Ⓐ Ⓑ Ⓒ Ⓓ	59	Ⓐ Ⓑ Ⓒ Ⓓ	89	Ⓐ Ⓑ Ⓒ Ⓓ	119	Ⓐ Ⓑ Ⓒ Ⓓ
30	Ⓐ Ⓑ Ⓒ Ⓓ	60	Ⓐ Ⓑ Ⓒ Ⓓ	90	Ⓐ Ⓑ Ⓒ Ⓓ	120	Ⓐ Ⓑ Ⓒ Ⓓ

PRAXIS MIDDLE SCHOOL MATHEMATICS

Part A

30 Multiple-choice Questions
(Suggested time—60 minutes)

Directions: Each of the questions or incomplete statements below is followed by four choices (A, B, C, and D). Choose the best response to each question and fill in the appropriate space for that question on your answer sheet.

Numbers: All numbers used are real numbers.

Figures: Figures that accompany questions are intended to provide information that is useful in answering the questions. They are drawn as accurately as possible except when it is stated in a specific question that its figure is not drawn to scale.

Lines shown as straight are straight and angle measures are positive. Positions of points, angles, regions, etc., exist in the order shown.

Rectangular coordinate systems are used unless otherwise stated.

Formulas: Infrequently used formulas will be provided in specific questions.

Notation: Specialized mathematical notation will be defined in specific questions.

Calculators: Graphing calculators and scientific calculators will be allowed; however, calculators that have QWERTY keyboards will not be allowed.

1. If $bd \neq 0$, then $\dfrac{a}{b} + \dfrac{c}{d} =$

    (A) $\dfrac{ac}{bd}$

    (B) $\dfrac{a+c}{b+d}$

    (C) $\dfrac{a+c}{bd}$

    (D) $\dfrac{ad+bc}{bd}$

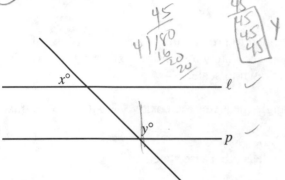

2. In the figure above, line ℓ and line p are parallel and $y = 3x$. What is the value of x ?

    (A) 30
    (B) 45
    (C) 60
    (D) 75

3. A 224-mile trip requires 6 gallons of gasoline. At this rate, how many gallons of gasoline would be required for a 168-mile trip?

    (A) 4
    (B) 4.5
    (C) 8
    (D) 8.5

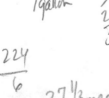

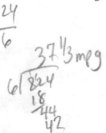

4. When Khalid solved a word problem, he correctly gave 84.8 as the answer. Which of the following could have been the question asked in the problem?

    I.   What was the number of students on the class trip?
    II. What was the average temperature in this city during the month of July?
    III. What is the product of the following two rational numbers?

    (A) I and II only
    (B) I and III only
    (C) II and III only
    (D) I, II, and III

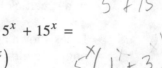

5. $5^x + 15^x =$

    (A) $5^x(1 + 3^x)$
    (B) $5(4^x)$
    (C) 20^x
    (D) 75^{2x}

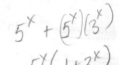

6. Which of the following defines y as a function of x ?

    (A) $x - y^2 = 4$
    (B) $x^2 + y^2 = 4$
    (C) $y = x^2 + 2$
    (D) $y < x + 1$

7. If a and b are integers, then all of the following must be true EXCEPT

    (A) $|a| = |-a|$

    (B) $|ab| = |a||b|$

    (C) $|ab| = \sqrt{a^2 b^2}$

    (D) $|a + b| = |a| + |b|$

    ```
    1 cup = 16 tablespoons
    1 tablespoon = 3 teaspoons
    ```

8. A certain recipe calls for $\frac{1}{4}$ cup of white sugar, $\frac{1}{2}$ cup of brown sugar, $2\frac{1}{4}$ cups of flour, $\frac{1}{4}$ teaspoon of salt, and 2 tablespoons of cornstarch. The amount of cornstarch called for is approximately what fraction of the total amount of sugar called for?

    (A) $\frac{1}{24}$

    (B) $\frac{1}{12}$

    (C) $\frac{1}{8}$

    (D) $\frac{1}{6}$

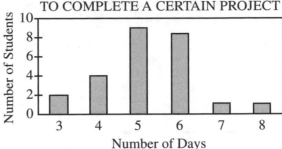

NUMBER OF DAYS TAKEN
TO COMPLETE A CERTAIN PROJECT

9. A certain project was given to 25 students in a club to complete. The graph above shows a distribution of the number of days it took the students to complete the project. What is the average (arithmetic mean) number of days it took the students to complete the project?

    (A) 5.0

    (B) 5.2

    (C) 5.4

    (D) 5.6

10. 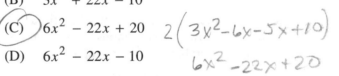 $2(x-2)(3x-5) =$

    (A) $2x^2 - 22x + 20$

    (B) $3x^2 + 22x - 10$

    (C) $6x^2 - 22x + 20$

    (D) $6x^2 - 22x - 10$

11. Jane withdrew half of the money from her savings account. She later withdrew an additional $5.00, leaving a $12.75 balance in the account. If no other transactions were performed, how much money was in Jane's account originally?

    (A) $35.50

    (B) $31.00

    (C) $30.50

    (D) $15.50

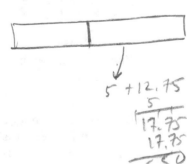

12. In a store, pencils can be bought only in packs of 5 or in packs of 8. If Annie bought 42 pencils, how many packs of 8 did she buy?

    (A) 2
    (B) 3
    (C) 4
    (D) 5

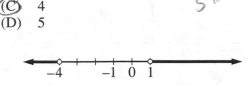

13. The graph shown on the number line above represents the set of values of x satisfying which of the following inequalities?

    (A) $(x - 1)(x + 4) < 0$

    (B) $(x - 1)(x + 4) > 0$

    (C) $(x + 1)(x - 4) < 0$

    (D) $(x + 1)(x - 4) > 0$

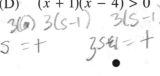

Step 1   Step 2   Step 3

14. If the pattern above continues indefinitely, which of the following expressions could be used to find the number of dots in step n ?

    (A) $2n - 1$

    (B) $\dfrac{n^2 + n}{2}$

    (C) $n^2 - n$

    (D) $\dfrac{n^2 + 3n + 2}{n}$

15. What is the negation of the following statement "All p is q"?

    (A) Some p is q.
    (B) Some p is not q.
    (C) If it is not q, it is p.
    (D) If it is not q, it is not p.

16. A taxi ride costs \$2.50 for the first $\frac{1}{4}$ mile or fraction thereof plus \$0.50 for each additional $\frac{1}{4}$ mile or fraction thereof. Which of the following graphs represents the total cost of the ride as a function of distance traveled?

    (A)

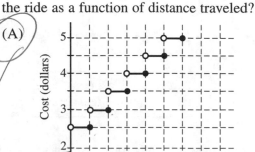

    (B)

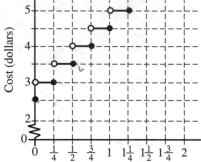

    (C)

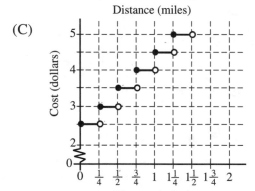

    (D)

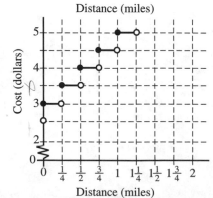

17. If $\dfrac{1}{1 - \frac{3}{7}} < \dfrac{1}{1 - x} < \dfrac{1}{1 - \frac{4}{7}}$, then x could equal

    which of the following?

    I. $\dfrac{1}{2}$

    II. $\dfrac{3}{5}$

    III. $\dfrac{5}{9}$

    (A) I only
    (B) II only
    (C) I and II only
    (D) I and III only

18. The original price of a certain car was 25 percent greater than its cost to the dealer. The actual selling price was 25 percent less than the original price. If c is the cost of the car and p is the selling price, which of the following represents p in terms of c ?

    (A) $p = 1.00c$

    (B) $p = 1.25c$

    (C) $p = 0.25(0.75c)$

    (D) $p = 0.75(1.25c)$

19. The following functions of x have the same domain (x values). Which of the functions have the same range (y values) ?

    I. $y = x^2 + 1$

    II. $y = 2|x| + 1$

    III. $y = 2^x$

    (A) I and II only
    (B) I and III only
    (C) II and III only
    (D) I, II, and III

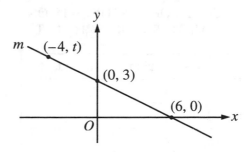

20. The point with coordinates $(-4, t)$ lies on the line m in the xy-plane, as shown above. What is the value of t ?

    (A) 4
    (B) 5
    (C) 9
    (D) 14

$32_4 = x_2$

21. In the equation above, the subscript of each number identifies the base in which the number is expressed. Which of the following values of x will satisfy the equation?

    (A) 1010
    (B) 1100
    (C) 1110
    (D) 1111

SCORES OF 23 STUDENTS ON
A MIDTERM FRENCH TEST

Scores	Number of Students
100	1
90–99	4
80–89	7
70–79	6
60–69	5

22. Which of the following statistics about the test
scores of the 23 students can be determined
using the information above?

    I. The range of the scores
    II. The median score
    III. The average (arithmetic mean) score

    (A) None
    (B) I only
    (C) II only
    (D) I and III only

23. Which of the following is an equation of a line
that is perpendicular to the line $y = 2x + 13$?

    (A) $y = -2x + 6$

    (B) $y = -\frac{1}{2}x + 3$

    (C) $y = \frac{1}{2}x + 3$

    (D) $y = 2x + 6$

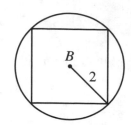

24. A square is inscribed in each of the circles
above. The radius of circle A is 1, and the
radius of circle B is 2. What is the ratio of the
area of the square inscribed in circle A to the
area of the square inscribed in circle B ?

    (A) $1 : \sqrt{2}$

    (B) $1 : 2$

    (C) $1 : 2\sqrt{2}$

    (D) $1 : 4$

✳	a	b
a	a	b
b	b	a

25. The table above defines an operation ✳ on the
set $S = \{a, b\}$. Which of the following
properties are satisfied by S under the
operation ✳ ?

    I. S is closed.
    II. S is commutative.
    III. S contains an identity.

    (A) I and II only
    (B) I and III only
    (C) II and III only
    (D) I, II, and III

Weights (pounds)	
Stem	Leaf
12	0, 2
13	1, 3, 3
14	2, 4, 5, 8
15	0, 1, 4, 7, 7, 9
16	2, 8, 8
17	1, 6, 9
18	0, 0, 1
19	5

26. The table above is a stem-and-leaf plot of the weights of the 25 members of a men's fitness club. What percent of the club members weigh less than 155 pounds?

(A) 36%
(B) 48%
(C) 52%
(D) 64%

27. A rectangular solid with dimensions 1, 2, and 3 is shown above. What is the area of the cross section *ABCD* ?

(A) $2\sqrt{10}$

(B) $2\sqrt{13}$

(C) $3\sqrt{5}$

(D) 8

28. According to a survey of 100 students, 73 students took a math course and 57 took a music course. Of those surveyed, 22 reportedly took a math course but not a music course. How many students took neither a music course nor a math course?

(A) 6
(B) 21
(C) 30
(D) 51

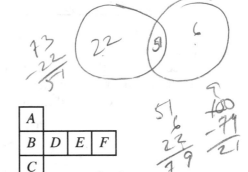

29 The *T*-shaped figure above consists of six congruent squares. A coin will be placed randomly on one of the squares. It will then be moved randomly to a square that is adjacent to the square on which it was originally placed. What is the probability that after the coin has been moved, it will be on square *E* ? (Two squares are adjacent if they share a common side.)

(A) $\frac{1}{3}$

(B) $\frac{1}{4}$

(C) $\frac{1}{6}$

(D) $\frac{1}{12}$

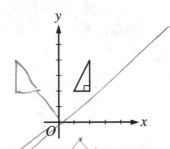

30. The triangle shown in the plane above is to be reflected about the y-axis and then reflected about the line $y = x$. Which of the following would be the result of these reflections?

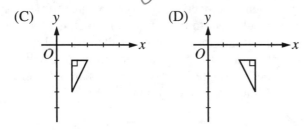

(C)

(D)

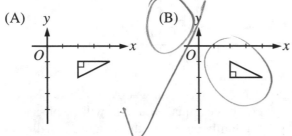

Part B

2 Constructed-Response Questions
(Suggested time—20 minutes)

General Directions for Questions 31–32: There are two constructed-response questions below. Write your answers to these questions in the space provided in the lined pages following the questions. If a question has more than one part, be sure to answer each part of the question.

Question 31

There are 100 lockers in a school corridor, numbered from 1 to 100, inclusive. Lily puts a red sticker on every locker; Kareem puts a yellow sticker on the even-numbered lockers, beginning with the one numbered 2; and Shahid puts a green sticker on every third locker, beginning with the one numbered 3. Answer the following questions using your knowledge of factors and multiples. The chart is for reference only; no work on it will be scored.

1	2	3	4	5	6	7	8	9	10
11	12	13	14	15	16	17	18	19	20
21	22	23	24	25	26	27	28	29	30
31	32	33	34	35	36	37	38	39	40
41	42	43	44	45	46	47	48	49	50
51	52	53	54	55	56	57	58	59	60
61	62	63	64	65	66	67	68	69	70
71	72	73	74	75	76	77	78	79	80
81	82	83	84	85	86	87	88	89	90
91	92	93	94	95	96	97	98	99	100

(A) How many lockers have a red sticker only? Explain your reasoning using the concepts of multiples and factors.

(B) How many lockers have three stickers—red, yellow, and green? Explain your reasoning using the concepts of multiples and factors.

(C) Suppose there were 1,000 lockers in the school and that Lily, Kareem, and Shahid continued the same pattern for all 1,000 lockers. Chris then puts a blue sticker on every fifth locker, beginning with the one numbered 5. What is the <u>last</u> locker that would have a red, a yellow, a green, and a blue sticker? Explain your reasoning.

You may use the space below for any notes you wish to make. The material on this page will NOT be used in scoring your response.

Question 32

At a certain theme park, a customer can buy an admission pass for $5.00 and then pay an additional $0.50 for each ride, or the customer can pay $3.00 for a pass and an additional $0.75 for each ride.

(A) Write an equation that represents the cost C of admission and rides at the park for each alternative. Define any variables that you use.

(B) In the xy-coordinate system, graph the cost (on the y-axis) *versus* the number of rides (on the x-axis) for each equation you wrote in part A.

(C) Write a sentence or two summarizing what you can observe from the graphs about the relative merits of each alternative.

You may use the space below for any notes you wish to make. The material on this page will NOT be used in scoring your response.

Begin your response to Question 31 here.

(Question 31 continued)

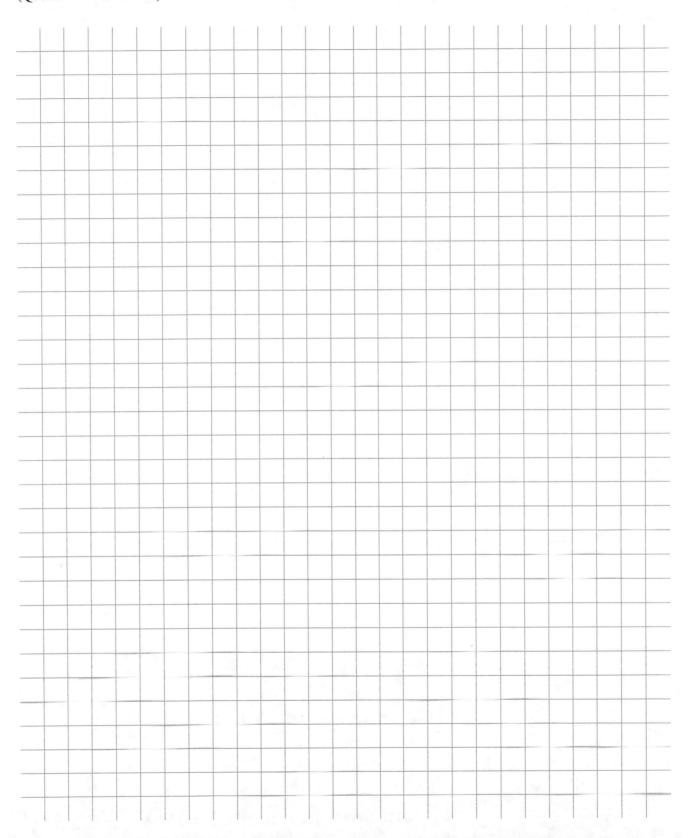

(Question 31 continued)

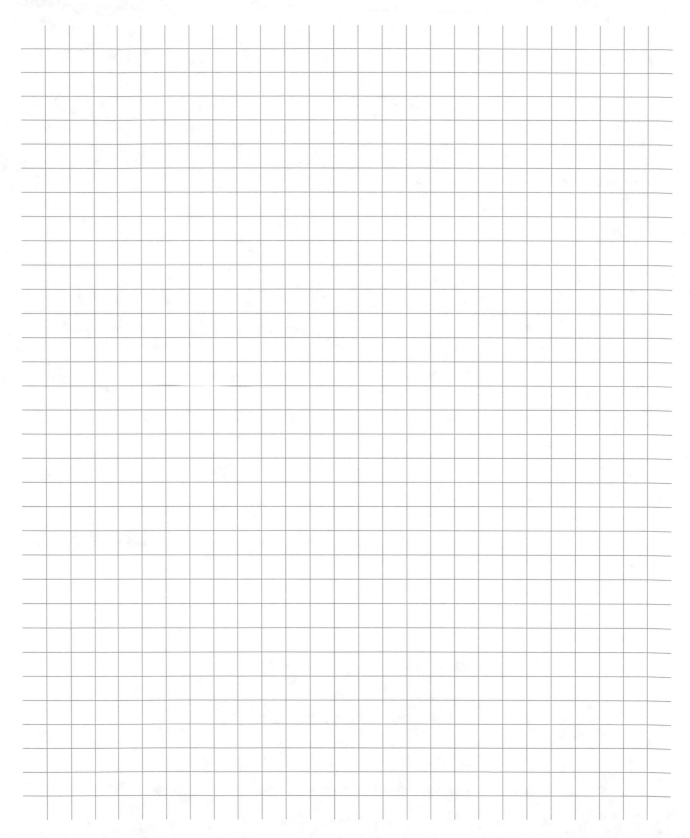

Begin your response to Question 32 here.

(Question 32 continued)

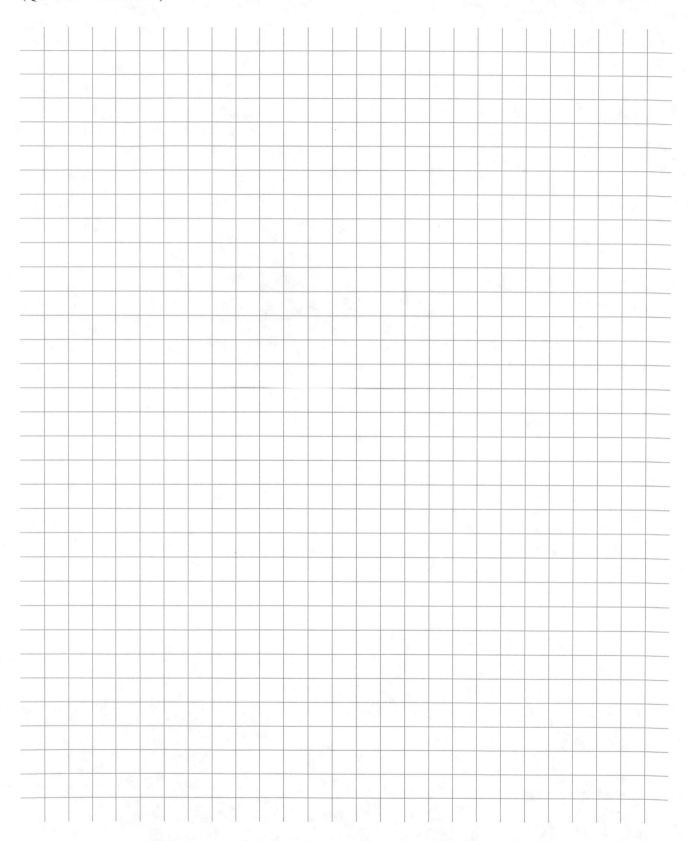

(Question 32 continued)

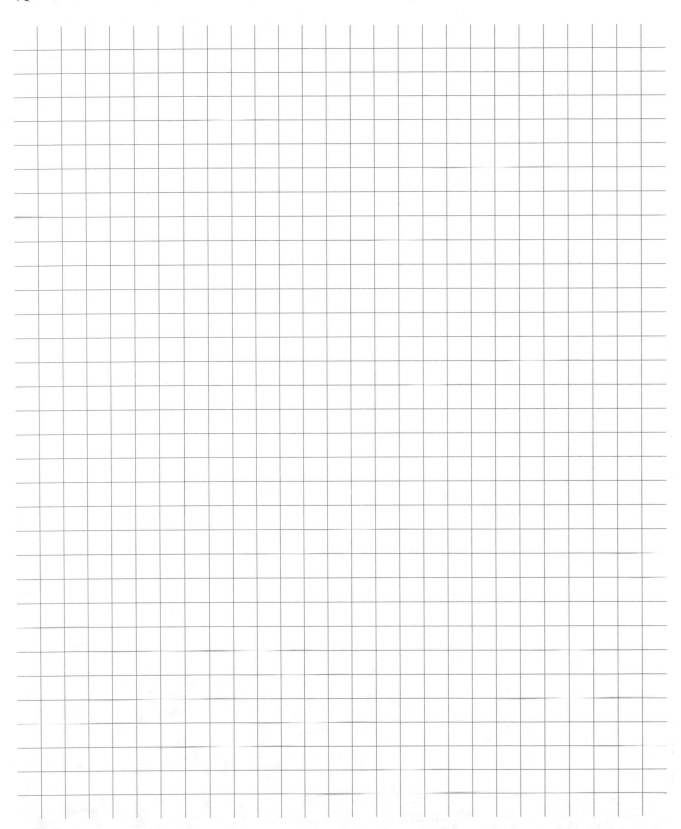

Chapter 10
Right Answers and Sample Responses for the *Middle School Mathematics* Practice Questions

▶ ▶ ▶ ▶ ▶ ▶ ▶ ▶ ▶ ▶ ▶ ▶

The first part of this chapter contains right answers and sample responses to the multiple-choice practice questions for the *Middle School Mathematics* test. The second part of this chapter contains scored sample responses to the constructed-response practice questions, along with explanations for why the responses received the scores they did.

Part One: Right Answers and Explanations for the Multiple-Choice Questions

Now that you have answered all of the practice questions, you can check your work. Compare your answers to the multiple-choice questions with the correct answers in the table below.

Question Number	Correct Answer	Content Category	Question Number	Correct Answer	Content Category
1	D	Arithmetic and Basic Algebra	17	D	Arithmetic and Basic Algebra
2	B	Geometry and Measurement	18	D	Arithmetic and Basic Algebra
3	B	Arithmetic and Basic Algebra	19	A	Coordinate Geometry, Functions and their Graphs
4	C	Arithmetic and Basic Algebra	20	B	Coordinate Geometry, Functions and their Graphs
5	A	Arithmetic and Basic Algebra			
6	C	Coordinate Geometry, Functions and their Graphs	21	C	Discrete Mathematics
7	D	Arithmetic and Basic Algebra	22	A	Data, Probability, and Statistical Concepts
8	D	Geometry and Measurement	23	B	Coordinate Geometry, Functions and their Graphs
9	B	Data, Probability, and Statistical Concepts			
10	C	Arithmetic and Basic Algebra	24	D	Geometry and Measurement
11	A	Arithmetic and Basic Algebra	25	D	Arithmetic and Basic Algebra
12	C	Arithmetic and Basic Algebra	26	B	Data, Probability, and Statistical Concepts
13	B	Coordinate Geometry, Functions and their Graphs	27	A	Geometry and Measurement
14	B	Discrete Mathematics	28	B	Discrete Mathematics
15	B	Discrete Mathematics	29	B	Data, Probability, and Statistical Concepts
16	A	Coordinate Geometry, Functions and their Graphs	30	B	Geometry and Measurement

1   (D). This question asks you to add algebraic fractions that have different denominators. You should recall that, as with adding numerical fractions, you first need to find a common denominator. Since the values of the denominators b and d are not given, the product bd is the most obvious common denominator to use. (That is, bd is clearly a multiple of both b and d. The product bd may not be the least common multiple, but the common denominator does not need to be the least common multiple.) In order to rewrite the fraction $\dfrac{a}{b}$ with denominator bd, you need to multiply by $\dfrac{d}{d}$. (Remember that multiplying by $\dfrac{d}{d}$ is the same as multiplying by 1, so the value of $\dfrac{a}{b}$ will not change.)

$$\frac{a}{b} = \frac{a}{b} \cdot \frac{d}{d} = \frac{ad}{bd}$$

Similarly, $\dfrac{c}{d} = \dfrac{c}{d} \cdot \dfrac{b}{b} = \dfrac{bc}{bd}$

Therefore, $\dfrac{a}{b} + \dfrac{c}{d} = \dfrac{ad}{bd} + \dfrac{bc}{bd} = \dfrac{ad + bc}{bd}$.

The correct answer is (D).

2. (B). This question asks you to apply your understanding of angles in a plane, and in particular, properties of angles associated with parallel and transversal lines. You should be able to show, using pairs of alternate interior angles and corresponding angles, that angle x and angle y are supplementary angles. Recall that the sum of the measures of supplementary angles is 180°. That is, $x + y = 180$. It is given that $y = 3x$. Substituting for y, you get $4x = 180$. Hence, $x = 45$. Therefore, the correct answer is (B).

3. (B). This question asks you to apply your knowledge of rate or proportional reasoning to a real-life situation. The following presents two ways to solve this problem, the first using rates and the second using proportional reasoning.

First solution: The question states that a 224-mile trip requires 6 gallons of gasoline. This is equivalent to a rate of gasoline use of $\dfrac{224}{6} = 37.3\overline{3}$ miles per gallon, or $\dfrac{6}{224} = 0.026786$ gallons per mile.

To find the total gallons used for a trip of 168 miles, you would multiply:
0.026786 gallons/mile $\times$ 168 miles $=$ 4.5 gallons. The correct answer is (B).

Second solution: Set up and solve a proportion expressing the relationship between the number of gallons used and the number of miles of the trip. For example, let g be the number of gallons of gasoline required for the 168-mile trip. Since the rate of miles per gallon for the 168-mile trip is equal to the rate of miles per gallon for the 224-mile trip, you can set up the proportion $\dfrac{224 \text{ miles}}{6 \text{ gallons}} = \dfrac{168 \text{ miles}}{g \text{ gallons}}$.

Solving the proportion gives $g = \dfrac{6 \times 168}{224} = 4.5$ gallons. The correct answer is (B).

4. (C). This question asks you to apply your understanding of decimal numbers to various situations. When asked a question such as this, in which a list of statements or questions is given (numbered using roman numerals), you must evaluate each of the statements or questions individually. This question is asking you to determine which of the three numbered questions (I, II, and/or III) could have 84.8 as an answer.

I.: The number of students must be a whole number. So, 84.8 <u>cannot</u> be the answer to question I.

II.: The temperature in some city in July could be 84.8 degrees Fahrenheit. So, 84.8 <u>could</u> be the answer to question II.

III.: The product of two rational numbers is a rational number, which could be 84.8. So, 84.8 <u>could</u> be the answer to question III.

Therefore, the correct answer is (C), "II and III only."

5. (A). This question asks you to apply your understanding of operations involving exponents in order to find an expression equivalent to $5^x + 15^x$. In order to find an equivalent form of the given sum, you might want to look at the answer choices given for suggestions of different ways in which one or more of the numbers given could be represented. In this case, choice (A) suggests using properties of exponents to rewrite 15^x as $15^x = (3 \times 5)^x = \left(3^x\right)\left(5^x\right)$. Then, substituting this expression into the original expression and factoring out the common term 5^x, gives

$$5^x + 15^x = 5^x + \left(3^x\right)\left(5^x\right) = 5^x\left(1 + 3^x\right).$$

Thus, the correct answer is (A). You should recall that the bases of numbers with exponents cannot be added, so choices (B) and (C) are not correct.

6. (C). This question asks you to identify a function by applying your understanding of function to different mathematical statements. To answer a question such as this, which asks "which of the following," you need to consider only the choices given. There are usually other correct answers to the question, as in this case, that you are not asked to consider. To answer this question, you should recall that if y is a function of x, each value of x (in the domain of the function) results in only one value of y. In choices (A) and (B), for each value of x there may be two different corresponding values of y. You can see this by solving the equations in (A) and (B) for y. In (A), $y = + \sqrt{4 - x}$ or $y = - \sqrt{4 - x}$.

Similarly, in (B), $y = \pm \sqrt{4 - x^2}$. So neither (A) nor (B) defines y as a function of x. In choice (D), for each value of x, there is more than one value of y that satisfies the inequality. So (D) does not define y as a function of x. In (C), however, there is only one value of y that corresponds to any given value of x. Thus, the correct answer is (C).

7. (D). This question asks you to apply your understanding of absolute value to find a property that is <u>not always</u> true. Recall that the absolute value of a number a, written $|a|$, is always positive and can be thought of as the distance a is from 0 on the number line. One way to solve this kind of problem is by trial and error. Try to find two numbers a and b that show a statement is not always true. Another way is to analyze each of the choices given by cases and use reasoning to prove the ones that are true and find a counterexample to identify the one that is not always true.

Choice (A):

<u>Case 1</u>: if $a \geq 0$, then $|a| = a$ and $|-a| = -(-a) = a$. So $|a| = |-a|$;

<u>Case 2</u>: if $a \leq 0$, then $|a| = -a$ and $|-a| = -a$. That is, $|a| = |-a|$.

So, choice (A) is true.

Choice (B):

Remember that if the product of two numbers is positive, then either both numbers are positive or both numbers are negative. If the product of two numbers is negative, then one of the numbers must be negative and the other must be positive.

<u>Case 1</u>: $ab \geq 0$. If $a \geq 0$ and $b \geq 0$, then $|ab| = ab = |a||b|$; if $a \leq 0$ and $b \leq 0$, then

$|ab| = ab = (-a)(-b) = |a||b|$.

<u>Case 2</u>. $ab \leq 0$. If $a \geq 0$ and $b \leq 0$, then $|ab| = -ab = a(-b) = |a||b|$; if $a \leq 0$ and $b \geq 0$,

$|ab| = -ab = (-a)b = |a||b|$.

Thus, for numbers a and b, $|ab| = |a||b|$, choice (B) is true.

Choice (C):

Based on choice (B), $|ab| = |a\|b| = \sqrt{|a|^2}\sqrt{|b|^2}$. Choice (C) is true.

Choice (D) is not always true because the equality fails when the signs of a and b are opposite. For example, if $a = 10$ and $b = -8$, then $|a + b| = |10 + (-8)| = |2| = 2$. But $|a| + |b| = |10| + |-8| = 10 + 8 = 18$. Therefore, the correct answer is (D).

8. (D). This question asks you to apply your understanding of measurement conversion to solve a problem using familiar ingredients used in cooking. To compare the amount of cornstarch to the total amount of sugar, you have to note the amount of each used and the unit that each is given in, and make sure that both are in the same units. The sugar is given in cups and the cornstarch is given in tablespoons (T). The total amount of sugar is $\frac{3}{4}$ of a cup (add the amounts of white sugar and brown sugar). Using the conversion table, you see that 2 T of cornstarch is equivalent to $\frac{1}{8}$ cup. Comparing $\frac{1}{8}$ to $\frac{3}{4}$ is the same as comparing $\frac{1}{8}$ to $\frac{6}{8}$, and this ratio is $\frac{1}{6}$. The best answer is therefore (D). Alternatively, you could have converted the amount of sugar into tablespoons ($\frac{3}{4}$ cups $= 12$ tablespoons). The ratio of cornstarch to sugar is then $\frac{2}{12}$ or $\frac{1}{6}$, and the correct answer is (D).

9. (B). This question asks you to apply your knowledge of the concepts associated with average, arithmetic mean, and weighted average to the data in a bar graph. According to the data, the 25 students took a total of 130 days to complete the project. This total is found by multiplying each of the numbers of days by the number of students who took that many days to complete the project. This can be written:

$$(3 \times 2) + (4 \times 4) + (5 \times 9) + (6 \times 8) + (7 \times 1) + (8 \times 1) = 130$$

The average number of days it took the students to complete the project can be found by dividing the total number of days by the total number of students.

$$130 \div 25 = 5.2$$

Therefore the correct answer is (B).

10. (C). This question asks you to apply your knowledge of basic algebraic computations to expand an expression given in factored form. You can answer this question in different ways. One way is to actually multiply the factors and combine like terms.

$$2(x - 2)(3x - 5)$$
$$= 2\left(3x^2 - 6x - 5x + 10\right)$$
$$= 6x^2 - 22x + 20.$$

You can see directly that the correct answer is (C).

Another way to answer this type of question is to mentally look for a match between the quadratic and constant terms of the expanded expression and those of the expressions in the answer choices. Recall that the quadratic term will contain x^2 and the constant term will contain no variables. For example, the coefficient of the quadratic term in the question has to be 6, which means (C) and (D) are possible; the constant term has to be 20, which eliminates (D). The correct answer is therefore (C).

11. (A). This question asks you to apply the basic problem-solving strategy of working backward to a familiar situation. Notice that the balance of $12.75 plus $5.00 equals $17.75, which is half of Jane's original savings. Thus, Jane originally had $35.50 in her account and the correct answer is (A).

12. (C). This question asks you to demonstrate your understanding of the concepts associated with multiples of integers. If x is the number of 5-pencil packs and y is the number of 8-pencil packs Annie bought, then you can set up an equation $5x + 8y = 42$ that will help you solve the problem. It now might help to make a table and list possible ways of finding two numbers whose sum is 42, keeping in mind that multiples of 5 must end in 0 or 5. Here are a few possible entries in such a table: 0 and 42, 5 and 37, 10 and 32, 15 and 27. Since $5x$ will always end in 0 or 5, then $8y$ must end in 2 or 7. However, no multiple of 8 can end in 7 because $8y$ is an even integer. Only $y = 4$ makes $8y$ an integer that has a ones digit of 2 and at the same time is not greater than 42. So, the correct answer is (C).

13. (B). This question asks you to apply your knowledge of solving inequalities to identify the solution set on the number line. In order to determine the graph, you need to solve each of the inequalities given in the choices. Once again, you need to remember that if the product of two numbers is positive, then both of the numbers must be positive or both of the numbers must be negative. If the product of two numbers is negative, then one of the numbers must be positive and one must be negative.

Choice (A): $(x - 1)(x + 4) < 0$. Since $(x - 1)(x + 4) < 0$, you need to consider

either $x - 1 > 0$ and $x + 4 < 0$ (Case 1) OR $x - 1 < 0$ and $x + 4 > 0$ (Case 2).

Case 1: $x - 1 > 0$ and $x + 4 < 0$. Solving these inequalities gives $x > 1$ and $x < -4$, which is impossible. No solutions.

Case 2: $x - 1 < 0$ and $x + 4 > 0$. Solving these inequalities yields $-4 < x < 1$.

The solution to (A) is then $-4 < x < 1$. But the graph of this set is not the same as that given.

Choice (B): $(x - 1)(x + 4) > 0$. Since $(x - 1)(x + 4) > 0$, you have either

$x - 1 > 0$ and $x + 4 > 0$ (Case 1) OR $x - 1 < 0$ and $x + 4 < 0$ (Case 2).

Case 1: $x - 1 > 0$ and $x + 4 > 0$. It follows from $x - 1 > 0$, i.e., $x > 1$, and from

$x + 4 > 0$, i.e., $x > -4$, that the set of x satisfying both inequalities is $x > 1$.

Case 2: $x - 1 < 0$ and $x + 4 < 0$. The solution to the first inequality is $x < 1$; the solution to the

second inequality is $x < -4$. The solution to the system of the inequalities is $x < -4$.

In summary, the solution set of $(x - 1)(x + 4) > 0$ is either $x > 1$ or $x < -4$, which is graphed as shown on the number line.

Therefore, the correct answer is (B).

Choice (C): $(x + 1)(x - 4) < 0$. Since $(x + 1)(x - 4) < 0$, you need to consider either

$x + 1 < 0$ and $x - 4 > 0$ (Case 1) OR $x + 1 > 0$ and $x - 4 < 0$ (Case 2).

Case 1: $x + 1 < 0$ and $x - 4 > 0$. The solution to $x + 1 < 0$ is $x < -1$; the solution to

$x - 4 > 0$ is $x > 4$. There is no value of x satisfying them both. No solution in this case.

Case 2: $x + 1 > 0$ and $x - 4 < 0$. The solution of $x + 1 > 0$ is $x > -1$; the solution of

$x - 4 < 0$ is $x < 4$. The solution to this case is $-1 < x < 4$.

The solution to (C) is $-1 < x < 4$. The graph of this solution set is not the same as that given.

Choice (D): $(x + 1)(x - 4) > 0$. Since $(x + 1)(x - 4) > 0$, you need to consider either

$x + 1 > 0$ and $x - 4 > 0$ (Case 1) OR $x + 1 < 0$ and $x - 4 < 0$ (Case 2).

Case 1: $x + 1 > 0$ and $x - 4 > 0$. The solution to $x + 1 > 0$ is $x > -1$; the solution to

$x - 4 > 0$ is $x > 4$. The set of x values satisfying them both is $x > 4$.

Case 2: $x + 1 < 0$ and $x - 4 < 0$. The solution of $x + 1 < 0$ is $x < -1$; the solution of

$x - 4 < 0$ is $x < 4$. The solution to this case is $x < -1$.

The solution to (D) is $x < -1$ or $x > 4$. The graph of this solution set is not the same as that given.

14. (B). This question asks you to observe a pattern and select a rule or formula that might be used to find any step in the pattern. From the figures, you can see that 2 dots are added at step 2, and 3 dots are added at step 3. Generalizing, you can say that n dots are added at step n for $n > 1$. The total number of dots at step 2 is $\frac{2 \times 3}{2}$, and the total number of dots at step 3 is $\frac{3 \times 4}{2}$. If you extend the pattern to step 4, there will be 10 dots, which can be written as $\frac{4 \times 5}{2}$, and at step 6 there will be $\frac{6 \times 7}{2}$ dots. If you put what seems to be happening into words, you might say: Multiply the step number by the step number plus 1 and divide by 2. Algebraically you would write this as $\frac{n(n + 1)}{2} = \frac{n^2 + n}{2}$.

The answer choice that seems to fit the pattern is (B). You should note that you have not proved that the rule is always true. You have just found a rule that works for the samples given.

Here is another way of seeing the pattern when the step number is 6:

Draw a grid of six rows and seven columns and fill in one dot in each cell of the grid. Then model step six of the pattern by circling the first dot in row 1, the first two dots in row 2, ... , the first six dots in row 6. You will notice that you have a 6×7 grid in which half of the dots have been circled, so that $\frac{6 \times 7}{2} = 21$ is the number of dots in step 6. This approach can also be used to suggest the generalization written algebraically above.

In problems like this, you can also substitute numbers into the rules or formulas given to see which one works. But be careful, since some rules work some of the time and you may have to check each one with several values.

15. (B). This question asks you to apply your understanding of logic to a statement ("All p is q") that we will call S_1. The negation of a statement S_1, sometimes called "not S_1," is another statement, S_2, that is false when S_1 is true and true when S_1 is false. Now, you may be looking for the statement "All p is not q," because in everyday language that is how you would negate the statement, but it is not one of the choices. There is something you need to understand about logic. When the logician says, "All p is q," she also means "Some p is q," and this is the statement you need to negate. This is easily done by saying, "Some p is not q." It often helps to draw a Venn diagram when solving logic problems that are not too complicated. Doing so will help you to visualize the relationships you are asked to think about. So the best answer is (B).

16. (A). This question asks you to apply your knowledge of graphing data in a coordinate plane to a situation involving graduated rate. You should notice that each of the choices given is the graph of a step function. You will need to identify the graph that includes the correct cost for the first step and the correct interval between steps. Since the cost for the first $\frac{1}{4}$ mile or less is $2.50, the cost for the first step (the value on the vertical axis) should be 2.5 over the horizontal interval from 0 to $\frac{1}{4}$ miles, with a solid dot at $\frac{1}{4}$ miles. (There should be no cost at a distance of 0 miles, since there is no charge if there is no ride.) In each of the subsequent horizontal intervals of $\frac{1}{4}$ miles, the cost value on the vertical axis should show an increment of $0.50 with a solid dot at the right end point of each interval. Only choice (A) illustrates this correctly. Choice (C) has the correct cost values for each step but does not represent the endpoints of each interval correctly. The correct answer, therefore, is (A).

17. (D). This question asks you to use your knowledge of fractions and reasoning skills to compare

fractions. Since $\dfrac{1}{1-\frac{3}{7}} < \dfrac{1}{1-x}$, the denominator $1 - \dfrac{3}{7}$ has to be greater than the denominator $1 - x$;

that is, $1 - \dfrac{3}{7} > 1 - x$. (This is because if two fractions have equivalent numerators, the fraction with the

larger denominator will have the smaller value.) Solving $1 - \dfrac{3}{7} > 1 - x$ yields $x > \dfrac{3}{7}$. Similarly,

$\dfrac{1}{1-x} < \dfrac{1}{1-\frac{4}{7}}$ implies that $1 - x > 1 - \dfrac{4}{7}$. Solving this for x yields $x < \dfrac{4}{7}$. Thus, the value of x

must be between $\dfrac{3}{7}$ and $\dfrac{4}{7}$. You should examine each of the fractions in I, II, and III to see if they are

between $\dfrac{3}{7}$ and $\dfrac{4}{7}$. This can be done by comparing fractions (by rewriting them with common

denominators) or by converting the fractions to decimals and comparing the decimal equivalents.

First, comparing fractions:

I. Compare $\dfrac{1}{2}$, $\dfrac{3}{7}$, and $\dfrac{4}{7}$:

$$\frac{3}{7} \cdot \frac{2}{2} = \frac{6}{14}$$
$$\frac{1}{2} \cdot \frac{7}{7} = \frac{7}{14}$$
$$\frac{4}{7} \cdot \frac{2}{2} = \frac{8}{14}$$

So $\dfrac{3}{7} < \dfrac{1}{2} < \dfrac{4}{7}$, and therefore $\dfrac{1}{2}$ could be a value of x.

II. Compare $\dfrac{3}{5}$, $\dfrac{3}{7}$, and $\dfrac{4}{7}$:

$$\frac{3}{5} = \frac{21}{35}$$
$$\frac{3}{7} = \frac{15}{35}$$
$$\frac{4}{7} = \frac{20}{35}$$

Since $\dfrac{4}{7} < \dfrac{3}{5}$, $\dfrac{3}{5}$ cannot be a value of x.

III. Compare $\frac{5}{9}$, $\frac{3}{7}$, and $\frac{4}{7}$:

$$\frac{5}{9} = \frac{35}{63}$$

$$\frac{3}{7} = \frac{27}{63}$$

$$\frac{4}{7} = \frac{36}{63}$$

So $\frac{3}{7} < \frac{5}{9} < \frac{4}{7}$, and $\frac{5}{9}$ could be a value of x.

The correct answer, then, is "I and III only," which is choice (D).

Alternatively, comparing decimals:

I. $\frac{1}{2} = 0.5$, $\frac{3}{7} = 0.428571$, and $\frac{4}{7} = 0.571429$. So $\frac{3}{7} < \frac{1}{2} < \frac{4}{7}$, and therefore $\frac{1}{2}$ could be a value of x.

II. $\frac{3}{5} = 0.6$ Since $\frac{4}{7} < \frac{3}{5}$, $\frac{3}{5}$ cannot be a value of x.

III. $\frac{5}{9} = 0.55\overline{5}$ So, $\frac{3}{7} < \frac{5}{9} < \frac{4}{7}$, and $\frac{5}{9}$ could be a value of x.

The correct answer, then, is "I and III only," which is choice (D).

18. (D). This question asks you to apply your knowledge of percent increase or decrease to determine a selling price based on cost c. In the question, the original price of the car was $c + 0.25c = 1.25c$. The selling price was $p = 1.25c - 0.25(1.25c) = 1.25c(1 - 0.25)$, which is equal to $(1.25c)(0.75)$. Thus, the correct answer is (D).

19. (A). This question asks you to apply your understanding of the concepts of domain and range to compare or determine the ranges of various functions. Recall that a function $f(x)$ can be thought of as a set of ordered pairs, no two of which have the same first component. The domain of a function $f(x)$ is the set of all possible values of x, the first component of the ordered pairs. The range of a function $f(x)$ is the set of all values of $f(x)$, the second component of the ordered pairs. By inspection, the domain of the function in I is all real numbers and the range is all real numbers greater than or equal to 1. The domain of the function in II is all real numbers, and the range is all real numbers greater than or equal to 1. The domain of the function in III is all real numbers, but the range includes numbers less

than 1. For example, $2^{-2} = \dfrac{1}{2^2} = \dfrac{1}{4}$. Thus, the ranges of the functions in I and II are the same. You

might recognize that the ranges of I and II are both $[1,\infty)$. The correct answer is (A).

20. (B). The question asks you to use the information in the graph to determine t, the y-coordinate of a point on the line m that has x-coordinate -4. There are several steps you must take in solving this problem.

■ First, find the slope of the line using the intercepts.
■ Second, write the slope-intercept form of the equation of the line.
■ Third, substitute -4 into the equation to find the value of t.

Line m has slope $-\dfrac{1}{2}$ since $\dfrac{3-0}{0-6} = \dfrac{3}{-6} = -\dfrac{1}{2}$. By inspecting the graph you can see that its

y-intercept is 3. Thus, the equation of the line m can be written as $y = -\dfrac{1}{2}x + 3$. Therefore, the value of t when $x = -4$ is 5. The correct answer is (B).

21. (C). This question asks you to apply your knowledge of the number system in base 10 to the number system in different bases. Recall that each digit in a number has a place value that can differ with the base the number is written in. In base 4, the number 32_4 is equal to $3 \times 4^1 + 2 \times 4^0$, which is 14 (in base 10); and in base 2, the number "14" can be expressed as $14 = 8 + 4 + 2 + 0 = 1 \times 2^3 + 1 \times 2^2 + 1 \times 2^1 + 0 \times 2^0$, which yields 1110. So, $32_4 = 1110_2$, and $x = 1110$. The correct answer is (C).

22. (A). This question asks you to apply your knowledge of range, median, and average to a data collection where only score ranges are given, except for the one score of 100.

I. Since the least score is not known, the range (greatest score minus least score) of the scores cannot be determined.

II. The median (the middle value when the 23 scores are arranged in order) is in the score group 80-89, but its value is not known either.

III. Since all scores except 100 are not specified, the average of the scores cannot be calculated.

Therefore, none of the statistics in I, II, and III can be determined, so the correct answer is (A).

23. (B). This question asks you to use your knowledge of the slope of a line to identify a property of perpendicular lines. It can be shown that the product of the slopes of two perpendicular lines is -1. Another way of saying this is that the slopes of perpendicular lines are negative reciprocals of one another. Since the slope of the line $y = 2x + 13$ is 2, the slope of a line that is perpendicular to this line has to be $-\frac{1}{2}$, which satisfies the requirement that $2\left(-\frac{1}{2}\right) = -1$.

Since the slope of the line $y = -\frac{1}{2}x + 3$ is $-\frac{1}{2}$, the correct answer is (B).

24. (D). This question asks you to apply your knowledge of circles, squares, and proportional reasoning to find the ratio of the areas of two squares. There are many ways in which you can approach this problem. One approach is to use the information given and many things you know about circles, squares, and triangles and do lots of computation. The other is to reason the answer by using your knowledge of what happens to area when you scale up corresponding linear dimensions in a figure. If you like to compute, here is what you might do. First consider circle A. The radius of circle A is 1 and its diameter is 2. This diameter is also the diagonal of the inscribed square and the hypotenuse of a right triangle with side a. By the Pythagorean theorem, $a^2 + a^2 = 2^2$, $2a^2 = 2 \times 2$, $a^2 = 2$, and a, the length of a side of square A, is $\sqrt{2}$. So the area of square A is $\left(\sqrt{2}\right)^2 = 2$. Likewise, the area of square B is $\left(2\sqrt{2}\right)^2 = 8$.

Thus, the ratio of the area of square A to the area of square B is 2:8, which is 1:4. The correct answer is (D).

Alternatively, you can recall that when you are comparing two similar figures and the ratio of corresponding linear dimensions is 1 to 2, as in this problem, the ratio of the areas of the figures is the ratio of the square of the linear dimensions or 1^2 to 2^2, which is 1 to 4. The correct answer is (D).

25. (D). This question asks you to demonstrate your understanding of the properties of closure, commutativity, and identity of a set under a certain operation. A set S is said to be closed under an operation $\circledast$ if the result of performing the operation on any two elements of the set (or on any element of the set with itself) is also an element of the set. Since $a \circledast a = a$, $a \circledast b = b$, $b \circledast a = b$, and $b \circledast b = a$, set S is closed under $\circledast$. It follows from $a \circledast b = b$ and $b \circledast a = b$ that the operation $\circledast$ is commutative. By observing that $a \circledast a = a$ and $a \circledast b = b$, it can be seen that a is the identity element for set S under operation $\circledast$. Hence, the properties in I, II, and III are all satisfied, and the correct answer is (D).

26. (B). This question asks you to apply your knowledge of how to interpret data in a stem-and-leaf plot and to find a new piece of information related to the data. The 12 in the stem column and the 0 in the leaf column taken together represent the weight 120 pounds. The 19 in the stem column and the 5 in the leaf column read together represent the weight 195 pounds. There are 12 weights that are less than 155 pounds: 120, 122, 131, 133, 133, 142, 144, 145, 148, 150, 151, and 154. Thus, the percent of the 25 club members who weigh less than 155 pounds is $\dfrac{12}{25}$ or 48%. The correct answer is (B).

27. (A). This question asks you to use your knowledge of spatial geometry to find the area of a slice of a rectangular solid. As shown in the figure, the section $ABCD$ is a rectangular region that has width AB and length BC. The width of AB is the same as the height of the solid, which is 2. The length of BC is the length of the diagonal of the top face of the solid, which has dimensions 1 by 3. By the Pythagorean theorem, $BC = \sqrt{1^2 + 3^2} = \sqrt{10}$. Therefore, the area of $ABCD$ is equal to $2\sqrt{10}$. The correct answer is (A).

28. (B).

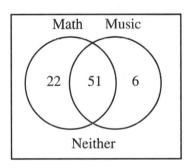

This question asks you to apply your knowledge of sets to solve a real-life problem. You can illustrate the data in a Venn diagram as shown above. The entire rectangular region represents the 100 students who were surveyed. The region of the rectangle that is outside the circles represents the students who took neither a music course nor a math course. From the diagram you can see that the number of students who took neither a music course nor a math course is $100 - (22 + 51 + 6) = 21$. When solving problems like this, you must recall that some students are counted twice and this count shows up in the intersection of the two circles. Therefore, the correct answer is (B).

29. (B). This question asks you to apply your understanding of the counting principle to the probability of a multistage event. In order for the coin to be moved to E, either

- it must be placed first on F and then moved to E or
- it must be placed first on D and then moved to E.

The probability of the first scenario occurring is $\dfrac{1}{6}$ (since the probability of the coin being randomly placed on square F is one out of the six possible squares).

It is more complicated to find the probability of the second scenario occurring. The probability that the coin will be placed first on D is also $\dfrac{1}{6}$. However, the probability that a coin placed on D will be moved to E is the same as the probability that a coin placed on D will be moved to B. Thus, the probability that a coin will be placed on D and then moved to E is $\left(\dfrac{1}{2}\right)\left(\dfrac{1}{6}\right) = \dfrac{1}{12}$.

The total probability of the coin being on E after it is moved is the sum of the probabilities of the two scenarios: $\dfrac{1}{6} + \dfrac{1}{12} = \dfrac{1}{4}$. The correct answer is (B).

30. (B). This question asks you to apply your knowledge of reflection with respect to a line to identify the placement and orientation of a triangle after two consecutive reflections. When the original triangle is reflected about the y-axis, it is moved to the second quadrant with the orientation shown in the figure below. (This reflection maps the point (x, y) to the point $(-x, y)$.)

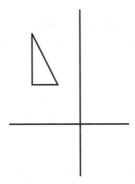

The reflection of this triangle in the second quadrant about the line $y = x$ moves the triangle to the fourth quadrant with the orientation shown below. (This reflection maps the point (x, y) to the point (y, x).)

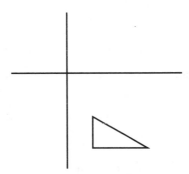

Therefore, the correct answer is (B).

Part Two: Sample Responses to the Constructed-Response Questions and How They Were Scored

This section presents actual scored sample responses to the constructed-response questions in the practice test in chapter 9 and explanations for the scores they received.

As discussed in chapter 4, each constructed-response question on the *Middle School Mathematics* test is scored on a scale from 0 to 3. The general scoring guide used to score these questions is reprinted here for your convenience.

Praxis *Middle School Mathematics* General Scoring Guide

Score	Comment
3	<ul><li>Responds appropriately to all parts of the question</li><li>Where required, provides a strong explanation that is well supported by relevant evidence</li><li>Demonstrates a strong knowledge of subject matter, concepts, theories, facts, procedures, or methodologies relevant to the question</li><li>Demonstrates a thorough understanding of the most significant aspects of any stimulus material presented</li></ul>
2	<ul><li>Responds appropriately to most parts of the question</li><li>Where required, provides an explanation that is sufficiently supported by relevant evidence</li><li>Demonstrates a sufficient knowledge of subject matter, concepts, theories, facts, procedures, or methodologies relevant to the question</li><li>Demonstrates a basic understanding of the most significant aspects of any stimulus material presented</li></ul>
1	<ul><li>Responds appropriately to some part of the question</li><li>Where required, provides a weak explanation that is not well supported by relevant evidence</li><li>Demonstrates a weak knowledge of subject matter, concepts, theories, facts, procedures, or methodologies relevant to the question</li><li>Demonstrates little understanding of significant aspects of any stimulus material presented</li></ul>
0	<ul><li>Blank, off-topic, or totally incorrect response</li><li>Does nothing more than restate the question or some phrases from the question</li><li>Demonstrates very limited understanding of the topic</li></ul>

Constructed-Response Question 1—Sample Responses

We will now look at three scored responses to the first constructed-response question and see comments from the scoring leader about why each response received the score it did.

Sample Response 1: Score of 3

A. Red sticker only = 33
- All the odd numbers from 1-100 that are <u>not</u> multiples of 3
  - b/c evens have yellow, multiples of 3 have green

B. Three stickers = 16
- All the even numbered multiples of 3
  - all have red, evens have yellow and multiples of 3 have green

C. Last locker w/ R, Y, G, + B = 990
- Has to be:

(1) Even

(2) Multiple of 3 ⎤
⎟———— Even multiple of 15
(3) AND multiple of 5 ⎦

  - If it's even and a multiple of 5 it's going to be a multiple of 10.
  - Worked back from 1000 (not divisible by 3)

$$1000 - 10 = 990 \longrightarrow \text{even}$$

$$990 \div 3 = 330$$
$$990 \div 5 = 198$$

√ Check

Commentary on Sample Response That Earned a Score of 3

This response received a score of 3 since it contains a correct answer to each part of the question along with strong explanations. In Part A, the correct answer of 33 is given with the explanation that these are the numbers that are odd and not multiples of three. In Part B, the answer of 16 lockers is correct. There are 16 even multiples of three, as explained. In Part C, the response includes a statement that the number must be divisible by 1, 2, 3, and 5 and a check that the correct answer is 990. This response shows strong conceptual understanding of the mathematics involved in this question.

Sample Response 2: Score of 2

A. 33 numbers only have a red sticker

B. 16 numbers have three stickers

These 16 numbers are all factors of 2 and 3.

C. 9990 would be the last number with a red, yellow, green and blue sticker. It is the last number that is a multiple of 2, 3 & 5.

Commentary on Sample Response That Earned a Score of 2

This response earned a score of 2. In Part A, the correct answer is given without any explanation. In Part B, the correct answer of 16 is given and the explanation is correct, with the exception of the use of the word "factor" instead of "multiple." In Part C, correct conceptual thinking is shown to find the right answer for 10,000 lockers. This response shows basic conceptual understanding, but is flawed by minor errors and a missing explanation.

Sample Response 3: Score of 1

Lily put red stickers on all the lockers. The even lockers have yellow. Every three beginning with 3 would be any factor of 3, (3, 6, 9, 12, ...) There would be 3 columns and 10 rows with red stickers, there would be 30 lockers with only red.

B. They have to be even and every 3 would have to be even. So using multiples of 3, these would be 14, with three red, yellow, and green stickers.

C. The locker would be 900, because it is even, 5 divides it, 3 divides it, so it is the one.

Commentary on Sample Response That Earned a Score of 1

This response received a score of 1. Parts A and B contain incorrect answers and show a rather vague understanding of the concept of multiples. In Part C, the response presents a number (900) that is even and divisible by 5 and 3, but this is not the largest such number less than or equal to 1,000. Overall, this response offers limited evidence of knowledge of the mathematical concepts involved in this question.

Constructed-Response Question 2—Sample Responses

Sample Response 1: Score of 3

A. Alternative 1 $C = 5.00 + .50\ (x)$

   Alternative 2 $C = 3.00 + .75\ (x)$

   C = Cost   x = number of rides

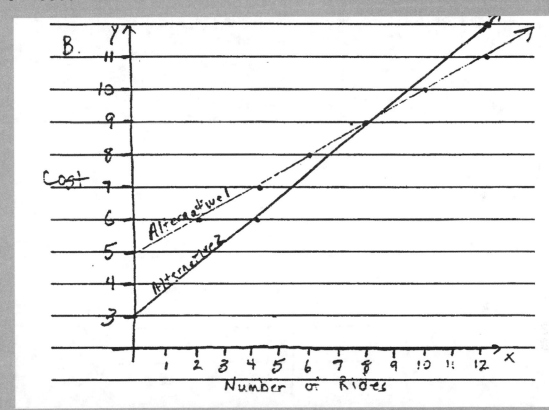

C. If you were planning to ride more than 8 rides, then it would be less expensive to select alternative 1. If you chose to ride less then 8 rides, then it would be less expensive to select alternative 2. If you choose to ride exactly 8 rides then the total cost would be 9 dollars with either alternative.

Commentary on Sample Response That Earned a Score of 3

This response received a score of 3 since all parts are answered correctly and explanations are complete. In Part A, correct equations are given, with the variables used clearly defined. The graph for Part B is drawn accurately, the axes and functions are properly labeled, and the intersection of the two functions is shown. The statements given in Part 3 correctly assess the merits of each pass, including the intersection point. This response offers clear evidence of strong conceptual understanding of the mathematics involved in this question.

Sample Response 2: Score of 2

A. 1. C = 5 + .5x   total cost equals five dollars plus fifty cents for each ride

2. C = 3 + .75x   total cost equals three dollars plus seventy-five cents for each ride

1.			2.		
	1 ride	5.50		1 ride	3.75
	2 rides	6.00		2 rides	4.50
	3 rides	6.50		3 rides	5.25
	4 rides	7.00		4 rides	6.00
	5 rides	7.50		5 rides	6.75
	6 rides	8.00		6 rides	7.50
	7 rides	8.50		7 rides	8.25
	8 rides	9.00		8 rides	9.00

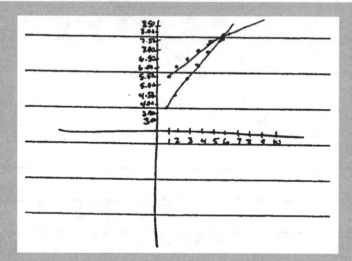

The second option of $3.00 admission and $.75/rides is a better bargain if you ride less than 9 rides. 9 is the break even point. If you plan to ride more than 9 rides — you should pay the $5.00 and then get each ride for only $.50.

Commentary on Sample Response That Earned a Score of 2

This response received a score of 2. In Part A, the equations are correct, but the *x* variable is not clearly defined. In Part B, the graph shown provides evidence of some understanding of how to graph the functions. However, neither the axes nor the functions are labeled, and the choice of a more appropriate scale certainly would have been helpful. For Part C, the statements offered are correct, with the exception of the break-even-point numbers. Although the tables in Part B show the correct break-even point, the response in Part C appears to have confused the cost and the number of rides at this point. Overall, this response shows basic conceptual understanding but also includes several minor errors and omissions.

Sample Response 3: Score of 1

$c = cost$ $b =$ each ride taken (4), Let $b = 4$
          $x =$ admission price $y =$ ride price

$c = 5.00 + .50 \,(b)$ $c = 5.00 + .50\,(4) = 5.00 + 2.00 = \$7.00$

$c = 3.00 + .75 \,(b)$ $c = 3.00 + .75\,(4) = 3.00 + 3.00 = \$6.00$

It is better to purchase the \$3.00 admission fee and pay \$.75 for each ride, you will save approximately \$1.00 for each 2 rides taken.

Commentary on Sample Response That Earned a Score of 1

This response earned a score of 1 since only Part A is answered correctly. The graph in Part B is incomplete and shows little evidence of knowledge of how to graph the two functions in the xy-coordinate system. The statements offered for Part C are only partially correct. This response shows little understanding of the mathematical concepts involved in this question.

Chapter 11
Preparing for the *Middle School Social Studies* Test

▶ ▶ ▶ ▶ ▶ ▶ ▶ ▶ ▶ ▶ ▶ ▶

The *Middle School Social Studies* test is designed to measure the subject-area knowledge and competencies necessary for a beginning teacher of social studies in a middle school. The test contains both multiple-choice and constructed-response questions.

The first part of this chapter focuses on the multiple-choice section of the test. The second part of the chapter contains information about the constructed-response section of the test.

Part One: Multiple-Choice Questions

This part of the chapter is intended to help you organize your preparation for the multiple-choice portion of the test and to give you a clear indication about the depth and breadth of the knowledge required for success on the multiple-choice questions.

The *Middle School Social Studies* test contains 90 multiple-choice questions that constitute approximately 75 percent of the test taker's total test score. It is expected that about 90 minutes will be spent on the multiple-choice questions.

Here is an overview of the areas covered on the test, along with their subareas:

United States History —

> Physical geography of North America
> Native American peoples
> European exploration and colonization
> Establishing a new nation (1776–1791)
> Early years of the new nation (1791–1829)
> Continued national development (1829–1850s)
> Civil War era (1850–1870s)
> Emergence of the modern United States (1877–1900)
> Progressive Era through the New Deal (1900–1939)
> The Second World War and the postwar period
> (1939–1963)
> Recent developments (1960s–present)

World History —

> Prehistory to 1400 C.E.
> World history 1400–1914
> 1914 to the present

Government and Civics ———

> Basic political concepts
> United States political system
> Other forms of government
> International relations

Geography ———

> Themes
> Map skills
> Physical geography
> Human geography
> Regional geography

Economics ———

> Microeconomics I
> Microeconomics II
> Macroeconomics I
> Macroeconomics II

Sociology ———

> Socialization
> Patterns of social organization
> Social institutions
> Study of populations
> Multicultural diversity
> Social problems

Anthropology ———

> How cultures change

The multiple-choice questions on the *Middle School Social Studies* test focus on understanding important social, economic, cultural, and political concepts, geographical thinking, the workings of government systems, important historical events, and contributions of notable individuals within their historical and cultural context. The areas within social studies are mutually enriching and interdependent, and many of the questions on the test will require knowledge and integration of two or more areas.

Using the topic lists that follow

You are not expected to be an expert on all aspects of the topics that follow. But you should understand the major characteristics or aspects of each topic and be able to relate the topic to various situations presented in the test questions, for example, a map, picture, graph, table, or quotation. For instance, here is one of the topic lists in "World History," under Prehistory to 1400 C.E.:

- The decline of classical civilizations and changes (circa 500-1400 C.E.)

  ▶ Nomadic migrations of Huns, Germanic peoples, Mongols

  ▶ Byzantine Empire, eastern Europe, and the emergence of Russia

  ▶ Rise and expansion of Islam and Islamic civilization

> ★ What factors led to the expansion of Islamic influence into India, North Africa, and sub-Saharan Africa?

  ▶ African kingdoms of Ghana, Mali, and Songhai

  ▶ Feudalism in western and central Europe and in Japan

> ★ What similarities and differences were there in the practice of feudalism in Europe and Japan?

  ▶ Mesoamerican and Andean cultures (Aztecs, Olmecs, Toltecs, Mayas, and Incas)

  ▶ Tang, Song, and Ming China

Referring to textbooks, state standards documents, or other sources as needed, make sure you can provide in your own words a brief explanation for the decline of each civilization or key changes that occurred during this time period. Find materials that will help you draw conclusions about the accomplishments of these civilizations in specific fields. You are likely to find that the topics above are covered by most world history or world civilization textbooks, but a single general survey textbook may not cover all of the topics. Consult multiple textbook sources and other materials and resources, including lecture notes from your social studies coursework. You should be able to match up specific topics and subtopics with what you have covered in your courses. Compare and contrast the information from different sources you consult in your search.

Special questions marked with stars

Interspersed throughout the list of topics are questions that are outlined in boxes and preceded by a star (★). These questions are intended to help you test your knowledge of fundamental concepts and your ability to apply fundamental concepts in particular content areas. Some of the starred questions require you to combine several pieces of knowledge in order to formulate an integrated understanding and response. If you spend time on these questions, you will gain increased understanding and facility with the subject matter covered on the test. You might want to discuss these questions and your answers with a teacher or mentor.

Note that the questions marked with stars are not short-answer or multiple-choice, and this study guide does not provide the answers. The questions marked with stars are intended as *study* questions, not practice questions. Thinking about the answers to them should improve your understanding of fundamental concepts and will probably help you answer a broad range of questions on the test.

Study Topics

United States History

★ Make your own timeline of United States history, starting with space for each century: 1400s, 1500s, 1600s, etc., (recognizing, of course, that Native Americans were here for thousands of years before that). Put the events listed in the study topics on your timeline in the correct century, then trace and describe in your own words important trends in cultural, intellectual, social, economic, political, and diplomatic history.

★ Other trends to identify and describe in your timeline might include

- Migration—patterns and effects
- Technology—important developments and their effects
- Urbanization—patterns and effects
- Religions—dominant religions, conflicts with each other and government, influence on society and politics
- The emergence of the United States as a world leader in the areas of military power, industry, finance, and politics
- The significance of the following dates in United States history: 1607, 1776, 1787, 1803, 1861–65, 1914–18, 1929, 1941–45

Physical geography of North America

- The physical characteristics of each major region of North America

- Broad climate patterns of each major region of North America

- Location of the main geographic features of the North American continent
  - ► Rivers
  - ► Lakes
  - ► Mountain ranges
  - ► Plains
  - ► Deserts

Native American peoples

- Important points in the early political, economic, social, and cultural histories of the following native North American peoples

  - ► Inuit (Eskimos)
  - ► Anasazi (cliff dwellers)
  - ► Northwest Indians (Kwakiutl)
  - ► Plains Indians
  - ► Mound Builders
  - ► Iroquois
  - ► Cherokee
  - ► Seminoles

★ What were the major similarities and differences in the economies, religions, governments, and cultures of native North American societies?

European exploration and colonization

- The causes of, purposes of, and different approaches to exploration and colonization of North America by Spain, France, Holland, and England

- Consequences of early contacts between Native Americans and Europeans (exchange of food, disease, culture, etc.)

- The major European explorers, the areas they each explored, and their reasons for exploration

★ What events occurring outside of the Americas caused Europeans and others to come to America?

- Names and locations of major colonies controlled by Spain, France, and England in North America

- Establishment and growth of the English colonies, including their political, economic, social, and cultural organization and institutions

★ How were the New England, the middle and the southern colonies different from each other? How were they similar?

Establishing a new nation (1776–1791)

- Sources of dissatisfaction that led to the American Revolution, including the role of mercantilism and British economic policies following the French and Indian War

    ▶ Proclamation of 1763

    ▶ Grenville Acts

    ▶ Stamp Act

    ▶ Townshend Acts

    ▶ Intolerable Acts

    ▶ The tax on tea

- Key individuals and their roles and major ideas

    ▶ King George

    ▶ John Adams

    ▶ George Washington

    ▶ Thomas Jefferson

    ▶ Benjamin Franklin

    ▶ Thomas Paine

- Major events of the war, including the battles of Lexington and Concord, Saratoga, and Yorktown, and the Treaty of Paris

- Major ideas in the Declaration of Independence

- The first government of the United States under the Articles of Confederation

★ What were the weaknesses in the Articles of Confederation that eventually led to its replacement by the Constitution? How were the colonists' problems and frustrations with the British reflected in the articles?

- How the United States Constitution came into being, including major points of debate and compromises (including the Great Compromise and the Three-Fifths Compromise)

★ What were the major differences between the Federalists and Anti-Federalists?

★ What are *The Federalist* papers and what are the most important principles expressed in them?

★ Read the Constitution carefully in its entirety if you have not already done so.

- The addition of the Bill of Rights to the Constitution; why it was added

★ How did the Constitution deal with the issues of representation of slaves and the importation of slaves?

Early years of the new nation (1791–1829)

- Early presidential administrations and their challenges, including

    ▶ Maintaining national security

    ▶ Creating a stable economy

    ▶ Establishing a court system

    ▶ Defining the authority of the central government

- Establishment of the federal judiciary and the principle of judicial review

- The inception and growth of political parties

- Economic development, including Hamilton's economic plan and tariffs

- Changes in agriculture, commerce, and industry during this period

- Foreign-policy issues and attempts to maintain neutrality

    ▶ Louisiana Purchase

    ▶ War of 1812

    ▶ The Monroe Doctrine

★ What were the political and economic causes and outcomes of the War of 1812?

- Social and cultural development in this period, including

    ▶ Immigration

    ▶ The frontier

    ▶ Family life and the role of women

    ▶ Religious life

    ▶ Slavery

    ▶ Nationalism and regionalism

Continued national development (1829–1850s)

- Origins of slavery in the United States and how it is addressed in the United States Constitution

- Slavery's effects on political, social, religious, economic, and cultural development among African Americans and American society generally

- The important elements of "Jacksonian Democracy"

    ▶ The spoils system

    ▶ Veto of the National Bank

    ▶ Policy of American Indian removal

    ▶ Opposition to the Supreme Court

★ How did Jacksonian Democracy influence United States social, political, and economic life?

- The nullification crisis (Calhoun and states' rights)

- Westward expansion

    ▶ The Lewis and Clark expedition

    ▶ The acquisition of Florida, Texas, Oregon, and California

- The story of the Indian Removal Act and the "Trail of Tears," including broken treaties, massacres, conflicts, and displacement of Native Americans

★ What was "Manifest Destiny" and how did it influence the expansion of United States territory?

★ What was the impact of westward expansion on the United States economy?

- Impact of technological and agricultural innovations before the Civil War

    ▶ Whitney's cotton gin

    ▶ McCormick's reaper

    ▶ Fulton's steamboat

    ▶ The steam locomotive

    ▶ Creation of a national transportation network of roads, canals, and railways

- Changing role of women to consumers and household managers

- Reasons for and consequences of waves of immigration from Europe in the first half of the nineteenth century

- The Second Great Awakening and reform movements

    ▶ Temperance

    ▶ Prison reform

    ▶ Early labor movement

- The Mexican War—major causes and outcomes

★ How did the outcome of the Mexican War affect sectionalism and the politics of western expansion and slavery between 1848 and 1860?

Civil War era (1850–1870s)

- The economic, philosophical, cultural, and political differences between the North, South, and West

★ What long-term trends or developments contributed to the growth of sectionalism?

★ How did the regions try to resolve differences? How and why did those efforts succeed or fail?

★ What were the roles of John C. Calhoun, Henry Clay, and Daniel Webster?

- Missouri Compromise and Compromise of 1850

- The abolitionist movement

★ What were the abolitionists' arguments? How did they pursue their agenda?

★ What was the role of women in the abolitionist movement?

★ What was the impact of the abolitionists' movement on the events of the period?

- The Underground Railroad

- The women's movement

- The Fugitive Slave Act and the Dred Scott case

- Key roles and actions of major figures in this time period, including

  ▶ Abraham Lincoln
  ▶ Ulysses S. Grant
  ▶ Jefferson Davis
  ▶ Robert E. Lee
  ▶ Frederick Douglass
  ▶ William Lloyd Garrison
  ▶ Harriet Tubman
  ▶ Harriet Beecher Stowe
  ▶ John Brown
  ▶ Clara Barton

- Key events leading to the declaration of secession and war

- Significance of major events during the war

  ▶ Capture of Fort Sumter
  ▶ Battles of Gettysburg and Vicksburg
  ▶ Sherman's march

★ What were the advantages that each side, the North and the South, enjoyed before the war began? What were each side's disadvantages? How did these shift during the war? How did they affect the outcome of the war?

  ▶ Lee's final surrender

- Major points and provisions in the Emancipation Proclamation, and the Thirteenth, Fourteenth, and Fifteenth Amendments to the United States Constitution

- Development and impact of Reconstruction policies on the South and the Compromise of 1877

★ What did Reconstruction plans and policies accomplish, and where did they fail?

★ What were the short- and long-term effects of the Compromise of 1877?

- The institution and effects of Jim Crow laws

Emergence of the modern United States (1877–1900)

- Displacement of Native Americans from western lands

- Growth and development of western states

- Segregation after the Civil War, including the Supreme Court decision in *Plessy* v. *Ferguson*

★ What did the court rule in the case of *Plessy* v. *Ferguson*? How did the outcome of this case affect Americans for the next 58 years? What case overturned *Plessy* v. *Ferguson*?

- Business and labor after the Civil War

  ▶ Tariffs, banking, land grants, and subsidies and how states and the federal government used them to encourage business expansion

  ▶ Bankers and entrepreneurs Andrew Carnegie, John D. Rockefeller, and J. P. Morgan—their industries and the changes in American business that they represented

  ▶ The dominance of sharecropping in the South

  ▶ The state of urban areas, especially those affected by renewed immigration, migration from rural areas, difficult working conditions (including child labor), and greater social stratification

  ▶ The beginnings of the labor movement, including the views and actions of Samuel Gompers, the Knights of Labor, and the American Federation of Labor

- Asian and European immigration

★ What were the "push" and "pull" factors that contributed to late-nineteenth-century immigration to the United States?

★ On your timeline of United States history, take particular care with the immigration patterns in the nineteenth century, noting the decades during which immigrants from various countries or regions came to the United States in large numbers.

★ Late-nineteenth-century immigration to the United States can be viewed in terms of creating a "melting pot" or a "pluralist" or "multicultural" society. What does this distinction mean, and why is it important?

- The Pendleton Act

- The Muckrakers

- Political, cultural, and social movements

  ▶ The Populist movement

▶ Social Darwinism

▶ Women's rights

▶ The Social Gospel

★ What reforms did Susan B. Anthony, W. E. B. DuBois, and Robert LaFollette lead?

★ Compare and contrast Populism and Progressivism.

- America's imperialism at the turn of the century as evidenced in the Spanish-American War, the building of the Panama Canal, Theodore Roosevelt's "Big Stick" diplomacy, and the Open Door policy

Progressive era through the New Deal (1900–1939)

- Political and social reforms, direct ballot, settlement-house movement

- Internal migration and Mexican immigration

- Causes of United States participation in the First World War

- Major actions by Woodrow Wilson

- The Treaty of Versailles and its impact on Germany

- The League of Nations

- Important developments in the 1920s

  ▶ The Harlem Renaissance (Zora Neale Hurston, Langston Hughes)

  ▶ Prohibition

  ▶ The Red Scare

  ▶ Women's suffrage (the movement and the amendment)

  ▶ The rise of mass-production techniques and new technologies with far-reaching effects (e.g., automobile and electricity)

  ▶ Immigration and the National Origins Act

- The Great Depression and the New Deal

  ▶ Causes of the Depression

  ▶ Impact of the Depression on various groups in the United States

  ▶ Franklin D. Roosevelt and the New Deal

    ◆ Works Progress Administration

    ◆ Social Security

    ◆ National Labor Relations Board

★ What were the major successes, failures, and legacies of the New Deal?

The Second World War and the postwar period (1939–1963)

- America's role in the Second World War and consequences at home and abroad

  ▶ Attempts to stay out of the war

  ▶ Attack on Pearl Harbor

  ▶ Internment of Japanese Americans

  ▶ Decision to drop atomic bombs on Hiroshima and Nagasaki and the consequences

- America's role in the Cold War; major provisions of the Marshall Plan

- Korean War—major causes and outcomes

- Important political, economic, social, and cultural events and trends in the 1950s, including

  ▶ *Brown* v. *Board of Education of Topeka*

  ▶ The "American dream"

  ▶ The baby boom

  ▶ The GI Bill

  ▶ The rise of suburbia

  ▶ Growth of the consumer society

- Red Scare and McCarthyism

- Cuban missile crisis

Recent developments (1960s–present)

- Vietnam War—major causes, events, and outcomes; student protests in the United States

---

★ How were the "domino theory" and the policy of containment applied to United States foreign policy from the 1950s through the 1970s?

- The African American Civil Rights movement; the leadership and assassination of Martin Luther King Jr.

- Other social reform movements, including

  ▶ The women's movement

  ▶ The peace movement

  ▶ The migrant farm workers movement

  ▶ The consumer movement

  ▶ The environmentalism movement

★ What roles did individuals such as Ralph Nader, Rachel Carson, Betty Friedan, Dennis Banks, and Cesar Chavez play in social reform movements of the period?

- Social policy initiatives: the "Great Society" and the "War on Poverty"

- Watergate scandal

- Increase in the number of working women and changes in family structure

- Changing demographics—subcultures and ethnic and cultural identities

- Conservative movements

  ▶ Religious conservatives

  ▶ Tax revolts

  ▶ The drive to reduce the size of government

★ Why did the voting blocs supporting the major political parties become realigned beginning in the 1960s?

- Industrial trends
  - ▶ The decline of unions
  - ▶ Growth of the service sector
  - ▶ Growth of the budget deficit
  - ▶ The impact of deregulation
  - ▶ Energy and environmental issues

- Energy policies and problems and their economic impact

- International relations, including United States relations with the Soviet Union and its successor states and the changing role of the United States in world political and economic affairs

- Development of computers and information systems and their impact on the economy and jobs

World History

★ Work with a globe or world map as you study and review world history. It would be especially useful to use a historical atlas so that you can see a place or region in its historical context. In addition, many recent world history textbooks have excellent maps. Find regions and places you are studying on the globe and make sure you understand the locations, movements, and relationships among the many societies you are reviewing.

★ Think carefully about the periods into which this history is divided. You will probably find alternative schemes—that is, different names and year spans—in the materials you use for review. Why do historians divide history into periods? Do they agree on the names and dates of some periods more than on others? What do the periods say about historical interpretation? How do periods relate to long-term trends?

★ Explain the significance of the following dates in world history: 220 C.E. and 476 C.E., 622 C.E., 1096-1099 C.E., 1200–1300, 1453, 1492, 1750–1780, 1789, 1870s, 1914–18, 1939–45, 1947, 1957, 1989. (If you cannot find these on your own, see the list at the end of this section.)

Prehistory to 1400 C.E.

- Major developments in human societies during the Paleolithic and Neolithic periods, including the development of settled agriculture, animal husbandry, and sedentary communities

- The development of city civilizations (circa 3000-1500 B.C.E.) in Mesopotamia, the Nile valley, Indus River valley, Huang He River valley, and Mesoamerica

- Ancient empires and civilizations (circa 1700 B.C.E.–500 C.E.)
  - ▶ India
    - ◆ Vedic age (foundation of Indian civilization)
    - ◆ Hinduism (origins and beliefs)
    - ◆ Buddhism (origins and beliefs)
  - ▶ China
    - ◆ Han dynasty (206 B.C.E.–220 C.E.)
    - ◆ Confucianism
    - ◆ Daoism
  - ▶ Ancient western Asia
    - ◆ Judaism and Israel
    - ◆ Assyria
    - ◆ Persia
  - ▶ Mediterranean
    - ◆ Early and Classical Greece (Athens, Sparta, Persian Wars, and Peloponnesian Wars)
    - ◆ Hellenistic world (influence of Greek culture on areas conquered by Alexander the Great)

- ◆ Roman Republic and Empire (republic to empire, Julius and Augustus Caesar, Pax Romana, major causes of the decline and fall)
  - ◆ Christianity (origins and spread, including the rule of Constantine)
- ▶ Africa
  - ◆ Kush, Axum, Nok culture, and Bantu migrations

★ How did geography influence the civilizations of Egypt, Greece, and Rome?

★ What similarities can you find in the establishment and influence of the Roman and Han empires? What factors led to the decline of these two empires?

- ■ The decline of classical civilizations and changes (circa 500–1400 C.E.)
  - ▶ Nomadic migrations of Huns, Germanic peoples, Mongols
  - ▶ Byzantine Empire, eastern Europe, and the emergence of Russia
  - ▶ The rise and expansion of Islam and Islamic civilization

★ What factors led to the expansion of Islamic influence into India, North Africa, and sub-Saharan Africa?

- ▶ African kingdoms of Ghana, Mali, and Songhai
- ▶ Feudalism in western and central Europe and in Japan

★ What similarities and differences were there in the practice of feudalism in Europe and Japan?

- ▶ Mesoamerican and Andean cultures (Aztecs, Olmecs, Toltecs, Mayas, and Incas)
- ▶ Tang, Song, and Ming China

World history: 1400–1914

- ■ Emerging global-wide interactions (circa 1400–1800 C.E.)
  - ▶ The transition from subsistence agriculture to a market economy
  - ▶ The rise of centralized states
  - ▶ The Renaissance (expansion of trade fostered by new practices in Italian city-states, contributions to the arts and sciences)
  - ▶ The Reformation (Martin Luther's Ninety-five Theses, Council of Trent)
  - ▶ The Scientific Revolution (scientific theories and discoveries of Newton, Copernicus, and Galileo)
  - ▶ The Enlightenment (major theoretical contributions of Voltaire and Rousseau)

★ How did the writings of Thomas Hobbes and John Locke influence the eighteenth-century Enlightenment philosophers?

- ▶ Movement of peoples, goods, and ideas
- ▶ Patterns of cultural contact
  - ◆ Destruction of cultures in Mesoamerica and South America
  - ◆ Colonization (economic and military competition for colonies)
  - ◆ Trans-Atlantic slave trade
  - ◆ Rejection of European culture by China and Japan
- ■ Political and industrial revolutions, nationalism (1750–1914)
  - ▶ American Revolution
  - ▶ French Revolution
  - ▶ Latin American independence movements
  - ▶ Industrialization, population expansion, and urbanization

★ What were the key inventions that contributed to the rapid technological change described as the Industrial Revolution?

★ What consequences did industrialization have for population distribution and the birth rates of industrializing nations?

► New ideologies, including liberalism, socialism, and Marxism

► Nationalism and imperialism
  ◆ The unification of Italy and Germany
  ◆ European commercial power expands in Asia and Africa
  ◆ China's resistance (Opium Wars) and revolution

► Reformist and revolutionary movements and conservative reactions
  ◆ Revolutions of the 1830s and 1848
  ◆ The Meiji Restoration in Japan

1914 to the present

■ Conflicts, ideologies, and changes in the twentieth century

  ► Causes, major events, and consequences of the First World War and the Russian Revolution

★ How did the treaties ending the First World War change the map of Europe?

  ► Interwar instabilities
    ◆ Political and economic instabilities in Europe and China
    ◆ The rise of fascism in Italy, Germany, and Japan
    ◆ Anticolonialism

★ What factors contributed to political and economic instability in the world between 1918 and 1939?

★ What similarities and differences are there in the causes and outcomes of the Chinese, Russian, and Mexican revolutions?

  ► Causes and consequences of the Second World War
    ◆ Holocaust and other cases of genocide
    ◆ The global impact of the Cold War
    ◆ Decolonization and neocolonialism

★ Why were the colonies of European powers in Africa and Asia more successful in gaining independence after the Second World War than after the First World War?

  ► The social and economic role of the state and movements to extend the rights of women, minorities, and classes

  ► The role of international organizations
    ◆ League of Nations
    ◆ United Nations

  ► The changing face of economic systems: communism, socialism, and capitalism

  ► Population growth and its impact

■ Contemporary trends (1991 to the present)

  ► Geopolitical changes, including the New Europe and the Pacific Rim

★ How did the end of the Cold War bring about changes in the political map of Europe?

  ► Regional and global economic and environmental interdependence

  ► Globalization: social and economic trends; global popular culture; new technologies

Significance of dates listed on p. 167

220 and 476   Fall of the Han dynasty and fall of the western Roman Empire

622   Flight of Muhammed to Medina (considered the beginning of Islam)

1096-1099   The First Crusade

1200-1300   Mongol domination of Asia

1453   The Fall of Constantinople to the Ottomans

1492   Columbus lands in the Americas

1750-1780   Height of the Atlantic slave trade

1789   The French Revolution

1870s   The scramble for Africa begins

1914-18   The First World War

1939-45   The Second World War

1947   Independence of India and Pakistan

1957   Sputnik launched

1989   Fall of the Berlin Wall

Government and Civics

Basic political concepts

- Reasons why government is needed (conflict resolution, collective decision-making, etc.); how governments are created and changed

- Political theory and major theorists such as Hobbes, Locke, Marx, and Lenin

★ What are the main ideas of each theorist as they contribute to the development of forms of government and their institutions?

★ Where did the ideas of sovereignty and social contract found in the United States Constitution come from?

★ Where did the concepts of checks and balances and the separation of powers come from?

★ How did the concepts of Marx and Lenin influence various forms of government in the twentieth century?

- Major political concepts such as citizenship, legitimacy, power, justice, authority, liberty, rights and responsibilities, federalism, and sovereignty

- Political orientations: radical, liberal, conservative, and reactionary

★ What are the core ideas of each political orientation?

★ What sorts of government or policy would each support, and why?

United States political system

- The content and structure of the United States Constitution and the Bill of Rights and the processes of constitutional interpretation and amendment

- The "separation of powers" among the three branches of the federal government and the relationship among them

★ What are the formal powers of each branch?

★ What are the functions of checks and balances and the separation of powers?

★ What are some examples of how the three branches check and balance each other?

▶ The processes contained in the Constitution for electing the president and vice president, passing legislation, removing federal officials from office, and selecting federal judges and cabinet officials

- The formation and operation of political institutions not established by the Constitution, such as political parties, political action committees, interest groups, and the federal bureaucracy; also, the role of the media and public opinion in American political life

- Relationships among federal, state, and local governments

> ★ What impact do these relationships have on policy, responsibility, and authority? How have the relationships developed and changed over time? What factors drove those changes?

- Individual and group political behavior, including voting behavior; changes in group opinion over time; interactions of race, class, and gender with political participation and opinion; and forms of political participation

  ▶ Hierarchy of the federal court system
  ▶ Landmark Supreme Court decisions, such as
    ♦ *Marbury* v. *Madison*
    ♦ *McCulloch* v. *Maryland*
    ♦ *Plessy* v. *Ferguson*
    ♦ *Brown* v. *Board of Education of Topeka*
    ♦ *Miranda* v. *Arizona*

> ★ What was the court's ruling in each of these cases? What were the short- and long-term effects of each?
>
> ★ How could the rulings in these cases be modified by later Supreme Court rulings? What would cause this to happen?

  ▶ Judicial activism *versus* judicial restraint

Other forms of government

- Classical republic

- Liberal democracy

- Federalism

- Absolute monarchy

- Dictatorship

- Parliamentary system

International relations

- Functions, powers, and problems of international organizations, such as the United Nations, and international law (human rights, world health, democratization)

Geography

Themes

- Relative and absolute location

- Physical and human characteristics of "place"

- Human-environment interactions

- Types of movement

Map skills

- Different types of maps

> ★ Be able to read and interpret various types of maps, including globe, climate, political, physical or topographic (including those with contour lines), thematic, and satellite maps.

- Distance and direction

- Purposes of latitude and longitude

★ How are the imaginary lines of latitude and longitude organized on Earth to identify the absolute location of a place?

- Location of physical features

- Spatial patterns

- Legends and keys

★ Locate maps with scales for miles and kilometers. Practice measuring distances using each measurement of distance.

★ Locate maps with keys for such factors as elevation, vegetation, climate zones. Practice drawing conclusions from the data illustrated by the key.

Physical geography

- Different types of landforms and water, climate, vegetation, and natural resources

★ Be able to define and distinguish between different types of landforms including continents, isthmuses, peninsulas, plains, plateaus, and steppes.

★ Be able to define and distinguish between different types of bodies of water and waterways, including oceans, seas, bays, estuaries, straits, canals, and rivers.

▶ Natural resources—what they are and why they matter
  ♦ Renewable and nonrenewable resources
  ♦ Energy, mineral, food, and land resources

★ How have the use, distribution, and importance of natural resources changed since the beginning of the twentieth century?

▶ Fundamental forces at work in weather systems, climate, and seasonal changes

★ What is the difference between weather and climate?

★ Explain how each of the following factors influences climate: latitude, ocean currents, winds, mountains, elevation, and proximity to water.

- Effects of human-initiated changes on the environment and community
  ▶ Water, air and ground pollution
  ▶ Deforestation and desertification
  ▶ Global warming
  ▶ Ozone depletion

Human geography

- Cultural geography

- Major cultural characteristics in the largest nations and regions of the world

★ What cultural factors are commonly used to organize the world into cultural regions?

- Economic geography
  ▶ Distinguish between developing and developed (industrialized) nations; the relative wealth of the most populous nations
  ▶ Major current trade relationships, especially between the United States and other nations
  ▶ Economic interdependence among major regions and nations

- Political geography
  ▶ Borders and political units

★ What are the types of natural and artificial boundaries?

★ What are the advantages and disadvantages of each type?

- Population geography

- Population movements, including basic concepts (push, pull factors); major trends in the population patterns of the world in the nineteenth and twentieth centuries and their causes (e.g., the Great Irish Famine)
- Consequences of overpopulation
- Factors affecting settlement patterns—why some places are densely populated and others are sparsely populated

Regional geography

- Location of major regions, countries, and cities of the world
- Ways in which regions are categorized for political, physical, or cultural reasons

★ Compare formal, or uniform, and functional regions.

Economics

Microeconomics I

- The basic economic problems of scarcity and opportunity cost

★ Why does the problem of scarcity force people to consider opportunity cost?

★ How does an increase or decrease in productivity affect efforts to overcome the problem of scarcity?

▶ How limited productive resources (land, labor, capital) force nations and individuals to deal with the issues of choice and cost

▶ The reasons for trade among nations and individuals; comparative advantage

▶ Impacts of trade barriers such as tariffs and quotas

▶ Pros and cons of protectionist policy

▶ How the different types of economic systems (command, traditional, free market, and mixed) attempt to deal with the economic problem

★ Why do people engage in exchange?

★ What are the sources of gain from trade?

★ What are the methods of economic organization? How do they differ?

★ Why do nations impose trade restrictions? What impact do trade restrictions have on the economy?

▶ The basic institutions that compose the market economy (e.g., businesses, households, and labor unions)

▶ How wages, profits, and interest rates act as economic incentives

- The determinants of supply and demand and the ways in which changes in these determinants affect equilibrium price and output

★ What are the laws of supply and demand?

★ How is the market price of a good determined?

★ How do markets adjust to changes in demand? How do markets adjust to changes in supply?

★ What happens when prices are set above the market equilibrium price?

★ What happens when prices are set below the market equilibrium price?

▶ Instances in which the private market may fail to allocate resources efficiently, as in the case of negative or positive externalities

▶ Examples of market failures

▶ The role of government and the type of taxes (e.g., sales, property, income)

★ How does the imposition of a tax affect a market?

★ What are the differences between progressive, proportional, and regressive taxes?

Microeconomics II

■ The characteristics and behavior of the product markets known as perfect competition and monopoly

★ What are the characteristics of perfect competition and of a monopoly? Compare and contrast in terms of the number of buyers and sellers, the type of product sold, degree of control over price, conditions of entry, and efficiency (allocative and productive).

★ How do government policies attempt to regulate pure competition and monopolies?

▶ Distribution of income, including the impact of the passage of minimum-wage laws

Macroeconomics I

■ Basic macroeconomic concepts, including

▶ Gross national product (GNP)

▶ Gross domestic product (GDP)

♦ Components that make up GDP

♦ The problems of calculating GDP

▶ Inflation

▶ Unemployment

▶ The role of money and exchange mechanisms

▶ Economic goals (e.g., growth, full employment, efficiency)

■ The use of the consumer price index (CPI) as a measure of the price level and the role of the CPI in making distinctions between nominal- and real-income values

★ What is gross domestic product (GDP)? What are the major components of GDP?

★ What is a price index? What do price indexes measure? How can they be used to adjust for changes in the general level of prices?

★ What are the causes of recessions and booms, sometimes accompanied by periods of inflation?

Macroeconomics II

■ The basic models of aggregate demand (AD) and aggregate supply (AS) and how the AS/AD model determines the equilibrium level of GDP

■ The use of fiscal and monetary tools to achieve price stability, full employment, and economic growth

★ What is the difference between fiscal and monetary policy?

★ What do economists expect the use of expansionary or contractionary policies to achieve?

★ What effect can government spending have on the economy?

★ What are the major functions of the Federal Reserve System?

★ What are the major tools the Federal Reserve can use to control the supply of money?

■ International trade and finance (trade balance, exchange rates, and balance of payments)

▶ Effects of international trade (net exports) on the domestic economy

▶ International currency fluctuation, appreciation and depreciation of a nation's currency and its effect on net exports and capital flows

■ The impact of international trade on other issues, including currency exchange rates and balance of payments

- The international aspects of growth and stability (e.g., economic development and foreign aid)

★ Why do nations trade? When can a nation gain from international trade?

★ Why do international exchange rates fluctuate?

★ What information is provided in the balance-of-payments account?

Current issues and controversies

- The protectionist arguments for tariffs, quotas, and restrictive immigration policies

- Government regulation of industry

- Protecting the environment versus stimulating economic growth

- The relative effectiveness of fiscal and monetary policies

- The impact of the national deficit and national debt

- The impact of an imbalance in the balance of trade

Sociology

Socialization

- The role of socialization in society

- Major agents of socialization

- The roles of positive and negative sanctions in the socialization process

★ How do social institutions take part in the socialization of an individual into society?

★ How does the socialization process change throughout the life cycle?

Patterns of social organization

- The concept of role

- The functions of primary and secondary groups and of group norms

- Folkways, mores, laws, beliefs, and values

- Social stratification

- Social mobility

★ What factors are commonly used in societies to establish social stratification?

★ What part does ascribed or achieved status play in the degree of social mobility for an individual?

Social institutions

- Including family, education, government, religion, clubs, ethnic communities, and the economy

Study of populations

- The impact on society of changes in population growth and distribution, migration, and immigration

Multicultural diversity

- The concepts of ethnocentrism, stereotypes, biases, values, ideals, prejudice, and cultural relativity

- Variation in race, ethnicity, and religion

- The prevalence and consequences of prejudice and discrimination

- The concepts of pluralism and multicultural diversity

★ How do advocates of multicultural diversity contrast its impact on society to traditional forms of amalgamation and assimilation of subcultures?

Social problems

- Contemporary social problems, including causes, consequences, and proposed solutions

Anthropology

How cultures change

- Invention

- Innovation

- Cultural diffusion

- Adaptation

- Acculturation

- Assimilation

- Retention

- Reinterpretation

- Extinction

Part Two: Constructed-Response Questions

This section of the chapter is intended to provide you with strategies for how to read, analyze, and understand the constructed-response questions on the Middle School Social Studies test and then for how to outline and write successful responses.

The test contains three equally-weighted constructed-response questions that assess the knowledge and skills necessary for a beginning middle school social studies teacher. The questions are based on the understanding and application of social studies knowledge, concepts, methodologies, and skills across the fields of United States History, World History, Government/Civics, Geography, Economics, Sociology, and Anthropology. All of the short-answer essays are interdisciplinary, reflecting the complex relationship among the social studies fields. Most questions are based on interpreting stimulus material such as written passages, maps, charts, graphs, tables, cartoons, diagrams, and paintings. The questions also ask you to draw inferences from such materials and place them in their historical, geographical, political, and economic contexts. The three equally-weighted constructed-response questions will focus on important historical events and issues as well as on fundamental social studies concepts. These questions, which should take about 10 minutes each to complete and will together comprise 25 percent of the total score, emphasize critical-thinking skills and interpretation of social studies content material. This test is designed to gather evidence about your knowledge of social studies and your ability to demonstrate your knowledge and skills in the fields that comprise the discipline.

What to Study

Success on this section of the test is not simply a matter of learning more about how to respond to constructed-response questions. It also takes real knowledge of the subject. It therefore would serve you well to review texts and notes relevant to the test's subject matter.

The following books, articles, and Web sites are particularly relevant to the types of topics and skills the test covers. Note, however, that the test is not based on these resources and that they do not necessarily cover every topic that may be included in the test. Most texts written for high school and college survey courses will provide a sufficient overview of the subjects. As you read, study how the primary sources, graphs, charts, and maps relate to the content of each chapter.

U.S. History

http://www.archives.gov/digital_classroom/lessons/analysis_worksheets/worksheets.html

The National Archives Administration has helpful checklists for what to look for in primary sources.

The following books provide an overview of United States history.

Davidson, James. 2001. *Nation of Nations*. Vols. I and II. Boston: McGraw-Hill.

Offers a concise narrative of United States history. It is a balanced text that carefully blends political and social history.

Divine, Robert. 1998. *America Past and Present*. 4th ed. Vols. I and II. Upper Saddle River, NJ: Longman.

Henretta, James. 2002. *America: A Concise History.* 2d ed. Vols. I and II. New York: Bedford-St. Martin's.

Nash, Gary. 1992. *American Odyssey: The US in the Twentieth Century.* Lake Forest, IL: Glencoe.

World History

http://www.phschool.com/curriculum_support/brief_review/global_history/index.html

This New York State Regents Web site offers practice tests containing questions based on stimulus material. Although these tests require the candidate to use several different stimuli while the Middle School Social Studies test questions usually use only one or two, they provide a good opportunity to practice using stimulus material when answering a question. There are also multiple-choice practice tests.

Stearns, Peter, Stephen Gosch, and Erwin Grieshaber. 2003. *Documents in World History.* 3d ed. Vol. I, *The Great Traditions: From Ancient Times to 1500* and Vol II, *The Modern Centuries: From 1500 to the Present.* New York: Longman.

A collection of primary sources for world history.

Wiesner, Merry, William Bruce Wheeler, Franklin Doeringer, and Kenneth Curtis. 2002. *Discovering the Global Past: A Look at the Evidence.* 2d ed. Vol I, *To 1650* and Vol II, *Since 1400.* Boston: Houghton Mifflin Company.

This collection of documents is organized by historical periods. Each includes the problem, background, method, and questions to consider, as well as the documents themselves.

The following books provide an overview of world history.

Stearns, Peter N. 1992. *World Civilizations: The Global Experience.* New York: Harper Collins.

Tignor, Robert, et al. 2002. *Worlds Together, Worlds Apart: A History of the Modern World (1300 to the Present).* New York: W.W. Norton.

Political Science

Burns, James MacGregor, J. W. Peltason, Thomas E. Cronin, David B. Magleby, David M. O'Brien, and Paul C. Light. 2003. *Government by the People.* 20th ed. New York: Prentice Hall.

Katznelson, Ira and Helen V. Milner. 2003. *Political Science: State of the Discipline.* New York: W.W. Norton & Company.

Economics

Baumol, William J. and Alan S. Blinder. 2002. *Economics: Principles and Policy.* 9th ed. Mason, Ohio: Thomson/South-Western.

Hall, Robert E. and Mark Lieberman. 2002. *Economics: Principles and Applications.* 2d ed. Mason, OH: Thomson/South-Western.

McConnell, Campbell R. and Stanley L. Brue. 2002. *Economics: Principles, Problems, and Policies.* 15th ed. Boston: McGraw-Hill.

Geography

Getis, Arthur, Judith Getis, and Jerome D. Fellmann. 2004. *Introduction to Geography.* 9th ed. Boston: McGraw-Hill Higher Education.

This source provides a solid introductory-level overview of physical and human geography.

Fellmann, Jerome D., Arthur Getis, and Judith Getis. 2003. *Human Geography: Landscapes of Human Activities.* 7th ed. New York: McGraw-Hill.

This is an introductory-level textbook for human and cultural geography. It also includes a section on human actions and environmental impacts.

Hudson, John C., and Edward B. Espenshade, Jr., eds. 2000. *Goode's World Atlas.* 20th ed. Skokie: Rand McNally.

Sociology

Andersen, Margaret L. and Howard F. Taylor. 2005. *The Essentials.* 3rd ed. Belmont, CA: Wadsworth.

Andersen, Margaret L. and Howard F. Taylor. 2004. *Sociology: Understanding a Diverse Society.* 3rd ed. Belmont, CA: Wadsworth.

Anthropology

Ember, Carol, Melvin Ember, and Peter Peregrine. 2005. *Anthropology.* 11th ed. Upper Saddle River, NJ: Prentice Hall.

What the Test Scorers Are Looking For

Even if you feel confident about your knowledge of the content to be tested, you still may wonder how you will be able to tell what the test scorers want.

In fact, you can find out what the test scorers want by looking at the questions themselves. The constructed-response test questions are crafted to be as clear as possible regarding what tasks you are expected to do. No expectations are hidden in the question or expressed in code words. The social studies educators who score your responses base your score on two considerations:

- Whether you do the tasks that the question asks for

- How well you do those tasks

So, to answer more specifically the question "What do the scorers want?" we should look at test questions, much like the ones on the test.

Understanding What the Questions Are Asking

It is impossible to write a successful response to a question unless you thoroughly understand the question. Often test takers jump into their written response without taking enough time to analyze exactly what the question is asking, how many different parts of the question need to be addressed, and how the information in the accompanying quotes, cartoons, charts, maps, or tables can be successfully incorporated. The time you invest in making sure you understand what the question is asking will very likely pay off in a better performance, as long as you budget your time and do not spend a large proportion of the available time just reading the question.

Examine the overall question closely, then identify what specific questions are being asked, mentally organize your response, and outline your key themes. Leave yourself plenty of time to write your answer. If you think out your response beforehand, your response will be stronger.

Sample Question

To illustrate the importance of understanding the question before you begin writing, let's start with a sample question.

COTTON PRODUCTION 1811

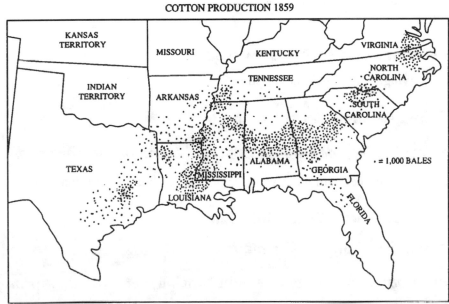

COTTON PRODUCTION 1859

(A) What do the two maps above reveal about the changes in cotton production in the United States between 1811 and 1859?

(B) Based on your knowledge of United States history, briefly describe two key developments—political, economic, or technological—that brought about these changes.

Identifying the Key Components of the Question

- Look carefully at the map and be sure you understand what it is showing; start by reading the title and the key.

- Identify the *changes in cotton production* in the United States between 1811 and 1859.

- *Identify* **two** key developments—political, economic, or technological—that brought about these changes.

- *Describe* how those factors contributed to the changes shown in the map.

Organizing Your Response

Successful responses start with successful planning, either with an outline or with another form of notes. By planning your response, you greatly decrease the chances that you will forget to answer any part of the question. You increase the chances of creating a well-organized response. Your note-taking space also gives you a place to jot down thoughts whenever you think of them—for example, when you have an idea about one part of the question while you are writing your response to another part. Planning your response is time well invested, although you must keep track of the time so that you leave sufficient time to write your response.

To illustrate a possible strategy for planning a response, let us focus again on the sample question introduced above. We analyzed the question and found that it asked for a two-part response. You might begin by jotting down those parts on your notes page, leaving space under each. This will ensure that you address each part when you begin writing.

Sample Notes—Main Parts to Be Answered

Here you start by identifying each part of the question:

> A. Identify changes shown in the maps.
>
> B. Describe how two key components brought about the changes.

You then might quickly fill out the main ideas you want to address in each part, like this:

Sample Notes—Ideas Under Each Main Part

> A. Identify changes shown in the maps.
>
> a. Cotton production increases substantially—more bales produced in more states
>
> b. Cotton production geographically more dispersed to more states

> B. Describe how two key components brought about these changes.
>
> a. Cotton gin
>
> b. Slave population
>
> c. Increase in markets

Now look at your notes and add any ideas that would address these characteristics. Notice below the additions that are made.

Sample Notes—With Added Ideas

This is where you use your knowledge of social studies. What you put here depends on how much you know. The following are some possible responses:

> A. Identify changes shown in the maps.
>
> a. Cotton production increases substantially—more bales produced in more states
>
> b. Cotton production geographically more dispersed to more states
>
> c. Cotton is a minor crop in 1811—harvested mostly in mid-Atlantic states—Carolinas, pockets in Tennessee, Virginia, Georgia
>
> d. By 1859—very large increase, most southern states growing cotton
>
> B. Describe how two key components brought about these changes.
>
> a. Cotton gin—revolutionized the way cotton was harvested
>
> b. Slave population—stabilized and grew
>
> c. Increase in markets—demand in northern United States and Europe

You have now created the skeleton of your written response.

Writing Your Response

Now the important step of writing your response begins. The scorers will not consider your notes when they score your paper, so it is crucial that you integrate all the important ideas from your notes into your actual written response.

Some test takers believe that every written response on a Praxis test has to be in formal essay form—that is, with an introductory paragraph, then paragraphs with the response to the question, then a concluding paragraph. This is the case for very few Praxis tests (e.g., *PPST Writing*). The Middle School Social Studies test does **not** require formal essays, so you should use techniques that allow you to communicate information efficiently and clearly. For example, you can use bulleted or numbered lists, or a chart, or a combination of essay and chart.

What follows is an actual response by a test taker.

Sample Response That Received a Score of 3

(A)   The two maps illustrate that cotton was a minor production crop in 1811 and confined to mostly the mid-Atlantic states. It was harvested in the Carolinas with pockets in Tennessee, Virginia and Georgia. Obviously, things had changed by 1859 with the most southern states producing the bulk of the cotton.

(B)   One reason for the increase in cotton production between 1811-59 was the introduction of the cotton gin. This machine revolutionized the way cotton was harvested. Another aspect was the stabilization of a larger slave population in the South. Cotton is labor intensive and the manpower was available through the use of African slaves. As the demand for cotton grew, slaveholders grew more dependent on slaves and were therefore less willing to set slaves free. They also sought to increase the number of slaves they held. Thirdly markets became larger for the cotton. Trade continued to increase within North America as well as with Europe because of increased demand for cotton in the textile mills in these areas.

Commentary on Sample Response That Earned a Score of 3

This response received a score of 3 because it answers all parts of the question clearly. It identifies the major changes shown on the map and uses some specifics from the map to do so. The response identifies and explains two key developments (stabilization of the slave population and the growth of the cotton trade) that brought about the changes shown on the map. A third factor is provided (the cotton gin) but not fully explained.

Also note that the two developments provided (demand and labor supply) are both economic. This question requires only that the factors be economic, political, or technological. Both may be economic, or one may be technological and one may be political. However, some questions state specifically that the factors must come from different fields (i.e., one political and one technological factor).

Sample Response That Received a Score of 1

(A)   From the 2 maps shown, cotton production in the United States more than quadrupled from 1811 to 1859. In 1811, cotton production in the USA was limited to South Carolina and Georgia and some in Virginia, but in 1859, all of the South has been "overcome" by cotton production. It has even stretched west to the eastern part of Texas. By 1859, cotton production which was formerly limited to 3 states has now spread to North Carolina, northern Florida, Alabama, Mississippi, Louisiana, Arkansas and Eastern Texas.

(B) In the 1811 period, cotton production was limited mostly due to limited labor. But as soon as slaves were brought from Africa, labor was abundant and cotton production spread like wild fire.

Commentary on Sample Response That Earned a Score of 1

This response received a score of 1 because it does not accurately address the second part of the question. It addresses the first part with a significant amount of detail and refers often to the map. It inaccurately states that cotton production "was formerly limited to three states." While a majority of the cotton production was located in three states, several others, such as North Carolina, Tennessee, and the Territory of Orleans, produced small amounts.

The second part of the response does not answer the question of what brought about the changes in cotton production shown on the map. The response also contains an important error in implying that the importation of African slaves did not begin until after 1811. In fact, the slave trade began in the early seventeenth century and continued until the early nineteenth century.

In Conclusion

Whatever format you select, the important thing is that your answer be thorough, complete, and detailed. You need to be certain to do the following:

- Answer all parts of the question.

- Give reasons for your answers.

- Demonstrate subject-specific knowledge in your answer.

- Refer to the data in the stimulus.

It is a good idea to use the practice test in the next chapter to help you develop a plan for how you will take the test on the actual testing day, especially if you tend to get nervous or freeze up in a testing situation. Some test takers prefer to start with the question with which they feel most confident. If you do this, make certain at the end of the test that you have answered all of the questions. Whatever format or order you select for your essays, the important thing is that your answers be thorough, complete, and detailed.

Chapter 12

Practice Questions for the *Middle School Social Studies* Test

▶ ▶ ▶ ▶ ▶ ▶ ▶ ▶ ▶ ▶ ▶ ▶

Now that you have studied the content topics in the six areas in social studies and have worked through strategies relating to multiple-choice and constructed-response questions, you should take the following practice test. You will probably find it helpful to simulate actual testing conditions, giving yourself a set amount of time to work on the questions. If you wish, you can cut out and use the answer sheet provided to answer the multiple-choice questions and write your responses to the constructed-response questions on the lined answer pages.

Keep in mind that the test you take at an actual administration will have different questions, although the proportion of questions in each area and major subarea will be approximately the same. You should not expect the percentage of questions you answer correctly for these practice questions to be exactly the same as when you take the test at the actual administration, since numerous factors affect a person's performance in any given testing situation.

When you have finished the practice questions, you can score your answers to the multiple-choice questions, see sample scored responses to the constructed-response questions, and read explanations of the answers and responses in Chapter 13.

Note: If you are taking these practice questions to help you prepare for the *Middle School: Content Knowledge* test, you should keep in mind that the test you take at the actual administration will have 120 multiple-choice questions, with 30 questions in each of the four content areas. You will be allowed 120 minutes to complete the test. The test does not contain any constructed-response questions.

THE PRAXIS
S E R I E S
Professional Assessments for Beginning Teachers ®

TEST NAME:

Middle School Social Studies

68 Practice Questions

Approximate time for the whole practice test—95 minutes

Suggested time for Part A (multiple choice)—65 minutes

Suggested time for Part B (constructed response)—30 minutes

(**Note:** At the official administration of this test, there will be 90 multiple-choice questions and 3 constructed-response questions. You will be allowed 120 minutes total to complete the test. The sections of the test will not be timed separately, though it is recommended that you spend 90 minutes on the multiple-choice questions and 30 minutes on the constructed-response questions.)

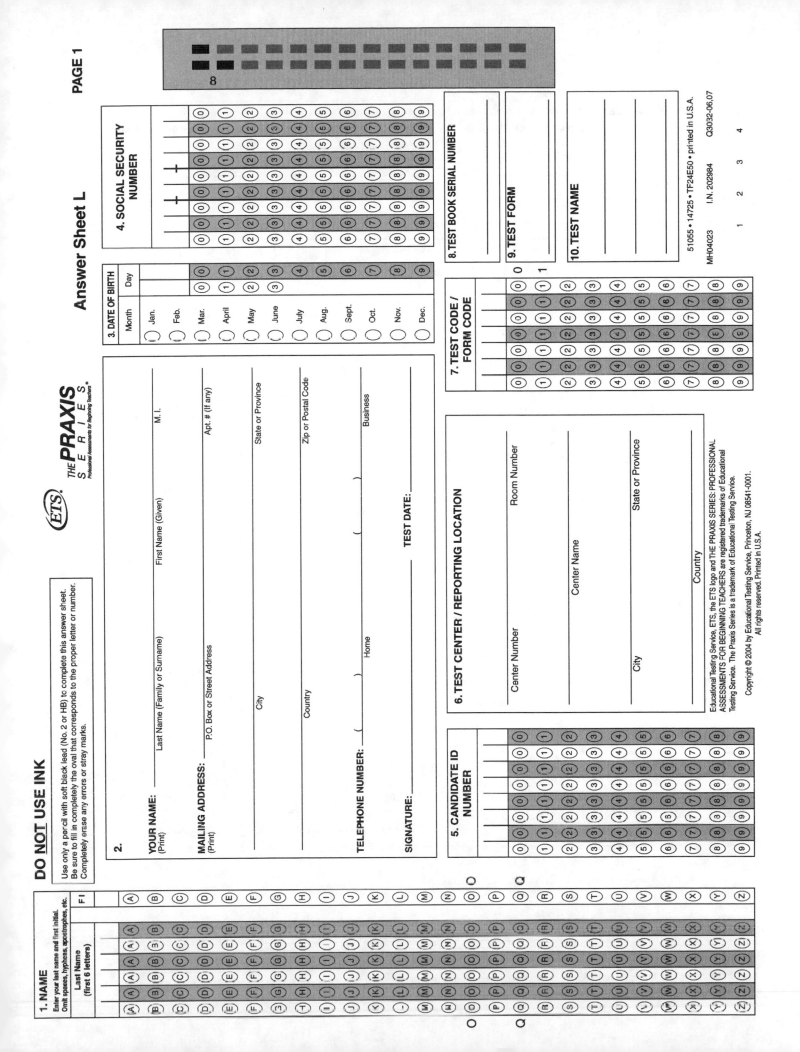

PAGE 2

BE SURE EACH MARK IS DARK AND COMPLETELY FILLS THE INTENDED SPACE AS ILLUSTRATED HERE: ● .

#		#		#		#	
1 Ⓐ Ⓑ Ⓒ Ⓓ		31 Ⓐ Ⓑ Ⓒ Ⓓ		61 Ⓐ Ⓑ Ⓒ Ⓓ		91 Ⓐ Ⓑ Ⓒ Ⓓ	
2 Ⓐ Ⓑ Ⓒ Ⓓ		32 Ⓐ Ⓑ Ⓒ Ⓓ		62 Ⓐ Ⓑ Ⓒ Ⓓ		92 Ⓐ Ⓑ Ⓒ Ⓓ	
3 Ⓐ Ⓑ Ⓒ Ⓓ		33 Ⓐ Ⓑ Ⓒ Ⓓ		63 Ⓐ Ⓑ Ⓒ Ⓓ		93 Ⓐ Ⓑ Ⓒ Ⓓ	
4 Ⓐ Ⓑ Ⓒ Ⓓ		34 Ⓐ Ⓑ Ⓒ Ⓓ		64 Ⓐ Ⓑ Ⓒ Ⓓ		94 Ⓐ Ⓑ Ⓒ Ⓓ	
5 Ⓐ Ⓑ Ⓒ Ⓓ		35 Ⓐ Ⓑ Ⓒ Ⓓ		65 Ⓐ Ⓑ Ⓒ Ⓓ		95 Ⓐ Ⓑ Ⓒ Ⓓ	
6 Ⓐ Ⓑ Ⓒ Ⓓ		36 Ⓐ Ⓑ Ⓒ Ⓓ		66 Ⓐ Ⓑ Ⓒ Ⓓ		96 Ⓐ Ⓑ Ⓒ Ⓓ	
7 Ⓐ Ⓑ Ⓒ Ⓓ		37 Ⓐ Ⓑ Ⓒ Ⓓ		67 Ⓐ Ⓑ Ⓒ Ⓓ		97 Ⓐ Ⓑ Ⓒ Ⓓ	
8 Ⓐ Ⓑ Ⓒ Ⓓ		38 Ⓐ Ⓑ Ⓒ Ⓓ		68 Ⓐ Ⓑ Ⓒ Ⓓ		98 Ⓐ Ⓑ Ⓒ Ⓓ	
9 Ⓐ Ⓑ Ⓒ Ⓓ		39 Ⓐ Ⓑ Ⓒ Ⓓ		69 Ⓐ Ⓑ Ⓒ Ⓓ		99 Ⓐ Ⓑ Ⓒ Ⓓ	
10 Ⓐ Ⓑ Ⓒ Ⓓ		40 Ⓐ Ⓑ Ⓒ Ⓓ		70 Ⓐ Ⓑ Ⓒ Ⓓ		100 Ⓐ Ⓑ Ⓒ Ⓓ	
11 Ⓐ Ⓑ Ⓒ Ⓓ		41 Ⓐ Ⓑ Ⓒ Ⓓ		71 Ⓐ Ⓑ Ⓒ Ⓓ		101 Ⓐ Ⓑ Ⓒ Ⓓ	
12 Ⓐ Ⓑ Ⓒ Ⓓ		42 Ⓐ Ⓑ Ⓒ Ⓓ		72 Ⓐ Ⓑ Ⓒ Ⓓ		102 Ⓐ Ⓑ Ⓒ Ⓓ	
13 Ⓐ Ⓑ Ⓒ Ⓓ		43 Ⓐ Ⓑ Ⓒ Ⓓ		73 Ⓐ Ⓑ Ⓒ Ⓓ		103 Ⓐ Ⓑ Ⓒ Ⓓ	
14 Ⓐ Ⓑ Ⓒ Ⓓ		44 Ⓐ Ⓑ Ⓒ Ⓓ		74 Ⓐ Ⓑ Ⓒ Ⓓ		104 Ⓐ Ⓑ Ⓒ Ⓓ	
15 Ⓐ Ⓑ Ⓒ Ⓓ		45 Ⓐ Ⓑ Ⓒ Ⓓ		75 Ⓐ Ⓑ Ⓒ Ⓓ		105 Ⓐ Ⓑ Ⓒ Ⓓ	
16 Ⓐ Ⓑ Ⓒ Ⓓ		46 Ⓐ Ⓑ Ⓒ Ⓓ		76 Ⓐ Ⓑ Ⓒ Ⓓ		106 Ⓐ Ⓑ Ⓒ Ⓓ	
17 Ⓐ Ⓑ Ⓒ Ⓓ		47 Ⓐ Ⓑ Ⓒ Ⓓ		77 Ⓐ Ⓑ Ⓒ Ⓓ		107 Ⓐ Ⓑ Ⓒ Ⓓ	
18 Ⓐ Ⓑ Ⓒ Ⓓ		48 Ⓐ Ⓑ Ⓒ Ⓓ		78 Ⓐ Ⓑ Ⓒ Ⓓ		108 Ⓐ Ⓑ Ⓒ Ⓓ	
19 Ⓐ Ⓑ Ⓒ Ⓓ		49 Ⓐ Ⓑ Ⓒ Ⓓ		79 Ⓐ Ⓑ Ⓒ Ⓓ		109 Ⓐ Ⓑ Ⓒ Ⓓ	
20 Ⓐ Ⓑ Ⓒ Ⓓ		50 Ⓐ Ⓑ Ⓒ Ⓓ		80 Ⓐ Ⓑ Ⓒ Ⓓ		110 Ⓐ Ⓑ Ⓒ Ⓓ	
21 Ⓐ Ⓑ Ⓒ Ⓓ		51 Ⓐ Ⓑ Ⓒ Ⓓ		81 Ⓐ Ⓑ Ⓒ Ⓓ		111 Ⓐ Ⓑ Ⓒ Ⓓ	
22 Ⓐ Ⓑ Ⓒ Ⓓ		52 Ⓐ Ⓑ Ⓒ Ⓓ		82 Ⓐ Ⓑ Ⓒ Ⓓ		112 Ⓐ Ⓑ Ⓒ Ⓓ	
23 Ⓐ Ⓑ Ⓒ Ⓓ		53 Ⓐ Ⓑ Ⓒ Ⓓ		83 Ⓐ Ⓑ Ⓒ Ⓓ		113 Ⓐ Ⓑ Ⓒ Ⓓ	
24 Ⓐ Ⓑ Ⓒ Ⓓ		54 Ⓐ Ⓑ Ⓒ Ⓓ		84 Ⓐ Ⓑ Ⓒ Ⓓ		114 Ⓐ Ⓑ Ⓒ Ⓓ	
25 Ⓐ Ⓑ Ⓒ Ⓓ		55 Ⓐ Ⓑ Ⓒ Ⓓ		85 Ⓐ Ⓑ Ⓒ Ⓓ		115 Ⓐ Ⓑ Ⓒ Ⓓ	
26 Ⓐ Ⓑ Ⓒ Ⓓ		56 Ⓐ Ⓑ Ⓒ Ⓓ		86 Ⓐ Ⓑ Ⓒ Ⓓ		116 Ⓐ Ⓑ Ⓒ Ⓓ	
27 Ⓐ Ⓑ Ⓒ Ⓓ		57 Ⓐ Ⓑ Ⓒ Ⓓ		87 Ⓐ Ⓑ Ⓒ Ⓓ		117 Ⓐ Ⓑ Ⓒ Ⓓ	
28 Ⓐ Ⓑ Ⓒ Ⓓ		58 Ⓐ Ⓑ Ⓒ Ⓓ		88 Ⓐ Ⓑ Ⓒ Ⓓ		118 Ⓐ Ⓑ Ⓒ Ⓓ	
29 Ⓐ Ⓑ Ⓒ Ⓓ		59 Ⓐ Ⓑ Ⓒ Ⓓ		89 Ⓐ Ⓑ Ⓒ Ⓓ		119 Ⓐ Ⓑ Ⓒ Ⓓ	
30 Ⓐ Ⓑ Ⓒ Ⓓ		60 Ⓐ Ⓑ Ⓒ Ⓓ		90 Ⓐ Ⓑ Ⓒ Ⓓ		120 Ⓐ Ⓑ Ⓒ Ⓓ	

PRAXIS MIDDLE SCHOOL SOCIAL STUDIES

Part A

65 Multiple-choice Questions
(Suggested time—65 minutes)

Note: The PRAXIS Social Studies tests now use the chronological designations B.C.E. (before the common era) and C.E. (common era). These designations correspond to B.C. (before Christ) and A.D. (anno Domini) respectively, which are also used in historical writing and sources.

Directions: Each of the questions or incomplete statements below is followed by four choices (A, B, C, and D). Choose the best response to each question and fill in the appropriate space for that question on your answer sheet.

1. The continental divide passes through which of the following states?

   (A) North Dakota
   (B) Kansas
   (C) Nevada
   (D) Colorado

2. Which of the following best describes the Piedmont region of the United States?

   (A) An area of higher elevations adjacent to the Gulf Coast plain
   (B) The intermontane basins and plateaus between the Rocky Mountains and the Pacific ranges
   (C) A wide area of low rolling hills between the Appalachian Mountains and the Atlantic coastal plain
   (D) A line of mountains and hills that separates the Great Plains from the Great Basin

3. The Anasazi culture most strongly influenced which of the following American Indian groups?

   (A) Seneca, Cayuga, and Onondaga
   (B) Cherokee, Chocktaw, and Chickasaw
   (C) Tlingit, Kwakiutl, and Salish
   (D) Hopi, Zuni, and Acoma

4. Which of the following was a major reason the population of the English colonies in North America grew more rapidly than the population of the French colonies in North America?

   (A) Unlike British ships, French ships carrying settlers had to avoid English warships blockading the coast of France.
   (B) Land for settlement was scarcer in the French colonies than in the English colonies.
   (C) Unlike the French Crown, the English Crown allowed religious dissenters to leave the homeland for North America.
   (D) The discovery of gold in the English colonies attracted settlers from several western European nations.

5. Which of the following was the most significant contribution of the Articles of Confederation government to the growth of the United States?

   (A) Providing an effective method for the taxation of the states by the national government
   (B) Passing the Northwest Ordinance of 1787 establishing the procedure whereby territories become states
   (C) Establishing the precedent that later allowed Thomas Jefferson to acquire the Louisiana Territory
   (D) Developing a system of tariffs that enabled the national government to meet its expenses by taxing imports

6. The principal source of opposition to the ratification of the Constitution during the years 1787–1788 came from a fear that ratification would

(A) lead to a large national debt
(B) weaken the power of the states
(C) put an end to majority rule among United States citizens
(D) be the first step in the establishment of a monarchy

7. Which of the following best describes Alexander Hamilton's economic plan?

(A) Assuming the debts of all the states and selling bonds to pay off previous debts
(B) Establishing state banks and honoring the debt owed to original debt holders but not to speculators
(C) Eliminating tariffs and assessing the national debt to the states
(D) Repealing the tax on whiskey and selling western lands to raise revenue

8. Which of the following best describes the Monroe Doctrine, promulgated by President Monroe in 1823 ?

(A) A publication from the first Continental Congress that outlined Federalist principles
(B) The first plan for self-government adopted in the English colonies
(C) A document intended to end European colonization in the Western Hemisphere
(D) One of the first documents to oppose slavery in the United States

9. Henry David Thoreau, Margaret Fuller, and Ralph Waldo Emerson were members of which of the following movements?

(A) Transcendentalism
(B) Utopianism
(C) The First Great Awakening
(D) Social Darwinism

10. Which of the following best describes a significant feature of the Waltham or Lowell factory system?

(A) Textile mill owners hired entire families, including children over seven years old, to work in the mills.
(B) Young women from neighboring farms were hired to work in the textile mills to earn money until they married.
(C) Textile mill owners paid the cost of passage for factory workers from Europe to the United States to guarantee a supply of labor.
(D) Textile mills printed their own scrip with which workers were paid for use in stores established by the owners.

11. Harriet Tubman made which of the following contributions to the abolitionist movement?

(A) Writing *Uncle Tom's Cabin,* a novel chronicling the abuses of slavery
(B) Editing *The Liberator,* an abolitionist newspaper
(C) Leading a slave rebellion in Virginia in 1831
(D) Acting as a "conductor" on the Underground Railroad

12. Which of the following best describes a consequence of including the principle of popular sovereignty in the Kansas-Nebraska Act of 1854 ?

   (A) It reopened the issue of slavery in the area closed to slavery north of the 36° 30' line of the Missouri Compromise.

   (B) It gave New Orleans the best chance of becoming the eastern terminus of the first transcontinental railroad.

   (C) It eliminated the possibility of extending slavery west of the Mississippi River.

   (D) It resulted in a repeal of the Fugitive Slave Act, thereby angering proslavery Southerners and increasing the chances of secession.

13. Which of the following was a major obstacle that had to be overcome before the Panama Canal could be successfully completed?

   (A) Several endangered species of plants and animals had to be moved away from the Canal Zone.

   (B) The Panamanian public had to be convinced the canal would benefit their country.

   (C) Doctors had to develop ways to combat malaria.

   (D) The American government had to revoke the Monroe Doctrine.

© CORBIS

14. A historian studying which of the following time periods would use the photograph above as a primary source?

   (A) Progressive Era
   (B) Civil War
   (C) Great Depression
   (D) Second World War

15. W. E. B. Du Bois' *The Souls of Black Folk* (1903) contained

    (A)   strong support for Marcus Garvey's Back-to-Africa movement

    (B)   a criticism of Booker T. Washington's approach to expanding the opportunities of African Americans

    (C)   an alternative to the plan for advancing the civil-rights movement advocated by the Niagara Movement

    (D)   a defense of the United States Supreme Court's decision in *Plessy v. Ferguson*

16. President Franklin D. Roosevelt's New Deal attempted to combat the economic problems of the Great Depression primarily by

    (A)   reducing government regulation of businesses

    (B)   providing funding for public-works projects

    (C)   lowering tariffs to encourage imports

    (D)   imposing wage and price controls to stop inflation

17. Which of the following best describes a major challenge that President Lyndon Johnson faced in 1968 as he completed his full term as president?

    (A)   He struggled to make the federal budget support both the Vietnam War and the "War on Poverty."

    (B)   He faced a Congress that was controlled by the Republican Party.

    (C)   The majority of the country felt that the nation was falling behind in the space race.

    (D)   His health insurance proposal for elderly Americans was stalled in Congress with little chance of passage.

EARLY CIVILIZATIONS
(3500–1000 B.C.E.)

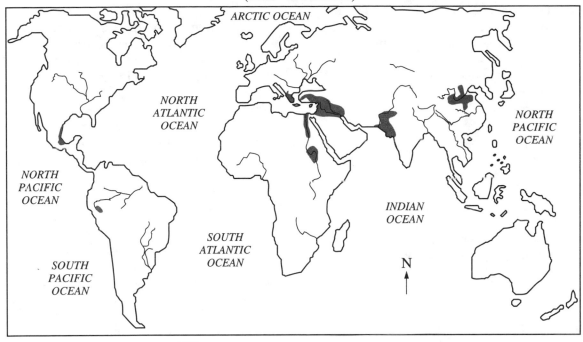

■ Locations of Early Civilizations

18. Which of the following can be concluded about most early civilizations from the map above?

(A) They tended to form in the east and spread west.
(B) They tended to form where irrigation would be unnecessary or easily accomplished.
(C) They tended to form adjacent to other civilizations with which they could trade.
(D) They tended to form in areas with tropical climates.

19. The Vedas and the Upanishads are associated with which of the following religious traditions?

(A) Islam
(B) Hinduism
(C) Judaism
(D) Daoism

20. Which of the following contributed most to the spread of Christianity in the fourth century C.E.?

(A) The decline of trade and industry in the Roman Empire
(B) A series of epidemic plagues
(C) The use of German mercenaries by the Roman army
(D) The support of the emperors Constantine and Theodosius

21. Which of the following was a central principle of feudal societies in Europe?

    (A) The absolute authority of the national monarch
    (B) The granting of land in exchange for military service
    (C) The separation of church and state
    (D) The primary importance of trade and merchants

22. Which of the following was a major accomplishment of China's Tang dynasty (618–907 C.E.)?

    (A) The first unification of China under one emperor
    (B) Reliance on a bureaucracy of merit
    (C) The introduction of Buddhism
    (D) The establishment of an overseas colonial empire

23. Which of the following postulated the theory of the heliocentric universe?

    (A) Copernicus
    (B) Aristotle
    (C) Hippocrates
    (D) Voltaire

24. Which of the following was a major effect of the Spanish conquest of Mesoamerica?

    (A) The decimation of native populations exposed to European diseases
    (B) The formation of alliances of native peoples to resist the Spanish invaders
    (C) The revival of Mayan culture
    (D) The expulsion of Catholic missionaries

25. The eighteenth-century invention of the steam engine had which of the following effects in Europe?

    (A) It led to the English victory over the Spanish Armada, ensuring the continuation of the Tudor dynasty.
    (B) It encouraged the invention of the spinning jenny and Arkwright's water frame.
    (C) It allowed weavers to increase their production of textiles in the home.
    (D) It provided a portable and relatively stable source of power, allowing factories to be located near urban centers.

26. "As every individual, therefore,…neither intends to promote the public interest, nor knows how much he is promoting it, he intends only his gain, and he is in this, as in many other cases, led by an invisible hand. By pursuing his own interest he frequently promotes that of the society more effectually than when he really intends to promote it."

    The quotation above expresses one of the major ideas in which of the following works?

    (A) Karl Marx and Friedrich Engels, *The Communist Manifesto*
    (B) Alexis de Tocqueville, *Democracy in America*
    (C) John Locke, *Second Treatise of Government*
    (D) Adam Smith, *The Wealth of Nations*

27. All of the following were characteristic of the interaction between China and Great Britain in the 1800s EXCEPT:

    (A) China used military means to resist the importation of opium.
    (B) China agreed to grant "treaty ports" to Great Britain.
    (C) Great Britain colonized large areas of southern and central China.
    (D) Great Britain joined with other Western powers to crush the Boxer Rebellion.

28. Which of the following was a major consequence of the treaties that ended the First World War?

    (A) The Romanov dynasty was overthrown in the first phase of the Russian Revolution, and the Bolsheviks took power in the second phase.
    (B) European powers applied the principle of national self-determination to their colonies.
    (C) The dismantling of empires in central, eastern, and southeastern Europe led to the creation of numerous unstable states.
    (D) Germany and Austria were admitted to the League of Nations with nonvoting status.

29. During the 1930s, Italy, Germany, and Japan had which of the following in common?

    (A) Highly industrialized societies
    (B) Rejection of the League of Nations
    (C) Cordial relations with the United States
    (D) Little participation in world markets

> *Glasnost*
>
> Solidarity Movement
>
> *Perestroika*

30. A discussion of the three terms above would most likely focus on explaining the

    (A) Soviet domination of Eastern Europe after the Second World War
    (B) collapse of the Soviet Union at the end of the Cold War
    (C) Cuban missile crisis and Bay of Pigs invasion
    (D) formation of NATO, the Warsaw Pact, and the Berlin Blockade

31. Which of the following has most accelerated the spread of a global popular culture?

    (A) The creation of the United Nations
    (B) The growth of world religions
    (C) New communications technologies
    (D) Increased access to air travel

32. In the United States, which of the following sets of policies is most likely to be supported by a political conservative and opposed by a political liberal?

    (A) Fewer restrictions on absolute freedom of speech, increased public funding for social-welfare programs
    (B) Greater restrictions on absolute freedom of speech, decreased government management of the economy
    (C) Decreased public funding for social welfare programs, increased government management of the economy
    (D) Decreased government management of the economy, fewer restrictions on absolute freedom of speech

33. Which of the following is true of a presidential system of government?

    (A) There is typically more party discipline than in a parliamentary system.
    (B) The executive is the head of government but not the head of state.
    (C) The executive is also a member of the legislature.
    (D) The executive serves a fixed term of office.

34. All of the following are accurate descriptions of the Security Council of the United Nations EXCEPT:

(A) The Security Council has five permanent member-states.
(B) The Security Council can authorize the use of United Nations peacekeeping forces.
(C) The Security Council is authorized to negotiate regional trade agreements among United Nations member states.
(D) Only permanent members of the Security Council have veto power.

35. The United States Supreme Court decision in the case of *Marbury* v. *Madison* was significant because it established the

(A) right of the Supreme Court to original jurisdiction in federal cases
(B) power of the Supreme Court to invalidate an act of Congress
(C) number of United States Supreme Court justices
(D) principle that presidents have the authority to expand United States territory by purchasing land

36. The United States Constitution permits both the federal and state governments to borrow money. Which of the following types of power best describes this arrangement?

(A) Concurrent powers
(B) Implied powers
(C) Expressed powers
(D) Reserved powers

37. The United States Senate and House of Representatives have passed a bill and forwarded it to the president. The president vetoed the bill. Congress is still in session. Under which of the following circumstances will the bill become a law?

(A) Congress appeals the veto to the Supreme Court, which rules in favor of Congress.
(B) Congress submits the bill to a conference committee of both houses, which passes the bill by a majority vote.
(C) The bill is returned to the Congress, and both houses pass the bill by a two thirds majority.
(D) The bill is submitted to the states, and a majority of the states' governors give their approval.

38. Which of the following diagrams most accurately depicts the process that has been used to amend the Constitution?

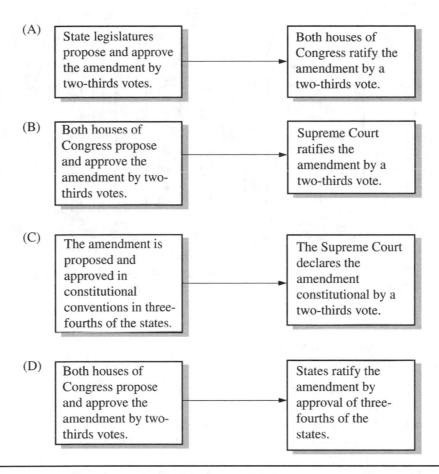

(A) State legislatures propose and approve the amendment by two-thirds votes. → Both houses of Congress ratify the amendment by a two-thirds vote.

(B) Both houses of Congress propose and approve the amendment by two-thirds votes. → Supreme Court ratifies the amendment by a two-thirds vote.

(C) The amendment is proposed and approved in constitutional conventions in three-fourths of the states. → The Supreme Court declares the amendment constitutional by a two-thirds vote.

(D) Both houses of Congress propose and approve the amendment by two-thirds votes. → States ratify the amendment by approval of three-fourths of the states.

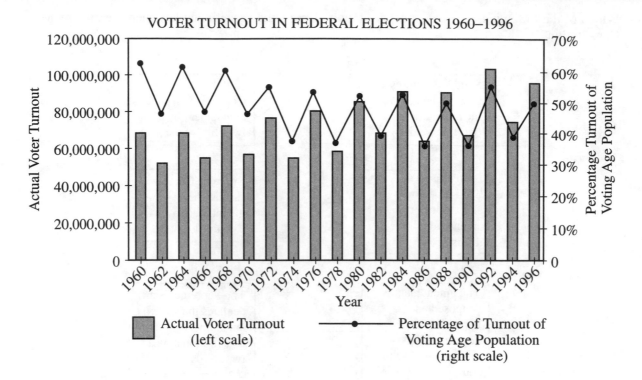

VOTER TURNOUT IN FEDERAL ELECTIONS 1960–1996

Actual Voter Turnout (left scale)

Percentage of Turnout of Voting Age Population (right scale)

39. All of the following conclusions about voter behavior in the United States can be made on the basis of the graph above EXCEPT:

(A) The percentage of voters turning out for both presidential and midterm elections has increased steadily since 1960.

(B) More voters turn out for presidential elections than for midterm elections.

(C) Since 1960 there has been a general upward trend in actual voter turnout in presidential elections.

(D) Since 1960 there has been a general downward trend in the percentage of voter turnout in presidential elections.

40. The president of the United States Senate is also the

    (A)   majority leader of the Senate
    (B)   majority whip of the Senate
    (C)   vice president of the United States
    (D)   secretary of state

41. Which of the following accurately describes the role of interest groups in the United States political system?

    (A)   They raise money to provide public funding for elections.
    (B)   Their membership generally includes a majority of potential beneficiaries of their efforts.
    (C)   They utilize lobbyists to provide policymakers with information on bills and issues.
    (D)   They hold national and state conventions to nominate candidates for political office.

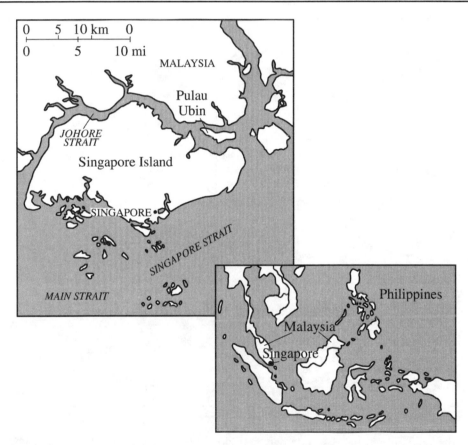

42. Singapore has become one of the outstanding centers of manufacturing, finance, and trade along the Pacific Rim. This is due in part to which of the following geographic advantages, as shown on the map above?

    (A)   Its relative location
    (B)   Its absolute location
    (C)   Its topography
    (D)   Its mineral resources

43. Which of the following best describes the Green Revolution?

   (A) The passage of international environmental agreements resulting from concerns about global warming

   (B) The creation of an international political organization to combat the depletion of the Amazon rain forest

   (C) The migration of work previously done in the world's developed nations to developing nations around the world

   (D) The development of new strains of grain and land-management strategies that have led to increased food production

44. Which of the following best describes the movement of a concept, innovation, or discovery from its area of origin to new areas?

   (A) Culture hearth
   (B) Cultural diffusion
   (C) Culture complex
   (D) Cultural realm

ALASKA

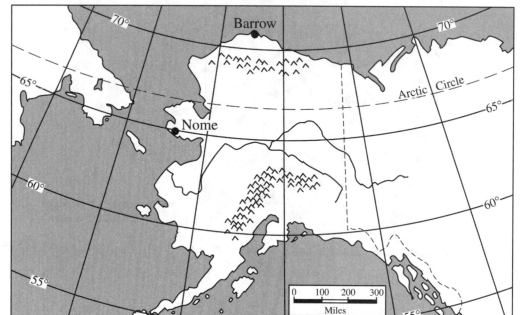

45. According to the map above, the distance between Nome and Barrow, Alaska, is approximately how many miles?

   (A) 25
   (B) 350
   (C) 450
   (D) 550

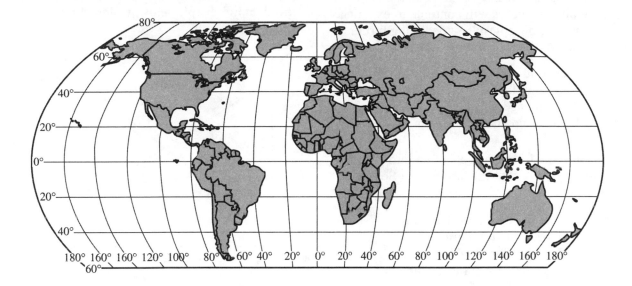

46. Which of the following are the approximate coordinates (latitude and longitude) for Japan?

    (A) 40° N, 140° E
    (B) 40° S, 140° W
    (C) 140° N, 40° E
    (D) 140° S, 40° W

47. Which of the following is the best example of a functional region?

    (A) The Rocky Mountain physiographic province
    (B) The New York metropolitan statistical area (MSA)
    (C) The ice-sheet climate
    (D) Siberia

48. All of the following contribute to desertification in a significant way, EXCEPT

    (A) clearing of original vegetation for cultivation
    (B) increased salinization of the soil
    (C) heavy rains on exposed soil
    (D) strip cropping and no-till farming

49. Which of the following is a result of a difference in air pressure in adjacent zones?

    (A) Precipitation
    (B) Temperature inversion
    (C) Drought
    (D) Wind

50. Which of the following climate types is found primarily in the low latitudes?

    (A) Moist subtropical
    (B) Wet equatorial
    (C) Mediterranean
    (D) Boreal forest

51. Many geographers have concluded that developing countries will continue to experience population growth despite a declining birth rate for which of the following reasons?

   (A) Increased urbanization
   (B) Migration from developed nations
   (C) A young age profile
   (D) Increased demand for labor

52. Which of the following sets of countries make up the region of the Andean West in South America?

   (A) Argentina, Paraguay, Uruguay
   (B) Bolivia, Ecuador, Peru
   (C) Colombia, Guyana, Venezuela
   (D) Guatemala, Honduras, Nicaragua

53. The fundamental economic problem stems from

   (A) high unemployment and inflation
   (B) scarce resources and unlimited wants
   (C) lack of economic growth
   (D) lack of competition and free markets

Questions 54 and 55 are based on the supply and demand graph below, which shows the market for grain.

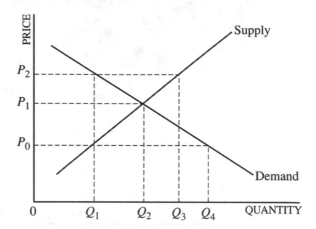

54. If the prevailing market price were at P_0, which of the following would be true?

   (A) The market would be in equilibrium at Q_1.
   (B) The quantity of grain demanded would be Q_1.
   (C) The quantity of grain supplied would be Q_4.
   (D) The quantity of grain demanded would exceed the quantity supplied.

55. Assume that the market for grain is in equilibrium. If the government imposes an effective price floor, the market price will

   (A) rise above P_1, helping grain farmers but creating a surplus of grain
   (B) rise above P_1, helping consumers but creating a shortage of grain
   (C) fall below P_1, helping grain farmers but creating a shortage of grain
   (D) fall below P_1, helping consumers but creating a surplus of grain

56. A market structure in which there is a single seller producing a product for which there are no close substitutes is known as

(A) perfect competition
(B) monopolistic competition
(C) monopoly
(D) oligopoly

57. The unemployment rate is a measure of the percent of the

(A) total population that is unemployed
(B) adult population that is unemployed
(C) labor force that is laid off from work
(D) labor force that is unemployed

58. Which of the following is an example of expansionary fiscal policy?

(A) The Federal Reserve lowers the federal funds rate to stimulate investment.
(B) The government raises taxes to finance its deficits.
(C) The government reduces taxes to increase aggregate demand.
(D) The government reduces spending to reduce inflation.

59. A fractional reserve banking system allows banks to

(A) create money and expand the money supply
(B) charge any interest rate on consumer loans
(C) limit the amount of cash deposits by customers
(D) limit the amount of cash withdrawals by customers

60. In one hour, a worker in Country X can produce either 5 shirts or 5 pairs of socks, whereas a worker in Country Y can produce 3 shirts or 2 pairs of socks. Which of the following statements regarding absolute advantage and comparative advantage is true?

(A) Country X has a comparative advantage in producing both shirts and socks.
(B) Country X has an absolute advantage in producing both shirts and socks and a comparative advantage in producing socks.
(C) Country Y has an absolute advantage in producing both shirts and socks.
(D) Country Y has an absolute advantage in producing socks and a comparative advantage in producing shirts.

61. If the international value of the United States dollar weakens in the foreign-exchange markets, which of the following will occur?

(A) United States exports will increase.
(B) United States imports will increase.
(C) The supply of the dollar will increase.
(D) The United States trade deficits will increase.

62. Which of the following best describes the fundamental purpose of social institutions in most societies?

(A) To provide a means for transmission of a society's characteristics or innovations to other societies
(B) To encourage the stratification of the society
(C) To operationalize a society's norms and roles to meet the needs and goals of the group
(D) To disperse power among a series of subcultures with the intention of minimizing exploitation of any individual group

63. According to demographic-transition theory, which of the following is a factor in declining birth rates?

   (A) Improvement of public health and sanitation
   (B) A reduced need for large numbers of children in urban, industrialized societies
   (C) A decrease in the mortality rate for women in their childbearing years
   (D) Faster-growing, higher-yielding, and more disease-resistant agricultural crops

64. Max Weber (1864–1920) argued that individuals band together based on such factors as race, ethnicity, religion, occupation, and gender to form

   (A) status groups
   (B) meritocracies
   (C) clans
   (D) egalitarian societies

65. Which of the following is an example of cultural diffusion?

   (A) The integration of Irish immigrants into the dominant culture of the United States
   (B) The intermarriage of immigrants of different ethnic and racial groups in Great Britain
   (C) The passage of gunpowder from China to Europe
   (D) Enforcement of an "English only" environment in government-run schools for Native Americans

Part B

3 Constructed-Response Questions
(Suggested time—30 minutes)

General Directions for Questions 66-68: There are three constructed-response questions in Part B. Write your answers to these questions in the space provided in the lined pages following the questions. If a question has more than one part, be sure to answer each part of the question.

Question 66

VALUE OF GOODS IMPORTED TO AMERICA FROM GREAT BRITAIN, 1764-1776

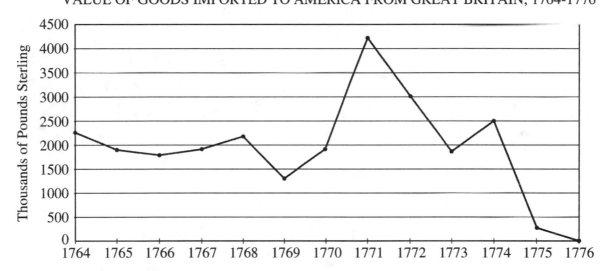

Source: *Historical Statistics of the United States*

Using your knowledge of North American colonial history and the information in the graph above

(a) describe the pattern of imports shown in the graph

AND

(b) explain how two historical factors contributed to the pattern you described

---

NOTES

Question 67

ÇATAL HÜYÜK: A NEOLITHIC VILLAGE, 6000 B.C.E.

Using specific examples from the drawing above and your knowledge of world history, describe two major developments in human life that marked the change from the Old Stone Age (Paleolithic) to the New Stone Age (Neolithic). (These developments are often referred to as the Neolithic Revolution.)

NOTES

Question 68

THE SPREAD OF THE BUBONIC PLAGUE, 1331-1353

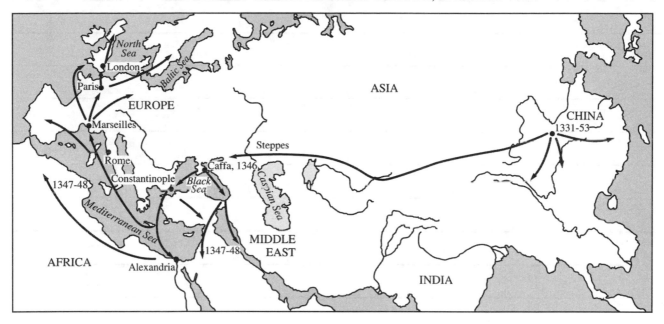

Using the map above and your knowledge of world history

(a) describe how socioeconomic factors contributed to the spread of the bubonic plague (the Black Death) throughout China and western Europe

AND

(b) explain its impact on the economies of the infected areas.

NOTES

Begin your response to Question 66 here.

_____

_____

_____

_____

_____

_____

_____

_____

_____

_____

_____

_____

_____

_____

_____

_____

_____

_____

_____

_____

_____

(Question 66 continued)

_____

_____

_____

_____

_____

_____

_____

_____

_____

_____

_____

_____

_____

_____

_____

_____

_____

_____

_____

_____

_____

_____

_____

_____

_____

(Question 66 continued)

_____

_____

_____

_____

_____

_____

_____

_____

_____

_____

_____

_____

_____

_____

_____

_____

_____

_____

_____

_____

_____

Begin your response to Question 67 here.

(Question 67 continued)

_____

_____

_____

_____

_____

_____

_____

_____

_____

_____

_____

_____

_____

_____

_____

_____

_____

_____

_____

(Question 67 continued)

_____

_____

_____

_____

_____

_____

_____

_____

_____

_____

_____

_____

_____

_____

_____

_____

_____

_____

_____

_____

_____

_____

_____

_____

Begin your response to Question 68 here.

_____

_____

_____

_____

_____

_____

_____

_____

_____

_____

_____

_____

_____

_____

_____

_____

_____

_____

_____

_____

_____

_____

(Question 68 continued)

_____

_____

_____

_____

_____

_____

_____

_____

_____

_____

_____

_____

_____

_____

_____

_____

_____

_____

_____

_____

_____

_____

_____

(Question 68 continued)

_____

_____

_____

_____

_____

_____

_____

_____

_____

_____

_____

_____

_____

_____

_____

_____

_____

_____

_____

_____

Chapter 13

Right Answers and Sample Responses for the *Middle School Social Studies* Practice Questions

▶ ▶ ▶ ▶ ▶ ▶ ▶ ▶ ▶ ▶ ▶ ▶

The first part of this chapter contains right answers and sample responses to the multiple-choice practice questions for the *Middle School Social Studies* test. The second part of this chapter contains scored sample responses to the constructed-response practice questions, along with explanations for why the responses received the scores they did.

Part One: Right Answers and Explanations for the Multiple-Choice Questions

Now that you have answered all of the practice questions, you can check your work. Compare your answers to the multiple-choice questions with the correct answers in the table below.

Question Number	Correct Answer	Content Category	Question Number	Correct Answer	Content Category
1	D	Physical Geography of North America	33	D	Other Forms of Government
2	C	Physical Geography of North America	34	C	International Relations
3	D	Native American Peoples	35	B	United States Political System
4	C	European Exploration and Colonization	36	A	United States Political System
5	B	Establishing a New Nation	37	C	United States Political System
6	B	Establishing a New Nation	38	D	United States Political System
7	A	Early Years of the New Nation	39	A	United States Political System
8	C	Early Years of the New Nation	40	C	United States Political System
9	A	Continued National Development	41	C	United States Political System
10	B	Continued National Development	42	A	Geographical Themes
11	D	Civil War Era	43	D	Geographical Themes
12	A	Civil War Era	44	B	Geographical Themes
13	C	Emergence of the Modern United States	45	C	Map Skills
14	A	Progressive Era through New Deal	46	A	Map Skills
15	B	Progressive Era through New Deal	47	B	Map Skills
16	B	Progressive Era through New Deal	48	D	Physical Geography
17	A	Recent Developments	49	D	Physical Geography
18	B	Prehistory to 1400 C.E.	50	B	Physical Geography
19	B	Prehistory to 1400 C.E.	51	C	Human Geography
20	D	Prehistory to 1400 C.E.	52	B	Regional Geography
21	B	Prehistory to 1400 C.E.	53	B	Fundamental Concepts
22	B	Prehistory to 1400 C.E.	54	D	Microeconomics
23	A	World History: 1400-1914	55	A	Microeconomics
24	A	World History: 1400-1914	56	C	Microeconomics
25	D	World History: 1400-1914	57	D	Macroeconomics
26	D	World History: 1400-1914	58	C	Macroeconomics
27	C	World History: 1400-1914	59	A	Macroeconomics
28	C	1914 to the Present	60	B	International Economic Concepts
29	B	1914 to the Present	61	A	International Economic Concepts
30	B	1914 to the Present	62	C	Sociology
31	C	1914 to the Present	63	B	Sociology
32	B	Basic Political Concepts	64	A	Sociology
			65	C	Anthropology

Explanations of Right Answers

1. In North America, the continental divide is the line that identifies the point in the Rocky Mountains at which streams and rivers flow either west or east. The streams and rivers to the west flow into the Pacific Ocean. The streams and rivers to the east flow into the Gulf of Mexico or the Atlantic Ocean. Among the choices given, Colorado is the only state intersected by the continental divide. The correct answer, therefore, is (D).

2. This question tests your knowledge of the physical geography of the United States. The Piedmont is a region of the foothills of the Appalachians that stretches from New Jersey south to Alabama. Therefore, the correct answer is (C).

3. The Anasazi and their descendants were noted for their large pueblos and sophisticated irrigation systems that allowed them to cultivate corn. They were also known for their pottery. Drought conditions destroyed the Anasazi culture in the twelfth century, but many Anasazi cultural forms were inherited by the Hopi, Zuni, and Acoma cultures that arose a few centuries later. The correct answer, therefore, is (D).

4. This question tests your knowledge of similarities and differences in the French and English colonies in North America. The principal religious dissenters in France were the Huguenots, French Protestants who had broken away from the Catholic Church. The French monarchy did not allow them to migrate to the North American colonies. In contrast, the British monarchy allowed religious dissenters to leave, and Puritans migrated to the Americas in large numbers. Therefore, the correct answer is (C).

5. This question tests your understanding of the United States government under the Articles of Confederation. The Northwest Ordinance of 1787 established a three step plan for territories to become states. The first step was the appointment of a governor, secretary, and three judges by Congress. Next, the territory was organized once it had a population of 5,000 free adult men, qualifying it to have a legislature. When the territory grew to 60,000 people, it could apply to Congress for admission as a state. The correct answer, therefore, is (B).

6. The Constitution was a highly controversial document and required several years to finally be ratified. Supporters of the Constitution's strengthening of the national government were called Federalists. Their opponents were called Anti-Federalists. One of the Anti-Federalists' great worries was that the independence and sovereignty of individual states would be eroded by a stronger national government. The correct answer is (B).

7. This question tests your knowledge of the financial plan developed after the adoption of the United States Constitution. As the first treasurer under the Constitution, Alexander Hamilton made it his main aim to establish faith in the financial stability of the new government. He advocated that the federal government assume the debts of all the states and sell new bonds to pay off the existing debt to all bondholders, including speculators. His plan also established a Bank of the United States. Therefore, the correct answer is (A).

8. The Monroe Doctrine was written in 1823 by Secretary of State John Quincy Adams and was made American policy by President James Monroe. Monroe declared that the United States would not interfere with any existing European colonies in the Americas but would oppose the establishment of any new colonies. (C) is therefore the correct answer.

9. The American Transcendentalist movement was centered in New England in the antebellum period of the early nineteenth century. Transcendentalists believed that individuals should look within themselves for truth and good and should not conform to rules and conventions if these went against their sense of right. Many of them also favored living simpler lives away from the pressures and distractions of cities and towns. Thoreau, Fuller, and Emerson were all famous transcendentalists. The correct answer is (A).

10. This question tests your knowledge of the nineteenth-century Industrial Revolution in the United States. In the early 1800s, Francis Cabot Lowell founded a factory in Massachusetts to produce cotton cloth. Lowell decided that it would be desirable to employ young women from New England farms to work in his mills until they married and started a family. He thought this would prevent the development of a permanent underclass of factory workers—which he had seen in England—in the United States. The correct answer, therefore, is (B).

11. This question asks you to identify the role Harriet Tubman played in the abolitionist movement. All of the choices were attempts to oppose slavery. Harriet Tubman, however, was a "conductor" on the Underground Railroad and helped hundreds of runaway slaves to escape to the North by hiding them in locations provided by abolitionist supporters. (D) is therefore the correct answer.

12. From 1820 to 1854, Congress passed a series of laws that admitted new states while maintaining the balance of slave and free states. Senator Stephen Douglas of Illinois wanted Chicago to be the eastern terminus of the transcontinental railroad. By introducing popular sovereignty into the Kansas-Nebraska bill, Douglas hoped to gain southern support. "Popular sovereignty" meant that residents could vote for their new state to be slave or free. In effect, the act reversed the Missouri Compromise (1820), which had barred slavery north of 36° 30' north latitude. The correct answer, therefore, is (A).

13. This question tests your knowledge of the basic events surrounding the building of the Panama Canal in 1904–1914. Early in the project, many workers died from malaria, also called yellow fever. Dr. William Gorgas traced the spread of the disease to mosquitoes and ordered the nearby swamps and ponds drained to prevent mosquitoes from multiplying. Within two years, malaria had disappeared. Therefore, the correct answer is (C).

14. The truck in the photograph clearly shows Woodrow Wilson's campaign positions on political issues, including his efforts to keep the United States out of the First World War. The banner also shows Progressive Era issues such as the 8-hour day and antitrust sentiment. The correct answer is (A).

15. This question tests your knowledge of the views of African American leaders in the late nineteenth and early twentieth centuries. W. E. B. Du Bois was a critic of Booker T. Washington's policies as spelled out in the Atlanta Compromise address in 1895. Du Bois believed that Washington was not a forceful advocate of total equality for African Americans. Du Bois made this criticism very strongly in The Souls of Black Folk. Du Bois was a founding member of the Niagara Movement, which led to the formation of the National Association for the Advancement of Colored People (NAACP). The correct answer, therefore, is (B).

16. This question focuses on the philosophy behind the New Deal. Faced with high unemployment, falling prices, and a major slowdown in business activity, Franklin Roosevelt took the economic approach of "priming the pump" in an effort to get the economy moving again. He created a series of federal agencies intended to fund public-works projects and put people back to work as soon as possible. Therefore, the correct answer is (B).

17. Despite the fact that the Democrats controlled both houses of Congress, by 1968 the Democratic Party was seriously divided over the war in Southeast Asia. President Johnson faced serious challenges from both pro-war and anti-war party members. Despite the passage of the Medicare Act (1965) to provide health care for elderly Americans, the key political problem facing President Johnson was how to afford the war as well as domestic programs. The correct answer is (A).

18. This question asks you to use a map of early civilizations to make a generalization. The map shows that most early civilizations were located in river valleys or along coasts. The correct answer, therefore, is (B).

19. The purpose of this question is to test your understanding of the practices and texts associated with the world's major religions. The Vedas are a collection of hymns and rituals transmitted orally by priests. Over time, the Vedas were written down along with a set of commentaries (the Upanishads). The Upanishads are a series of dialogues between teachers and disciples about religious issues. Sometimes referred to as the Vedic religion, these dialogues became part of the Hindu tradition. They were written in Sanskrit and date back to the sixth century B.C.E. Therefore, the correct answer is (B).

20. The events described in (A), (B), and (C) may have contributed to the spread of Christianity in the third and fourth centuries because of people's fear of disorder and need for a positive religious message, but the contribution was indirect. The Emperor Constantine issued the Edict of Milan in 313, officially tolerating Christianity. He also supported the Christian Church organization. Emperor Theodosius made Christianity the official religion of the Roman Empire; as a result, Christianity became a major force in the Empire. The correct answer, therefore, is (D).

21. This question tests your understanding of the system of feudalism that developed in Europe in the early Middle Ages (the seventh to eleventh centuries C.E.). Monarchs gained the support of vassals who served them. In its basic form, feudalism involved warriors who placed themselves under the protection of more powerful warriors in return for the use of land. The latter built up armies and controlled large areas and, in turn, pledged loyalty to a prince or king. All who pledged loyalty were known as vassals. A vassal was granted a fief, or land, in exchange for military service. The correct answer is (B).

22. The first unification of China under a single emperor (A) came under the Qin dynasty (221-207 B.C.E.). Buddhism (C) first came to China in the first or second century C.E. During the period of the Sui (581-618 B.C.E.) and Tang dynasties, China had great influence on its neighbors but did not establish overseas colonies, (D). Implementing Confucian principles, the Tang dynasty adopted and enforced the earlier practice of selecting government officials on the basis of performance on civil-service examinations. (B) is therefore the correct answer.

23. This question tests your ability to distinguish between well-known thinkers from different time periods. The theory of the heliocentric, or "Sun-centered" universe came from Copernicus, a Polish monk and astronomer. His theory created the groundwork for criticism of the commonly held sixteenth-century belief that the Earth was at the center of the universe. The works of Brahe, Kepler, Galileo, and Newton completed the proofs of Copernicus' work *On the Revolution of the Heavenly Spheres,* published in 1543, the year of his death. The correct answer, therefore, is (A).

24. The Spanish conquest of Mesoamerica (what is today Mexico and Central America) in the early sixteenth century had many significant effects, many of which were global in nature. The relative isolation of the Americas from the rest of the world made the native peoples of the Americas extremely susceptible to European or Old World diseases, and later to African diseases. Therefore, the correct answer is (A).

25. The steam engine as a source of power was invented too late to assist in the defeat of the Armada in 1588 (A). The spinning jenny and the Arkwright water frame (B) were invented at roughly the same time as the steam engine but did not create an incentive for its invention. The steam engine made it possible for mill owners to establish mills without being nearly as reliant on streams or rivers for water power. The correct answer, therefore, is (D).

26. This question tests your understanding of one of the major theorists who shaped the ideas of free trade and laissez-faire economics. The Scottish economist Adam Smith published *The Wealth of Nations* in 1776. Smith's description of the "invisible hand" supported the concept of laissez-faire. He argued that governments should allow individuals to act in their self-interest and that this would produce the greatest good for the society. (D) is therefore the correct answer.

27. This question tests your knowledge of the relationship between European powers and Asia in the period of nineteenth-century European imperialism. Note that this is an EXCEPT question, which means you are looking for the single choice that is *not* characteristic of the interaction between China and Great Britain. Great Britain imported large quantities of tea and other products from China, but China imported little from the British Empire. The British encouraged the export of opium from India to China in order to correct the trade imbalance. When China resisted, the first Opium War (1839-1842) broke out, as suggested by (A). At the end of the war, Great Britain imposed harsh conditions on China, including the acquisition of treaty ports (B). European powers acted at the end of the nineteenth century to repress the antiforeign movement of the Boxers. European powers, including Great Britain, did *not* colonize large portions of China. The correct answer, therefore, is (C).

28. The treaties following the First World War applied the principle of national self-determination to some areas of Eastern Europe but not to European colonies, as suggested in (B). The tsar had already been deposed in 1917 and Germany and Austria were not admitted to the League of Nations, as suggested by (A) and (D), respectively. The fall of the German, Austro-Hungarian, Russian, and Ottoman empires resulted in the creation of many nations: Poland, Yugoslavia, Finland, the Baltic States, Romania, Czechoslovakia, Bulgaria, and a much-reduced Hungary, Austria, Germany, and Russia. With few exceptions, these nations suffered grave economic and political crises in the interwar years. (C) is therefore the correct answer.

29. In the 1930s, Italy, Germany, and Japan all rejected the efforts by the League of Nations to restrain their aggressive territorial expansions. After Japan's invasion of Manchuria in 1931, the league recommended that Japan leave Manchuria and that no nation recognize Japan's puppet state of Manchukuo. Japan withdrew from the League in 1933. Germany also withdrew in 1933. Hitler then embarked on a policy to reverse the provisions of the Treaty of Versailles and to expand German territory and rearm. Italy invaded Ethiopia in 1935, and the League called for economic sanctions against Italy, but Mussolini ignored them. The correct answer, therefore, is (B).

30. This question tests your understanding of the different phases of the Cold War. Options (A), (C), and (D) all deal with events in earlier phases of the Cold War. The Solidarity movement sprang up in Poland in the 1980s to challenge Soviet control. *Perestroika* (restructuring of the economy) and *glasnost* (openness to allow criticism) were policies Mikhail Gorbachev tried to implement in a failed attempt to reform the Soviet Union in the late 1980s. The correct answer, therefore, is (B).

31. This question asks you to show your knowledge of contemporary trends and to assess the factors encouraging a specific trend: the diffusion of popular culture globally. All of the choices offered have had some effect on the creation and spread of a worldwide popular culture, but new communications technologies, such as computers, the Internet, cell phones, CDs, DVDs, instant messaging, and communications satellites, have accelerated a global popular culture. Access to music, news, movies, and so on, have made the spread of popular culture, much of it based on United States popular culture, very fast and worldwide. (C) is therefore the correct answer.

32. This question tests your knowledge of the premises of two important political ideologies, conservatism and liberalism. In contemporary American political thought, conservatives favor expanded personal economic freedom but are willing to limit individual social freedom, while liberals prefer expanded individual social freedom but are willing to limit personal economic freedom. The correct answer, therefore, is (B).

33. This question tests your knowledge of the presidential and parliamentary forms of government. Options (A), (B), and (C) are true of parliamentary systems. The correct answer, therefore, is (D), as presidents serve a fixed term, as opposed to prime ministers, who are subject to votes of confidence and who can control the timing of elections.

34. This question tests your knowledge of the composition and function of the Security Council of the United Nations. Notice that this is an EXCEPT question, asking you to determine the choice that is *not* an accurate statement about the Security Council. (A) is accurate, as these members are China, France, Russia, the United Kingdom, and the United States. (B) is also accurate, as evidenced in Afghanistan, Sierra Leone, and elsewhere. (D) is accurate, as the other ten members of the Security Council serve on a rotating basis. The correct answer, therefore, is (C), as the primary function of the Security Council is to maintain international peace and security and not to promote trade.

35. Chief Justice John Marshall in the case of *Marbury* v. *Madison* claimed judicial review, one of the most important powers of the Supreme Court, for the Court. The correct answer, therefore, is (B).

36. This question tests your knowledge of the division of power between the national and state governments under the United States Constitution. Expressed and implied powers are limited to the national government. Powers restricted to the states are referred to as reserved powers. Any powers shared by the federal and state governments are referred to

as concurrent powers. (A), therefore, is the correct answer.

37. The Supreme Court (A) only rules on bills that have been passed into law. Conference committees, as suggested by (B), meet to reconcile differences in Senate and House versions of bills. Governors of states (D) have no say in the matter, as the override of a presidential veto is strictly a federal matter. The correct answer, therefore, is (C), as a two-thirds vote of approval for a vetoed bill in both Houses of Congress is needed to override a presidential veto.

38. The United States Constitution provides two methods by which it may be amended. This item helps to evaluate your understanding of the only one of these methods which has actually been employed. An amendment may be proposed either by both Houses of the United States Congress or two-thirds of the states calling conventions for that purpose. No amendment has ever been proposed by two-thirds of the states calling conventions, however. Once proposed, a potential amendment must be ratified by the legislatures of three-fourths of the states or conventions called by the states for the purpose of ratification. The correct answer, therefore, is (D).

39. This question tests your understanding of voter turnout in the context of different types of national elections. This question also tests your ability to draw meaningful conclusions from political data. Since it is an EXCEPT question, you are looking for the choice that is *not* accurate. Choice (B) is accurate, as voter turnout is lower in years when there is no presidential election, whether percentages or actual turnout is considered. Choices (C) and (D) are both accurate and illustrate that the same data expressed as both absolute numbers and percentages can demonstrate different trends. Percentage voter turnout has generally declined for both presidential and midterm elections since 1960. Therefore, the correct answer is (A).

40. Article I, Section 3, Paragraph 4, of the United States Constitution states that the vice president shall preside over the United States Senate as its president and vote only in case of a tie vote in the Senate. The correct answer, therefore, is (C).

41. This question tests your knowledge of the influence of unelected individuals representing special interests in the political process. A wide range of groups have formed organizations that seek to influence the wording and passage of legislation on specific matters that impact directly on their interests. Choices (A) and (D) are functions performed by political parties, and research has shown (B) to be false. Interest groups hire lobbyists to present information in the hope of influencing legislators' votes. The correct answer, therefore, is (C).

42. This question tests your knowledge of relative and absolute location. The inset shown on the map clearly shows Singapore's relative location as a major entrepôt, or trade center, among the islands and peninsulas of Southeast Asia. This location enables Singapore to conduct trade with a vast regional hinterland. (A) is therefore the correct answer.

43. This question tests your knowledge of the human impact on the environment, which is one of the geographical themes included in the National Geography Standards. Important contemporary issues related to geographical themes are mentioned in (A), (B), and (C). However, the Green Revolution refers to the dramatic increase in crop production in locations such as China, India, and South America resulting from the development of new strains of grain and better land-management strategies. The correct answer, therefore, is (D).

44. This question tests your knowledge of the means by which discoveries, innovations, and other achievements of individual cultures are transmitted to neighboring societies. The origin of the ideas to be transmitted from an early civilization is sometimes referred to as a culture hearth, (A), but the process of spreading those ideas to other locations and societies is an example of cultural diffusion. Therefore, the correct answer is (B).

45. The distance from Nome to Barrow is greater than the maximum distance represented by the scale on the map. To answer the question, it is necessary to measure the scale with a ruler or use the edge of a piece of paper to replicate the scale and then apply it to the map so that the entire distance can be measured. The closest approximation to the distance is 450 miles. The answer, therefore, is (C).

46. This question tests two skills: your knowledge of basic geographical locations and your ability to read maps. Lines of latitude range from 0° to 90° north and south of the Equator. Lines of longitude range from 0° to 180° east and west of the prime meridian. Japan's approximate location is in the Northern and Eastern Hemispheres at 40° north and 140° east. (A) is therefore the correct answer.

47. This question tests your knowledge of the geographic theme of region as a tool to analyze spatial pattern. Identifying regions simplifies the study of geography. A formal region is marked by some degree of homogeneity in one or more phenomena, such as mountains, (A), climate, (C), or area, (D). A functional region is characterized by a core area with surrounding territory that acts as a dynamic organizational unit and as an integrated whole. The correct answer, therefore, is (B).

48. Take note that this is an EXCEPT question. Three of the choices are causes of desertification. You are looking for the choice that is *not* one of its causes. Desertification may come from forces in nature such as droughts. Human activity, however, accelerates the process of desertification when the original vegetation is cleared, (A), and damaged soil is exposed to heavy rains, (C), causing runoff into lakes and streams. Salinization, (B), occurs as moisture evaporates from the soil and leaves salt deposits behind. Strip cropping and no-till farming are two techniques used to maintain soil productivity. In no-till farming,

crop residue, such as corn stalks, is allowed to stay on the soil surface between plantings. Therefore, the correct answer is (D).

49. Atmospheric pressure is unequal between places. Pressure-gradient forces push air from one place to another, producing wind. The greater the pressure difference between two locations, the greater the force, and the stronger the wind. The correct answer, therefore, is (D).

50. This question tests your knowledge of climate patterns around the globe. Moist subtropical, (A), and Mediterranean, (C), are mid-latitude climates. Boreal forest, (D), is a high-latitude climate. Low-latitude climates lie for the most part between the tropic of Cancer and the tropic of Capricorn. They include wet equatorial, monsoon and trade winds, coastal, dry tropical and wet-dry tropical. The correct answer is (B).

51. The nations that are considered by geographers to be developed have a demographic profile that shows an older population. In many industrialized nations, the number of people receiving government-sponsored pensions is growing while the number of workers is declining as a result of a low birth rate. By contrast, many developing nations have large populations that will continue to grow because the average age in those nations is so much lower than in the previously industrialized nations. Therefore, the correct answer is (C).

52. Establishing regions helps to organize spatial areas that are similar in some important characteristics and distinct in some feature or features from surrounding areas. Bolivia, Ecuador, and Peru are characterized by physical geography dominated by the Andes Mountains, low gross domestic products (GDP), and large Amerindian populations. The correct answer, therefore, is (B).

53. This question tests your understanding of the economic problem that is the central focus of economics. All of the choices deal with economic problems related to inefficiencies, but the fundamental economic problem arises because of scarcity and the unlimited nature of human wants. (B) is therefore the correct answer.

54. The supply-and-demand graph is used to explain how competitive markets work in allocating resources and distributing output. In this question, the prevailing market price, P_0, is below the market equilibrium price, P_1. At P_0, the quantity demanded exceeds the quantity supplied, resulting in a shortage of grain in the market. The correct answer, therefore, is (D).

55. This question tests your understanding of how a price control, in this case a price floor, can affect price and the supply of and demand for the good. An effective price floor must be set above the market equilibrium. As a result of the effective price floor, the price will rise above P_1, creating a surplus in the market. (A) is therefore the correct answer.

56. This question tests your knowledge of the different types of market structures. A monopoly is described by the three characteristics of a single seller, a product for which there is no close substitute, and barriers to entry. The other options all describe market structures in which there is more than one seller. The correct answer, therefore, is (C).

57. The unemployment rate is the ratio of the number of people unemployed to those in the labor force. Those individuals employed and seeking employment are considered to be in the labor force. The unemployed consist of those laid off and those persons who are entering the labor market for the first time, and those who are returning after additional training and education. (D) is therefore the correct answer.

58. The focus of this question is the key economic instrument of fiscal policy. Fiscal policy can be either expansionary or contractionary. Choices (B) and (D) are contractionary policies. They may be used to reduce deficits or inflation but generally slow down the economy. An expansionary policy, such as reducing taxes, encourages economic expansion by injecting more spending directly

or indirectly by increasing disposable income, which leads to increased aggregate demand and output. Therefore, the correct answer is (C).

59. This question tests understanding of how banks create money and help to expand the money supply. The ability to create money derives from the fact that banks are required to keep available only a small fraction of their deposits, to meet their liabilities. This fraction is called the reserve requirement and is set in the United States by the Federal Reserve Bank. The correct answer, therefore, is (A).

60. This question tests knowledge and understanding of the principles of comparative advantage and absolute advantage. Absolute advantage occurs when a country or a person can produce a unit of a given good using fewer resources than another country or person can. Comparative advantage is based on comparison of opportunity costs. Country X has an absolute advantage in the production of both goods, since it requires fewer resources than Country Y to produce either of the two goods. However, Country X has a comparative advantage in the production of socks only, since its opportunity cost of producing a pair of socks (gives up 1 shirt) is lower than Country Y's (gives up 1.5 shirts). A country may have an absolute advantage in producing both goods but cannot have a comparative advantage in producing both goods. The correct answer, therefore, is (B).

61. This question tests your understanding of how fluctuations in currency values, either weakening or strengthening, will affect the international flow of goods and financial assets. A weak dollar will make imported goods more expensive for Americans, resulting in Americans' buying fewer imported goods and lowering the trade deficit. A weak dollar makes United States goods and services relatively cheaper in the world market, and therefore it tends to encourage United States exports. Therefore, the correct answer is (A).

62. This question tests your knowledge of some basic concepts in sociology. (A) addresses the process of cultural diffusion. (B) relates to social stratification. (D) represents the goal of creating a pluralistic society. The family, economy, religion, education, and political order are all social institutions that are created to fulfill the needs of society. The correct answer, therefore, is (C).

63. The demographic-transition theory of population moves through stages beginning with a high birth rate and a high death rate moving toward a low birth rate and a low death rate. The first stage is characterized by high birth and high death rates. In the second stage, birth rates remain high, but death rates decline. Options (A), (C), and (D) by themselves are all reasons for a continuation of a higher birth rate. Large families are characteristic of agrarian societies, but the need for and desirability of large numbers of children disappears with urbanization and industrialization. (B) is therefore the correct answer.

64. This question tests your knowledge of one of the key factors leading to social stratification. The German sociologist Max Weber believed that people come together to achieve aims based on cultural identities or interests. The existence of these status groups normally leads to the creation of a hierarchical order in the form of social stratification. The correct answer, therefore, is (A).

65. This item tests your knowledge of a key sociological concept that leads to the sharing of innovations and inventions around the world. Both (A) and (B) describe examples of assimilation. (B) also suggests cultural diversity. (D) is an example of forced enculturation. Cultural diffusion occurs when an innovation or invention is passed along to another culture or cultures. The correct answer, therefore, is (C).

Part Two: Sample Responses to the Constructed-Response Questions and How They Were Scored

This section presents actual scored sample responses to the constructed-response questions in the practice test in chapter 12 and explanations for the scores they received.

As discussed in chapter 4, each constructed-response question on the *Middle School Social Studies* test is scored on a scale from 0 to 3. The general scoring guide used to score these questions is reprinted here for your convenience.

Praxis *Middle School Social Studies* General Scoring Guide

Score	Comment
3	<ul><li>Shows a thorough understanding of the stimulus (where appropriate)</li><li>Provides an accurate and complete response</li><li>Provides the analysis required by the question</li><li>Applies appropriate subject matter knowledge</li><li>May contain minor errors</li></ul>
2	<ul><li>Shows an adequate understanding of the stimulus (where appropriate)</li><li>Provides a mostly accurate and complete response</li><li>Provides most of the analysis required by the question</li><li>Applies mostly appropriate subject matter knowledge</li><li>May contain significant errors</li></ul>
1	<ul><li>Shows little understanding of the stimulus (where appropriate)</li><li>Provides a basically inaccurate and incomplete response</li><li>Provides little of the analysis required by the question</li><li>Applies mostly inappropriate subject matter knowledge</li></ul>
0	<ul><li>Blank, off-topic, or totally incorrect response; rephrases the question</li></ul>

Constructed-Response Question 1—Sample Responses

We will now look at three scored responses to the first constructed-response question and see comments from the scoring leader about why each response received the score it did.

Sample Response 1: Score of 3

Part A:

During the period of 1764 to 1768 the level of imported goods into the American colonies from Great Britain was pretty level, showing a slight decline in 1766 but a rise in 1768. The value of goods imported in 1768 was very close to those in 1764. A sharp decline in imports occurred during the year 1769. Imports steadily increased with a sharp increase from 1770 to 1771. Following this period of increase, imports fell rapidly until they reached zero in 1776, with only one brief period of increase between 1773 and 1774.

The pattern of imports reported generally corresponds with the population remaining relatively steady from 1764 to 1768, 1769. The sudden downturn in imports in 1771 reflects the colonists' dissatisfaction with the British levying of taxes on imports and the move towards independence of the colonies.

Part B:

The colonists' response to Great Britain levying taxes on goods imported into the colonies and the general desire of the colonist towards more market independence caused a rapid decline in the level of imports. The colonists reacted strongly to the British taxation and many demonstrations followed. The Boston Tea Party was a result of such resentment of taxes on imported goods, especially tea. The colonists also reacted strongly to the Townshend Acts by boycotting them. This can be seen on the graph in the first major drop in imports.

The rise of anti-British sentiment and the actual process that lead the colonies towards independence also greatly reduced the demand for imported goods. Colonists refused to buy imported goods or to pay the imposed taxes. Thus, they were forced to find other sources for these goods or make the goods themselves. This lead to further self-reliance and a lack of dependency on Britain. Slogans such as "no taxation without representation" and "give me liberty or give me death" swelled anti-British sentiment to the point that the colonies declared their independence from Great Britain and set off to fight the American Revolutionary War in 1776, at which point the level of imports reached zero.

Commentary on Sample Response That Earned a Score of 3

This thorough, detailed, and accurate response received a score of 3. In responding to Part A, the response cites specific dates to carefully describe the rises and declines in imports from Great Britain to America. The description in the response accurately uses the dates to reflect the pattern of imports shown in the graph.

The response to Part B provides a detailed discussion of historical events to explain the pattern of imports shown in the graph. The two factors offered are the colonists' response to taxes and American desire for increased market independence. The response offers specific examples of one factor and a thorough but more general explanation for the second factor. When discussing the growing resentment of British taxes as a factor, two examples are mentioned: the Boston Tea Party and the boycott of the Townshend Acts. The response then links the boycott of the goods taxed under the Townshend Acts directly to the graph when it states: "The colonists also reacted strongly to the Townshend Acts by boycotting British goods. This can be seen on the graph in the first major drop in imports." The second factor—increasing self-reliance—is also clearly explained: the response points out that the colonists found other sources for goods or made goods themselves to decrease their reliance on British imports. The response then links the first and second factors together at the end of the last paragraph and refers specifically to the graph when it states that in 1776 "the level of imports reached zero."

Sample Response 2: Score of 2

The pattern of growth in the number of imports to colonial America during the 1760s to 1776 reflects important moments in colonial history.

The pattern, for the most part, shows a growth in imports as the colonies grew, became established, and increased in wealth and stability. The dips in the graph depict a time of consumer lack of confidence or productivity.

The most likely explanation for the growth early on would be that the colony was becoming more populated and established. With these factors in place productivity would cause profit and profit would cause a greater demand for imports. The first of the dips was most likely caused by the French and Indian War. To fund this war colonist lost spendable cash in taxes to support their security. This would explain the dip in the late 60s. In the 70s things were better than ever economically and the British, now in debt, began to impose more tariffs. With each new tariff, Americans had less money to buy British goods, but more importantly, less patience with Britain due to lack of American representation over the tax issue. They began to protest and boycott. These tensions led to the signing of the Declaration of Independence in 1776, which effectively shut down all trade between the colonies and British.

Commentary on Sample Response That Earned a Score of 2

This response received a score of 2 because it describes at least two trends in the graph (the dip in the late 1760s and the decline in the 1770s) and identifies at least one relevant historical factor contributing to the trends—the anti-British sentiment, protests, and boycotts of the 1770s. However, the response is less detailed than the response that received a score of 3, and it also contains some historical inaccuracies. The response does not discuss many of the rises and declines in imports in specific detail. It does address at least two aspects of the graph—the dip in the late 1760s and the decline in the 1770s. However, the explanation provided for the dip in the late 1760s is not completely accurate. Also incorrect is the first part of the response, which describes an increase in the value of imports early on as a result of population growth. The graph does <u>not</u> show growth in imports from 1764 to 1768, and, in fact, there is a slight decrease during this period. In addition, while it is true that the population of the colonies certainly increased during this period, this growth does not account for the peaks and valleys shown in the graph.

The discussion of the French and Indian War (1754-1763) is also rather jumbled. The War was a direct factor in the patterns shown on the graph but not in the way the response describes. The dip in the late 1760s was not a result of a lack of spendable cash caused by the taxes but was a result of the protests that resulted from these taxes. The boycott of items taxed under the Townshend Acts accounts for the dip in 1769.

The response does show basic understanding in its discussion of the tariffs imposed by the British in the 1770s. It explains that the colonists lost patience with the British and mentions taxation without representation, protests, and boycotts as examples. While the explanation does not offer specific examples of protests and boycotts (such as the Boston Tea Party), the mention of the factor is sufficient for a score of 2. The response is strengthened by directly linking the explanation to the graph at the end of the paragraph: ("These tensions led to the signing of the Declaration of Independence in 1776, which effectively shut down all trade between the colonies and British").

Sample Response 3: Score of 1

> As imported goods from Great Britain to America began in 1764, the two nations held stable exchanges of goods through 1768. In 1769, about 1,000 pounds of sterling was lost in imports from Great Britain due to the war and other economical factors that contributed to the loss. A dramatic rise took place from 1770 through 1771 as the economy began to rise and the relationship between Great Britain and the U.S. picks up as well. From 1772 until 1776 the relationship completely stopped due to war and differences that these countries faced during this time.

Commentary on Sample Response That Earned a Score of 1

This response received a score of 1 because it describes the graph but does not explain how historical factors contributed to the pattern of imports. In addition, the details mentioned in the response are vague and/or unsupported by evidence. For example, the response mentions war as one factor in 1769, but it is unclear which war is being referred to. The candidate then states that the relationship between Great Britain and the United States "picks up" but provides no evidence to support this assertion; the phrase "picks up" is too vague to count as one of the factors. In the last sentence, the response states: "From 1772 to 1776 the relationship completely stopped due to war and differences that these countries faced during this time." This is misleading because although conditions were deteriorating in this period, the Battle of Bunker Hill, which began the war, did not take place until April 17, 1775. In addition, the reasons for the decline in imports are not fully explained.

Constructed-Response Question 2—Sample Responses

Sample Response 1: Score of 3

One major development in human life from the Paleolithic age to the Neolithic age was the introduction of agriculture and farming. As seen in the picture, the men have cows and are plowing gardens. This was a major development because the people had additional resources and ways to get food. Instead of simply hunting and gathering their food, they could now grow gardens and raise livestock.

Another major development was how they began to build villages. This was made possible because they could now farm and no longer had to wander to hunt and gather food. As seen in the picture, all of their houses and gardens are all in very close proximity. This was great because it brought a sense of community. The children could now play together and everyone could help each other out.

Commentary on Sample Response That Earned a Score of 3

This response earned a score of 3 because it describes the two major developments that marked the change from the Old Stone Age to the New Stone Age: the ability to farm and the establishment of permanent settlements. (Many of the questions on this test require that the response identify a number of historical factors. In some cases there may be a variety of correct answers and the candidate needs to choose only two or three to identify and discuss. However, for this question, there are two specific correct answers that must be described to earn a score of 3.) This response clearly identifies and explains both farming and permanent settlement while also making specific reference to the drawing. Although the response is brief, it is sufficient because the question only asks the candidate to describe the changes—a detailed explanation is not required.

Sample Response 2: Score of 2

Many developments marked the change from the Old Stone Age to the New Stone Age. In the drawing there are many examples of these developments.

The people of this age were able to develop new methods of agriculture. They were no longer only able to hunt and gather food. In the drawing you see two men plowing a field. This shows that these people were able to plant and harvest their own crops. You also see three men herding cattle. They were capable of raising livestock for labor and food purposes.

In the drawing you also see several people carrying storage containers about the area. This proves that the people were capable of storing food for future use. They were able to produce a surplus and keep it for use in times of need or for trade as well.

These are just two of the many examples of how people of this age were developing from the Paleolithic age to the Neolithic age.

Commentary on Sample Response That Earned a Score of 2

This response received a score of 2 because it describes only one development of the Neolithic Revolution: the development of agriculture. It does not mention the development of permanent settlements. The second factor given, the ability to store food for future use, is important but is not one of the two major factors. This response would have received a score of 3 if it had gone on to explain how the ability to farm and store surplus food allowed for the establishment of permanent settlements.

This response also receives credit because it refers to the drawing several times. In doing so, it does not simply state what is in the drawing but explains it. ("In the drawing you see two men plowing a field. This shows that these people were able to plant and harvest their own crops. You also see three men herding cattle.")

Sample Response 3: Score of 1

> The drawing highlights a village of people using what means of survival possible for the development of human life. They use what tools and materials are necessary to live. They grow their own food and make their own tools and cooking utensils in the Old Stone Age.
> Changes were made when the people became more modernized and made new developments in the Neolithic Revolution.

Commentary on Sample Response That Earned a Score of 1

This response earned a score of 1 because it does not show an accurate understanding of the Neolithic Revolution. It describes some of the activities shown in the illustration but does not use outside knowledge to explain how any specific activities were developed in the Neolithic period. Although it mentions growing food, this response incorrectly identifies that activity as taking place in the Old Stone Age. The other information provided, "they made their own tools and cooking utensils" is not specific enough to count as a development. In the Paleolithic period, humans were making their own chipped-stone tools. In the Neolithic period, humans were able to polish or grind stones to make stronger and more sophisticated tools.

Constructed-Response Question 3—Sample Responses

Sample Response 1: Score of 3

> The Bubonic Plague devastated Western Europe as it spread from China. Looking at the spread of the plague one can see how Europeans traveled and traded. Trade between countries was beginning to increase greatly but as the trade continued, it spread the plague with it. The European countries were trading with the Middle Eastern countries and also began receiving goods from China. The goods spread through Europe to the north. Most of the goods were rare and expensive but it brought the plague with them. The poorer people were more affected because of the overcrowding and unclean conditions in which they lived. That is not to say the upper class were not

444444

4444

Sample Response 1: Score of 3 (continued)

affected, the plague spared no one, regardless of class or income. With millions of people sick and dying, there may have been more work for people but the plague made it difficult for people to work. Whole towns were wiped out by the plague. Travel was not always a good idea because no one knew where the plague would strike. The economies suffered from the lack of workers and wariness of the people to travel. It made people not want to trade anymore. Plague was spread very easily through the increasing trade and then through the unclean and crowded conditions of the lower classes. It also hurt the economies because millions of workers died and fear of death by the plague was felt by those still alive. But those who were left could now ask for higher wages because there were fewer workers.

Commentary on Sample Response That Earned a Score of 3

This response earned a score of 3 because it thoroughly and accurately responds to all parts of the question. It describes two or more factors contributing to the spread of the plague: increasing trade of expensive goods and crowded, unsanitary living conditions among the poor. It also provides two accurate examples of how the plague impacted the economies of the affected areas: lack of workers and less trade. The response links the reluctance to travel to a decrease in trade. In the last line, the response explains how fewer workers led to higher wages. Lastly, the response demonstrates a clear understanding of the routes depicted on the map. It identifies China as the place of origin for the plague. It also states that, "The European countries were trading with the Middle Eastern countries and also began receiving goods from China. The goods spread through Europe to the north."

Sample Response 2: Score of 2

The Black Death was the result of disease carried by the fleas often found on rats. These rats were often found on sailing ships and traveling caravans that visited many cities and ports along their trade routes. The strong desire for increased trade and distribution brought many into contact with the diseases as goods were transported and the disease spread.

Societies were decimated by the effects of the plague. Travel restrictions were imposed as well as restrictions on goods being processed. People were afraid to travel or to allow travelers to enter areas based on fears of allowing the disease in. Economies were greatly reduced by these restrictions and fears. Goods from the Far East and from European areas could not travel along the well-established trade routes.

Commentary on Sample Response That Earned a Score of 2

This response earns a score of 2 because it explains one factor relating to the spread of the plague—trade—and one way in which the economies were affected—less trade—but it does not discuss the routes depicted on the map. The response explains that the disease was spread through the goods that were being traded. It goes on to explain that travel restrictions were imposed and people were afraid to travel. This hurt the economies of the affected areas because goods were no longer being traded. It should be noted that although the explanation of the economic impact—less trade—is not very thorough, it is enough to be given credit. A stronger response would include an additional socioeconomic factor contributing to the spread of the disease and further discussion of the effects of decreased trade on the economies.

The response also lacks specific references to the map provided. This response states: "Goods from the Far East and from European areas could not travel along the well-established trade routes." There is no clear discussion of how the map illustrates the impact of the disease's spread on the economies of the infected areas.

Sample Response 3: Score of 1

China was once a country that was not known. It made everything from food jewelry, clothing, etc. It did not know about the other countries and did not trade with them. Then one day it was discovered. They started to travel to other parts of the world. They had silk, pottery, jewelry, etc. Everyone from other countries wanted to have some of the rich cloth. However, since the Chinese had not been around other cultures and people there were not immune to the illnesses and diseases that were in the other countries. Therefore, a lot of people got sick and since it was new to them they did not know how to treat these diseases. So many people became sick. So as people came in and out of the country they spread the disease. People became sick.

Commentary on Sample Response That Earned a Score of 1

This response earned a score of 1 because it does not accurately explain any factors relating to the spread of the plague or its economic impact. The response identifies trade with China as one of the factors contributing to the spread of the disease, but it does not provide an accurate explanation. The response erroneously concludes that the Chinese were the ones infected while traveling outside China when it states: "However, since the Chinese had not been around other cultures and people there were not immune to the illnesses and diseases that were in the other countries. Therefore, a lot of people got sick…" The plague originated in China, and it was usually the European and Middle Eastern traders who picked up the disease and brought it back to their countries.

Chapter 14

Preparing for the *Middle School Science* Test

The *Middle School Science* test is designed to measure the subject-area knowledge and competencies necessary for a beginning teacher of science in a middle school. The test contains both multiple-choice and constructed-response questions.

The first part of this chapter focuses on the multiple-choice section of the test. The second part of the chapter contains information about the constructed-response section of the test.

Part One: Multiple-Choice Questions

This section of the chapter is intended to help you organize your preparation for the multiple-choice portion of the test and to give you a clear indication about the depth and breadth of the knowledge required for success on the multiple-choice questions.

The *Middle School Science* test contains 90 multiple-choice questions that constitute approximately 75 percent of the examinee's total test score. It is expected that about 90 minutes will be spent on the multiple-choice questions.

Here is an overview of the areas covered on the test, along with their subareas:

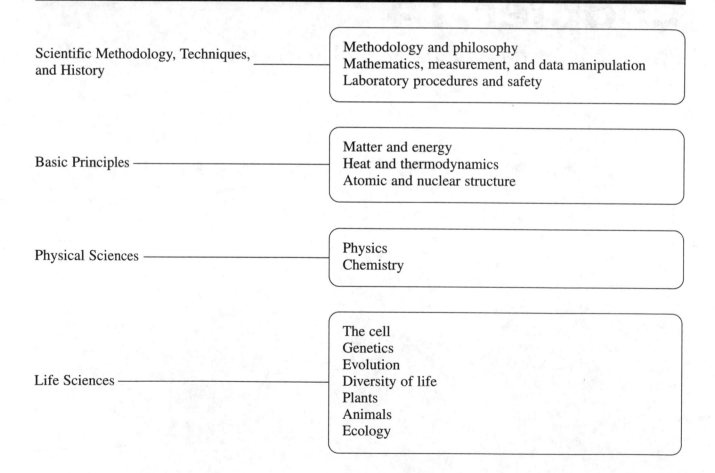

Scientific Methodology, Techniques, and History
- Methodology and philosophy
- Mathematics, measurement, and data manipulation
- Laboratory procedures and safety

Basic Principles
- Matter and energy
- Heat and thermodynamics
- Atomic and nuclear structure

Physical Sciences
- Physics
- Chemistry

Life Sciences
- The cell
- Genetics
- Evolution
- Diversity of life
- Plants
- Animals
- Ecology

Earth/Space Sciences ——————
Physical geology
Historical geology
Oceanography
Meteorology
Astronomy

Science, Technology, and Society ——————
Uses and applications of science and technology
Social, political, ethical, and economic issues

The Middle School Science test measures the knowledge and competencies necessary for a beginning teacher of middle school science, such as knowledge of scientific principles, facts, methodology, philosophy, and scientific concepts, as well as an ability to integrate basic knowledge from all of the sciences. Teachers need to understand the subject matter from a more advanced viewpoint than is actually presented to the students. Accordingly, some questions of a more advanced nature are included. These questions deal with topics typically introduced in introductory college-level courses in chemistry, physics, life sciences, and Earth/space sciences. The questions require a variety of abilities, including definition of terms, comprehension of critical concepts, application, and analysis, to address and solve problems. Some questions may require the test taker to integrate concepts from more than one content area.

Examinees will not need to use a calculator in taking this test. The test book contains a periodic table and a table of information that presents various physical constants and a few conversion factors among SI units. When necessary, additional values of physical constants are printed with the text of a question.

The test is designed to reflect current standards for knowledge, skills, and abilities in science education. Educational Testing Service (ETS) has aligned this test closely with the National Science Education Standards and works in collaboration with teacher educators, higher education content specialists, and accomplished practicing teachers in science to keep the test updated and representative of current standards.

Using the topic lists that follow

You are likely to find that the topics below are covered by most introductory textbooks in the fields of biology, chemistry, physics, and Earth and space sciences, but general survey textbooks may not cover all of the subtopics. Consult materials and resources, including lecture and laboratory notes, from all your science coursework. You should be able to match up specific topics and subtopics with what you have covered in your courses in chemistry, biology, physics, Earth and space science, and so on.

Try not to be overwhelmed by the volume and scope of content knowledge in this guide. An overview such as this that lists science topics does not offer you a great deal of context. Although a specific term may not seem familiar as you see it here, you might find you could understand it when applied to a real-life situation. Many of the items on the actual Praxis test will provide you with a context in which to apply these topics or terms, as you will see when you look at the practice questions in chapter 15.

Special questions marked with stars

Interspersed throughout the list of topics are questions that are outlined in boxes and preceded by a star (★). These questions are intended to help you test your knowledge of fundamental concepts and your ability to apply fundamental concepts to situations in the laboratory or the real world. Most of the questions require you to combine several pieces of knowledge in order to formulate an integrated understanding and response. If you spend time on these questions, you will gain increased understanding and facility with the subject matter covered on the test. You might want to discuss these questions and your answers with a teacher or mentor.

Note that the questions marked with stars are not necessarily short-answer or multiple-choice, and that this study guide does not provide the answers to these questions—they are intended as study questions, not practice questions. Thinking about how to answer them should improve your understanding of fundamental concepts and will probably help you answer a broad range of questions on the test. For example, the following box with a star appears in the list of study topics under the "Mechanics" topic within Physics:

★ What variables affect the period of a pendulum?

If you think about this question, perhaps jotting down some notes on the variables and how they relate to motion of a pendulum, you will review your knowledge of the subject and you will probably be ready to answer multiple-choice questions similar to the one below:

A simple pendulum has period T on Earth. Which of the following would decrease the period of the pendulum if the pendulum were kept at the same location?

(A)   Increasing the length of the pendulum

(B)   Increasing the mass of the pendulum bob

(C)   Decreasing the length of the pendulum

(D)   Decreasing the mass of the pendulum bob

The correct answer is (C). The period of a simple pendulum is dependent on the length and the acceleration due to gravity. The period of the pendulum does not depend on the mass of the pendulum bob. Acceleration due to gravity does not change because the location did not change. A long pendulum has a greater period than a short pendulum.

Study Topics

Scientific Methodology, Techniques, and History

Methodology and Philosophy

- Scientific method of problem solving
  - Making observations, formulating and testing hypotheses, drawing conclusions, and communicating findings
  - Understanding that scientific knowledge is consistent with evidence, subject to change, open to criticism, predictive, and subject to independent verification

- Comparing and contrasting facts, hypotheses, models, theories, and laws

- The use of science process skills in experiments and investigations, and to solve problems

- Experimental design
  - Choice of dependent (response) variable
  - Choice of independent variables
  - Use of controls
  - Hypothesis testing
  - Observations
  - Data collection and processing

- Historical roots of science
  - Historical figures (e.g., Einstein, Bohr, Curie, Mendel, Darwin, Watson and Crick, Newton, Copernicus, Galileo, Hutton, Mendeleev, Dalton)
  - Landmark events and discoveries (e.g., DNA structure, theory of evolution, radioactivity, atomic structure, Newton's laws of motion, big bang theory)

- Understanding of the unified, integrative nature of the various disciplines and concepts in science

Mathematics, Measurement, and Data Manipulation

- Scientific measurement and notation systems

  ▶ Metric and U.S. standards for volume, mass, length, molarity, time, and temperature

★ What unit is equivalent to 1/1,000th of a gram?

  ▶ Significant figures

★ What is the area, to the correct number of significant figures, of a rectangle having a width of 2 cm and a length of 6.7 cm?

- Processes involved in scientific data collection, analysis, interpretation, manipulation, presentation, and the critical analysis of sources of data

- Interpreting and drawing conclusions from data, including that presented in tables, graphs, maps, and charts

  ▶ Titles, legends, units
  ▶ Dependent versus independent variables

- Identifying sources of error in data, procedures, or processes

  ▶ Precision and accuracy

Laboratory Procedures and Safety

- Safety procedures involved in the preparation, storage, use, and disposal of laboratory and field materials

  ▶ Acids, bases, toxins, microbiological samples, fire hazards, etc.
  ▶ Ability to prepare reagents, materials, and apparatuses correctly for classroom use

★ How would you prepare 500 mL of a 3 *M* NaCl solution?

- Identifying laboratory and field equipment appropriate for scientific procedures

★ What is a graduated cylinder used for?

- Safety and emergency procedures for the science classroom and laboratory, including the teacher's legal responsibilities

Basic Principles

Matter and Energy

- Structure and properties of matter

  ▶ Atomic, molecular, and ionic nature of matter
  ▶ Physical and chemical properties of matter

    ♦ Melting point, boiling point, color, density, etc.
    ♦ Combustibility, oxidation potential, reactivity, etc.
    ♦ Organization of matter
      — Elements, compounds, solutions, mixtures

- Elements

  ▶ Names and symbols
  ▶ Factors that influence their occurrence and relative abundance

- Physical and chemical changes of matter

  ▶ Change in form versus change in composition
  ▶ Separation versus decomposition

★ How are physical changes in a substance different from chemical changes?

- Conservation of mass/energy

► Conservation of energy

► Relationship between conservation of matter and atomic theory

► Fusion and fission reactions

► Conversion of mass to energy

■ Energy transformations

► Kinetic-potential, electrical-mechanical, chemical-heat, etc.

★ How are kinetic energy and potential energy different?

★ What energy changes occur to a mass that starts from rest and slides without friction from the top to the bottom of an inclined plane? What additional energy changes occur when there is friction between the mass and the inclined plane?

Heat and Thermodynamics

■ The distinction between heat and temperature

► Molecular behaviors and interactions

► Heat as a form of energy

► Temperature as a measure of the average kinetic energy of a sample of molecules

■ Measurement, transfer, and effects of thermal energy on matter

► Heat exchange

♦ Heat lost equals heat gained

♦ Change in temperature and/or phase change

♦ Quantitative problems

— Change in temperature using specific heat capacity

★ If 100 g of water at 20°C absorbs 5 kJ of heat, by what amount will the temperature of the water increase?

■ First and second laws of thermodynamics

► Conservation of energy

★ When a reaction in solution produces energy, what happens to the temperature of the solution?

► Entropy

★ What entropy changes occur when a substance melts?

Atomic and Nuclear Structure

■ Atomic models and their experimental bases

► Cathode rays and electrons

► Alpha-scattering experiment and the nuclear atom

► Atomic spectra and electron energy levels

★ What changes in an atom produce an atomic spectrum?

► Bohr model of the atom

■ Atomic and nuclear structure and forces

► Protons, neutrons, and electrons

► Nuclear atom

► Electron configuration

★ How many neutrons are in $^{14}_{6}C$?

■ Relationship of electron configuration to the chemical and physical properties of an atom

► Chemical reactivity

★ What are the formulas of compounds that form between Cl and elements that have one electron in their outer electron shell?

► Atomic size

★ Of the atoms He, H, Li, and Be, which is the smallest?

- Radioisotopes and radioactivity
  - ► Types of radioactivity, such as alpha, beta, and gamma radiation

★ What is an example of a nuclear reaction involving beta decay? Alpha decay?

- ► Properties
  - ◆ Half-life

★ If a 100 g sample of a radioactive element decays to 25 g in 4 days, what is the half-life of the element?

- ◆ Nuclear stability
- ► Products of nuclear reactions
  - ◆ Conservation of mass number and charge number in reactions
  - ◆ Predicting products

Physical Sciences

Physics

- Mechanics
  - ► Motion in a straight line
    - ◆ Displacement, velocity and acceleration vectors, distance, speed, average speed, average acceleration, instantaneous velocity and acceleration, relative motion
    - ◆ Free fall

★ How does mass affect the acceleration of a falling object?

★ What is meant by the term "terminal velocity"?

- ► Projectile Motion

★ A ball is dropped and another ball of smaller mass is fired horizontally from the same height. Which ball has a greater acceleration when it hits the ground? Which ball hits the ground first?

- ► Circular and periodic motion
  - ◆ Frequency and period

★ What variables affect the period of a pendulum?

- ◆ Angular velocity
- ◆ Centripetal force
- ► Newton's laws of motion
  - ◆ Relate mass to inertia (first law)
  - ◆ Force and acceleration (second law)
  - ◆ Balanced and unbalanced forces

★ What forces act on a frictionless air puck as it moves across a table at constant speed in a straight line?

- ◆ Action and reaction forces (third law)
- ► The distinction between weight and mass
- ► Friction

★ Why is it more difficult to slide a crate starting from rest than it is to keep it moving once it is sliding?

- ► Work, energy, and power
  - ◆ Kinetic energy

★ If the speed of an object is doubled, by what factor does its kinetic energy change?

- ◆ Work and kinetic energy

★ Which requires more work: lifting a 100-kilogram sack a vertical distance of 2 meters or lifting a 50-kilogram sack a vertical distance of 4 meters?

▶ Simple machines and torque
  ◆ Pulleys, levers, gears, and inclined planes
  ◆ Mechanical advantage
▶ Linear momentum

★ If the momentum of a 2,500 kg car is equal to the momentum of a 1,500 kg car moving at 5 m/s, what must be the speed of the 2,500 kg car?

▶ Conservation of energy and conservation of linear momentum
  ◆ Kinetic energy
  ◆ Potential energy
  ◆ Energy transformations
  ◆ Collisions

★ When a moving object collides with an object at rest, is it possible for both objects to be at rest after the collision?

— Elastic collisions
— Inelastic collisions

★ What is the difference between an elastic collision and an inelastic collision?

▶ Angular momentum and torque
  ◆ Angular velocity
  ◆ Conservation of angular momentum

★ What happens to the angular velocity of a rotating platform as a person walks from the outer rim of the platform toward the center of the platform?

  ◆ Angular acceleration
▶ Force of gravity
  ◆ Newton's law of universal gravitation

★ If the distance between two masses is doubled, what happens to the gravitational force between the two masses?

  ◆ Kepler's laws of planetary motion
  ◆ Satellites
▶ Fluids
  ◆ Pressure and Pascal's principle

★ What is the absolute pressure at the bottom of a lake that is 25 m deep?

  ◆ Archimedes' principle (buoyancy)
  ◆ Bernoulli's principle

★ Why does a sheet of paper on a table rise when air is blown across the top surface of the paper?

■ Electricity and Magnetism
  ▶ Repulsion and attraction of electric charges
    ◆ Coulomb's law and the electrostatic force between charges

★ If the distance between two charges is halved, what happens to the electrostatic force between the two charges?

  ◆ Electric field
    — Electric field lines
    — Electric flux
  ◆ Electric potential
    — Potential difference between parallel plates
    — Potential difference and work

★ What happens to the electric potential between two positive charges when the distance between the charges decreases?

★ What is the electric field between two oppositely charged parallel plates separated by 0.05 m and having a potential difference of 50 V between them?

► Characteristics of current electricity and simple circuits (e.g., resistance, electromotive force, potential difference, and current)

- ♦ Resistance and Ohm's law
  - — Power dissipated by a resistor

★ What is the power dissipated by a 10-ohm resistor through which a 2-ampere current is flowing?

- ♦ Electromotive force (emf)
- ♦ Potential difference
- ♦ Capacitance and stored electric charge
- ♦ Current
- ► Series and parallel circuits
  - ♦ Resistors

★ If three 10-ohm resistors are connected in parallel, what is the equivalent resistance of the parallel combination?

- ♦ Capacitors

★ If a 10-microfarad capacitor and a 20-microfarad capacitor are connected in series, what is the equivalent capacitance of the series combination?

- ► Conductors and insulators

★ Why are metals good conductors of heat and electricity?

- ♦ Charging by friction, conduction, and induction
- ► Direct current and alternating current
- ► Sources of emf (e.g., batteries, photocells, and generators)
- ► Magnets, magnetic fields, and magnetic forces
  - ♦ Magnetic field lines
    - — Magnetic field lines around bar magnets

★ Describe the orientation of the magnetic field lines of a bar magnet.

- — Magnetic flux
- ♦ Magnetic force on a current-carrying wire (Biot-Savart law)

★ Is the magnetic force between two parallel wires carrying currents in opposite directions attractive or repulsive?

- ♦ Magnetic fields produced by currents (Ampere's law)
  - — Straight wire
  - — Coil of wire
- ♦ Electromagnetic induction (Faraday's law)
  - — Induced emf
  - — Induced current
- ♦ Lenz's law

★ When a bar magnet is moved toward a stationary conducting loop, in which direction does the induced current in the loop flow?

- ♦ Magnetic force on a moving charge (Lorentz force)

★ What factors determine the magnetic force on a moving charge?

- ♦ Magnetic dipoles and magnetic materials
- ► Transformers and motors

★ What is the basic difference between an electric motor and a generator? What is the basic similarity?

- ■ Waves
  - ► Wave characteristics, phenomena, models, and applications
    - ♦ Speed, amplitude, wavelength, and frequency

- Reflection, refraction, dispersion, absorption, transmission, and scattering

★ Why does the sky appear blue when viewed from the surface of Earth?

- Superposition
  — Standing waves
- Interference and diffraction

★ What is the fundamental difference between interference and diffraction?

— Constructive and destructive interference

★ For two waves to interfere constructively, what must be the path-length difference between the waves?

— Interference in thin films
— Double-slit interference (Young's experiment)
— Single-slit diffraction
— Diffraction gratings
- Transverse and longitudinal waves and their properties
  — Polarization

★ How do polarized sunglasses reduce the glare from reflective surfaces, such as the surface of a lake?

- Doppler effect
▶ Characteristics of sound waves
  - Speed
  - Pressure variations
  - Pitch and loudness
  - Beats
  - Vibrations of air columns and strings
    — Resonance and standing waves

★ When you blow over a bottle, what happens to the frequency of the sound produced as you fill the bottle with water?

▶ Characteristics of the electromagnetic spectrum
  - Gamma rays to radio waves
  - Visible spectrum

★ What is the range of wavelengths of visible light?

- Color

★ What color light is transmitted through a piece of blue glass? Why?

- Geometric optics
- Thin lenses
  — Convex and concave lenses

★ What is always true of the images formed by concave lenses?

— Lens equation
— Real and virtual images
— Magnification
- Plane mirrors and spherical mirrors

★ Describe image formation in a plane mirror.

— Convex and concave spherical mirrors
— Mirror equation
— Real and virtual images
— Magnification

★ Does the size of the image in a plane mirror change as the object moves away from the mirror?

- Prisms
- Fiber optics

Chemistry

- Periodicity
  - ► Meaning of chemical periodicity

★ What is the relationship between the position of an element on the periodic table and the distribution of electrons in the atoms of the element?

  - ► Periodic trends in chemical and physical properties
    - Ionization energy, atomic size, electronegativity

★ Of the elements Na, Mg, Al, P, S, and Cl, which has the highest first ionization energy?

    - Chemical reactivity

★ Of the elements K, Fe, Cu, and Ag, which will react most readily with Cl?

- The mole and chemical bonding
  - ► The mole concept, chemical composition, and stoichiometry

★ How many oxygen atoms are in 3 moles of CO_2?

  - ► Chemical formulas

★ How many H atoms are in calcium hydroxide, $Ca(OH)_2$?

  - ► Systematic nomenclature of inorganic and simple organic compounds
    - Binary compounds

★ What is the formula for cupric oxide, also known as copper (III) oxide?

    - Polyatomic ions and associated acids

- Prefix and suffix utilization, including -ic, -ous, per-, hypo-, -ide, -ate, -ite

★ Of the compounds Na_2S, Na_2SO_4, and Na_2SO_3, which is called sodium sulfate?

  - IUPAC nomenclature of simple organic compounds according to their functional groups
    - Alkanes, alkenes, alkynes, alcohols, carbohydrates, carboxylic acids, and amines

★ What are the molecular formulas for ethanol, ethanal, and butane?

  - ► Ionic, covalent, and metallic bonds
    - The differences between these basic types of bonds
      - Valence electron behavior
      - Electron pairing, sharing, or transfer

★ What kinds of bonding are exhibited by the compounds KCl, MgO, CO_2, and H_2?

  - ► Lewis electron dot and structural formulas

★ What are both the electron dot and structural formulas for methane, CH_4?

- The kinetic theory and states of matter
  - ► Kinetic molecular theory
    - Relationship among phases of matter, forces between particles, and particle energy

★ What are the arrangement and motions of molecules of substances in the solid phase? Liquid phase? Gaseous phase?

    - Phase changes

— The differences in intermolecular interactions among different states

— Conversion between molecular potential energy and molecular kinetic energy

— The special properties of water

♦ Relationships among temperature, pressure, volume, and number of molecules of an ideal gas

★ If a sample of gas is heated at a constant pressure, what will happen to the volume of the gas?

▶ Characteristics of crystals

♦ Crystal lattice of ionic salts and metals

★ What effect does the rate of evaporation have on the size of salt crystals that form when water evaporates from a saltwater solution?

■ Chemical Reactions

▶ Balancing chemical equations

★ Balance the following equation:
$Na + MgSO_4 \rightarrow Mg + Na_2SO_4$.

▶ Types of chemical reactions

♦ Single replacement, double replacement, combustion, combination (synthesis), and decomposition

▶ Endothermic and exothermic chemical reactions

♦ Energy absorbed or released

♦ Changes in the temperature of the surroundings

▶ Effects of temperature, pressure, concentration, and the presence of catalysts on chemical reactions

♦ Reaction rates

♦ Equilibrium shifts

★ In general terms, what will happen to the chemical equilibrium $2 NO_2(g) \rightleftharpoons N_2O_4(g) + 58$ kJ if the temperature, pressure, or concentration of one of the reactants is changed?

▶ Practical applications of electrochemistry

♦ Oxidation-reduction processes, voltaic cells, and/or electroplating

★ In an electrochemical cell, $Cd \rightarrow Cd^{2+}$, is Cd oxidized or reduced?

■ Solutions and Solubility

▶ Terminology and types of solutions

♦ Solute, solvent, saturated, unsaturated, supersaturated, electrolytes, and nonelectrolytes

★ If a solute is completely dissolved in a solvent, is the solution saturated or unsaturated?

▶ Types of solvents and factors affecting the dissolving process

♦ Selectivity of solvents

★ Why is ammonia gas very soluble in water while oxygen, O_2, is only slightly soluble?

♦ The dissolving process, and factors affecting the rate of dissolution

★ Will a substance dissolve faster if it is ground into a powder first?

♦ The effects of temperature and pressure on the solubility of a solute

★ Will increasing temperature always increase solubility?

▶ Physical and chemical properties of acids, bases, and salts

♦ pH scale

◆ Identify acids, bases, and salts

◆ The effects of buffers

★ What is the general function of buffer mixtures?

★ What will happen to the pH of an aqueous solution of HCl when a base such as NaOH is added?

Life Sciences

The Cell

■ Structure and function of cells

▶ Organelles and other subcellular structures (e.g., Golgi apparatus, nucleus, mitochondria, endoplasmic reticulum, chloroplasts)

★ What structures would you expect to find in a typical plant cell but not in an animal cell? What functions do these unique structures carry out for the plant?

▶ Biological membranes

◆ Fluid mosaic model

◆ Transport mechanisms (e.g., diffusion, osmosis, passive transport, active transport, exocytosis, endocytosis)

★ If you were stranded in a lifeboat on the ocean, why would drinking the ocean water be more harmful than not drinking the water?

▶ Biologically important inorganic and organic molecules and macromolecules

◆ Gases (carbon dioxide, oxygen, etc.)

◆ Water

◆ Proteins and amino acids

◆ Nucleic acids and nucleotides

◆ Fats/lipids, glycerol, and fatty acids

◆ Carbohydrates (starch, cellulose, glycogen) and monosaccharides (sugars)

■ Prokaryotic and eukaryotic cells

▶ Cellular level comparison (e.g., presence/absence of membrane enclosed organelles, DNA organization, methods of cell division)

▶ Cell theory

■ Cell cycle and cytokinesis

▶ Events of interphase and the mitotic phases

▶ Cytokinesis

★ What are the major differences between "normal" cells and cancerous cells? Chemotherapy is the use of chemicals to kill rapidly dividing cells. In addition to killing many types of cancer cells, why does chemotherapy treatment cause side effects such as anemia, gastrointestinal distress, and hair loss?

▶ Events during meiosis I and meiosis II

▶ Comparison of mechanisms (e.g., number of cell divisions, genetic makeup of daughter cells, and cell types in which each event occurs)

■ Chemical reactions in respiration and photosynthesis

▶ Metabolism

◆ Anabolic versus catabolic pathways

◆ Role of enzymes

▶ Photosynthetic reactions (overall equation)

◆ Pigments, wavelengths of light, location within eukaryotic cells

▶ Aerobic cellular respiration reactions (overall equation)

◆ Aerobic versus anaerobic reactions (fermentation)

★ At the cellular level, what is the benefit of exercising aerobically? Why do muscles become "sore" after excessive exercise?

★ What makes bread "rise" before it is baked?

- Mitosis and meiosis

Genetics

- DNA replication

  ► Structure of DNA and RNA nucleotides (e.g., A, C, G, T, and U bases, ribose and deoxyribose sugars)

★ Describe Watson and Crick's model for DNA structure.

  ► Mechanism of semiconservative, antiparallel replication, base pairing

- Protein synthesis

  ► Transcription (DNA-directed mRNA synthesis)

  ► Translation (mRNA-directed protein synthesis)

    • Functions of ribosomes, mRNA codons, tRNA anticodons

- Mutation

- Mendelian inheritance

  ► Monohybrid and dihybrid crosses, pedigree analysis, probability analysis

  ► Dominant and recessive alleles

  ► Law of segregation, independent assortment

★ How are Mendel's laws related to the behavior of chromosomes during the formation of gametes?

- Non-Mendelian inheritance

  ► Complete dominance, epistasis, incomplete dominance, multiple alleles, polygenic inheritance

★ What percentage of offspring will have blood type A if the parents have blood types AB and O? What percentage will have blood type O?

★ Why are there more color-blind males than color-blind females?

  ► Linkage and crossing over
  ► Sex-linkage

- Recombinant DNA

  ► Cloning and gene splicing

    • Restriction enzymes, vectors

  ► Diagnostic, medical, forensic, and agricultural applications

★ How has recombinant DNA technology been used to solve criminal cases? To treat diabetes?

- Interaction between heredity and environment

- Chromosomal and gene aberrations leading to some common human genetic disorders (e.g., Down syndrome, sickle cell disorder, cystic fibrosis)

★ A small percentage of individuals with Down syndrome possess a chromosomal translocation in which a copy of chromosome 21 becomes attached to chromosome 14. How does this translocation occur?

Evolution

- Scientific evidence supporting the theory of evolution

  ► Biogeography, comparative anatomy and embryology, fossil record, molecular evidence

  ► Key historical figures (e.g., Cuvier, Lyell, Darwin, Lamarck)

- Mechanisms and rate of evolution

  ► Natural selection

- ▶ Gradualism versus punctuated equilibrium
- ▶ Introduction of variation and changes in a gene pool's allele frequency

★ A radioactive meteorite falls to Earth and kills 90 percent of a secluded population of salamander. What mechanisms are in action changing allelic frequency in this population's gene pool?

- ■ Isolating mechanisms and speciation
  - ▶ Biological definition of species
  - ▶ Process of speciation due to geographical barriers isolating populations
  - ▶ Darwin's theory of the origin of species

★ Explain the following concepts relative to Darwin's theory of the origin of species: a) Descent with modification, b) Struggle for existence, and c) Survival of the fittest

- ■ Scientific hypotheses for the origin of life on Earth
  - ▶ Earth's age
  - ▶ Abiotic synthesis
  - ▶ Endosymbiotic theory

★ How would the presence of molecular oxygen, O_2, in the atmosphere affect early living things?

Diversity of Life

- ■ Levels of organization and characteristics of life
- ■ Biological classification systems
  - ▶ Five-kingdom system (Monera, Protista, Fungi, Plantae, and Animalia)

★ What are the limitations of the five-kingdom system? Current debates about revising the five-kingdom system center mainly on which groups of organisms?

- ▶ Nomenclature schemes organizing life from the most broad to the most specific (kingdom, phylum/division, class, order, family, genus, and species)
- ■ Characteristics of viruses, bacteria, protists, fungi, plants, and animals (e.g., unicellular versus multicellular, modes of nutrition, and energy sources)
  - ▶ Symbiotic and phylogenetic relationships

Plants (Form and Function)

- ■ Characteristics of vascular and nonvascular plants
  - ▶ Pterophytes (ferns)
  - ▶ Gymnosperms (conifers)
  - ▶ Angiosperms (flowering plants)
- ■ Structure and function of roots, stems, and leaves
- ■ Control mechanisms
  - ▶ Hormones
    - ◆ Auxin
    - ◆ Cytokinins
  - ▶ Photoperiods
  - ▶ Tropisms
    - ◆ Phototropism
    - ◆ Gravitropism/geotropism

★ Consider a seed planted upside down three inches under the soil. When the seed germinates, why does the root grow downward into the soil while the shoot grows upward?

- ■ Water and nutrient uptake and transport systems

- ▶ Role and location of xylem and phloem
- ▶ Role of roots, stems, and leaves in transport
- ▶ Transpiration

★ Under what environmental conditions would you expect the transpiration rate to be the highest in an average-sized oak tree? The lowest?

- ■ Sexual and asexual reproduction in plants
  - ▶ Vegetative propagation
- ■ Growth
  - ▶ Seedling germination, differentiation, and development
  - ▶ Root and shoot meristems

Animals (Form and Function)

- ■ Anatomy and physiology of structures associated with life functions of organisms in the animal kingdom.
  - ▶ Digestion
    - ◆ Nutritional requirements (e.g., food sources, calories)

★ Why must the human body digest large macromolecules into small monomers before it can use them? What enzymes does the human body use to digest these macromolecules?

★ Of proteins, carbohydrates, fats, and alcohols, which type of nutrient has the highest caloric value per gram?

- ▶ Circulation
- ▶ Respiration
- ▶ Excretion
- ▶ Nervous control
- ▶ Musculoskeletal system

★ What are the structural and functional differences between the three muscle types, i.e., skeletal, smooth, and cardiac?

- ▶ Immunity
- ▶ Endocrine control
- ▶ Reproduction and development
  - ◆ Sexual (gametogenesis, fertilization, zygote and embryo development)
  - ◆ Asexual (e.g., budding, parthenogenesis, self-fertilization)
- ▶ Changes in anatomy or physiology that may lead to human disease
  - ◆ Mechanisms (e.g., heart disease, gastrointestinal ulcers, emphysema)

★ What are some genetic, lifestyle, and internal physiological factors that can lead to hypertension (high blood pressure)? If hypertension is uncontrolled, what health problems can occur? What types of treatments exist to help control hypertension?

- ■ Homeostasis

★ Why are insulin and glucagon considered "antagonistic" hormones? Are there other such hormone pairs in the human body?

- ■ Animal response to stimuli
  - ▶ Innate/instinctual behaviors
  - ▶ Learned behaviors

Ecology

- ■ Population dynamics
  - ▶ Intraspecific competition
  - ▶ Population growth

★ Explain J-shaped and S-shaped population growth curves in terms of biotic potential and carrying capacity.

- ■ Social behaviors (e.g., territoriality, dominance, altruism, threat display)
- ■ Intraspecific competition
  - ▶ Niche concept
  - ▶ Competition

★ What is the principle of competitive exclusion?

- Interspecific relationships

  ▶ Predation, parasitism, commensalism, mutualism

- Succession

- The stability of ecosystems and the effects of disturbances

  ▶ Human impact (e.g., acid precipitation, ozone depletion, deforestation, agriculture, cultural eutrophication, urbanization)

★ How have humans accelerated the process of the greenhouse effect? What is the environmental impact of this accelerated greenhouse effect?

- Energy flow

  ▶ Trophic levels and energy loss between levels (10% rule)

  ▶ Food webs

  ▶ Food chains

  ▶ Productivity

  ▶ Biomagnification

★ Create a food web, with organisms placed within an appropriate trophic level, with the following organisms: zooplankton, eagle, freshwater shrimp, green algae, goose, mouse, beetle, bacteria, trout, bear, and mushroom. What would the pyramids of number, biomass, and energy look like for this ecosystem? Describe the levels of DDT you would find in the tissues of the members of the community, if the pesticide DDT were introduced into this food web.

- Biogeochemical cycles (e.g., nitrogen, carbon, water)

- Types and characteristics of biomes

  ▶ Aquatic (e.g., wetland, estuary, lake, oceanic pelagic)

  ▶ Terrestrial (e.g., temperate deciduous, tundra, chaparral)

★ Compare the types of vegetation encountered with increasing altitude (e.g., traveling up a mountainside) and with increasing latitude (i.e., traveling from the Equator toward the North Pole).

Earth/Space Sciences

Physical Geology

★ What makes a topographic map different from any other map? Why is a topographic map useful to a geologist?

- Processes of mineral and rock formation

★ What are the source materials for the ingredients of sedimentary rocks?

- Methods used to identify and classify different types of minerals, rocks, and soils

- Structure of Earth and the physical characteristics of Earth's various layers

★ What does the behavior of seismic waves reveal about the structure and physical characteristics of Earth's interior?

- Internal processes and resulting features of Earth (e.g., folding, faulting, earthquakes, and volcanoes)

- Plate tectonic theory and the evidence that supports this theory

★ What evidence exists for "continental drift" and how is continental drift different from plate tectonics?

★ What processes occur at plate boundaries?

■ Hydrologic cycle and the processes by which water moves through the cycle

■ Processes of weathering, erosion, and deposition

★ What are the major agents of erosion?

Historical Geology

■ The principle of uniformitarianism

■ Basic principles of stratigraphy
  ▶ Law of superposition

■ Relative and absolute time
  ▶ The geologic time scale and how it was developed
  ▶ Dating techniques

★ What is radioactive dating and how is it used to provide dates for the geologic time scale?

■ Processes involved in the formation of fossils

■ Types of information fossils provide

★ How can fossils be useful to a geologist in correlating the north and south walls of the Grand Canyon?

■ Important events in Earth's history
  ▶ Formation of the atmosphere
  ▶ Formation of the hydrosphere
  ▶ Mass extinction

Oceanography

■ Geographic location of oceans and seas

■ Processes involved in the formation and movement of ocean waves

★ Why do waves break as they approach the shore?

■ Primary causes and factors that influence tides

★ How do the Sun and Moon influence tides? Why, in general, do two high tides occur at a given location every day?

■ Major surface and deep-water currents in the oceans and the causes of these currents

★ What is the Coriolis effect and how does it affect Earth's surface waters?

■ Processes that influence the topography and landforms of the ocean floor and shorelines

★ What are black smokers and how do they form?

★ What is seafloor spreading? Explain the origin of the rift valley in the center of the mid-oceanic ridge.

  ▶ Shore processes (e.g., formation of dunes, beach profiles, wave effects)

■ Factors that influence the physical and chemical properties of seawater and nutrient cycles of the ocean

Meteorology

■ Structure of the atmosphere and physical, thermal, and chemical properties of atmospheric layers

★ List the layers of the atmosphere and discuss the temperature changes within each.

- Chemical composition of the atmosphere

- Factors influencing seasonal and latitudinal variation of solar radiation

- Causes of winds and of global wind belts

- Factors that contribute to small-scale (local and regional) atmospheric circulation
  - ▶ Monsoons
  - ▶ Land and sea breezes
  - ▶ Desert winds

★ How does the Sun influence global and local winds?

- Relative humidity, absolute humidity, dew point, and frost point
  - ▶ Associated saturation processes (e.g., dew, frost, and fog)

- Cloud and precipitation types and their formation

- Major types of air masses in terms of temperature, moisture content, and source areas

- High- and low-pressure systems
  - ▶ Storms

★ Why do weather systems generally move across the United States from west to east?

★ Compare and contrast tornadoes and hurricanes.

- Structure and movement of frontal systems (e.g., cold, warm, stationary, occluded) and the air circulation around and weather associated with frontal systems

★ What weather would you predict for the next day if you observed a lowering sequence of stratiform clouds over a day or two?

- Information on weather maps

- Analyses needed to perform short-term weather forecasting

- Methods used to perform long-term weather forecasting

- Regional and local natural factors that affect climate
  - ▶ Topography
  - ▶ Latitude

★ What influence does one or more of the following have on the climate of a region: ocean currents, landforms, and world wind belts?

★ How does a volcanic eruption affect both regional and worldwide climate conditions?

- ▶ How humans affect and are affected by climate (e.g., desertification, greenhouse effect and global warming, volcanic ash effect, El Niño)

Astronomy

- Major theories of the origin and structure of the universe
  - ▶ Galaxies
  - ▶ Novas
  - ▶ Black holes
  - ▶ Quasars
  - ▶ Stars

- Large units of distance (e.g., astronomical unit, light-year, parsec)

★ How far does light travel in a light-year?

- Origin and lifecycle of stars

★ What information about stars and their life cycle can be obtained form a Hertzsprung-Russell (H-R) diagram?

■ Major theories involving the origin of the solar system

■ Major features and characteristics of the Sun and the source of the Sun's energy

★ How do the Sun and other stars generate their energy?

■ Components of the solar system (planets, moons, asteroids, comets, and other solar system components) and their physical features and movements

■ Geometry of the Earth-Moon-Sun system and the cause of lunar and solar eclipses

► Phases of the Moon
► Lunar eclipses
► Solar eclipses

★ Why do lunar and solar eclipses not occur every month?

■ Causes of Earth's seasons

★ Compare the temperature and length of the day at the North Pole, the midlatitudes, and the Equator on June 21 and on December 21.

■ Earth's motion and the basis of units of time (e.g., year, day, hour)

★ Why does the length of daylight change from day to day?

■ Time zones on Earth

★ What is the relationship between a time zone, longitude, and Earth's rotation?

■ Geosynchronous orbits

■ Contributions of satellites to science and technology

■ Contributions of manned and unmanned space missions

■ Present limitations of space exploration

★ What limitation of Earth-based telescopes has been solved by the Hubble space telescope?

■ Scientific contributions of remote sensing

Science, Technology, and Society

Uses and applications of science and technology in daily life

■ Production, transmission, and use of energy

★ Compare the availability and limitation of the following sources of power: geothermal, nuclear, hydroelectric, solar, and fossil fuel.

■ Production, storage, usage, management, and disposal of consumer products

★ Since plastic products do not readily decompose in waste sites, what is an alternative for plastic disposal?

■ Management of natural resources

► Environmental quality
► Wetland conservation
► Soil erosion control
► Mining

★ Compare and contrast the depletion of mineral resources with that of fossil fuels.

■ Nutrition and public health issues

■ Agricultural practices

Impact of science and technology on the environment and human affairs

- Nuclear energy and radioactive waste

- Air pollution

- Global warming

- Agricultural pollutants

- Fossil fuels

- CFCs and ozone depletion

- Aerosol cans

- Logging

★ Give examples of how events such as the clear-cutting of the tropical rain forests and building of nuclear energy plants have had both positive and negative impacts on humans and the environment.

Social, political, ethical, and economic issues arising from the use of certain technologies

- Recycling

- Biotechnology

- Cloning

- Prolonging life

- Prenatal testing

- Miniaturization

- Nuclear power

- Manned space missions

- Nutrition

Part Two: Constructed-Response Questions

This section of the chapter is intended to provide you with strategies for reading, analyzing, and understanding the constructed-response questions on the *Middle School Science* test and for writing successful responses.

The test contains three equally weighted constructed-response questions that assess your ability to use and analyze critical concepts in science. One question deals with a topic in physical sciences (chemistry/physics), the second with a topic in life sciences, and the third with a topic in earth/space science. One question will assess your understanding of concepts and models, the second will assess your skills in data analysis and experimental design, and the third will assess your understanding of patterns and processes that occur in natural systems. Within the framework of these questions, one question will contain a component that assesses your understanding of issues concerning science, technology, and society. This test is designed to gather evidence about your knowledge of scientific principles, facts, methodologies, philosophy, and scientific concepts as well as your ability to integrate basic knowledge from all of the sciences.

It is expected that about 30 minutes will be spent on the three constructed-response questions. These questions constitute approximately 25 percent of the total test score.

What to Study

Success on this section of the test is not simply a matter of learning more about how to respond to constructed-response questions. It also takes real knowledge of the field. As mentioned above, the test is designed to gather evidence about your knowledge of scientific principles and concepts, and your ability to integrate knowledge from all of the sciences. It therefore would serve you well to review texts and notes relevant to the subject matter of the test. Any general, college-level textbooks in biology, chemistry, earth/space science, and physics would be appropriate for review. In addition, the following Web site links to subject-specific professional organizations may be useful resources for information about science and science instruction at all levels in the different content areas.

> The National Science Teachers Association
>> www.nsta.org
> The American Institute of Biological Sciences
>> www.aibs.org
> American Chemical Society
>> www.acs.org
> American Geological Institute
>> www.agiweb.org
> American Physical Society
>> www.aps.org
> American Association of Physics Teachers
>> www.aapt.org

What the Test Scorers Are Looking For

Even if you feel confident about your knowledge of the content to be tested, you still may wonder how you will be able to tell what the test scorers want.

In fact, you can find out what the test scorers want by looking at the questions themselves. The constructed-response test questions are crafted to be as clear as possible regarding what tasks you are expected to do. No expectations are hidden in the question or expressed in code words. The science educators who score your responses base your score on two considerations:

- Whether you do the tasks that the question asks for

- How well you do those tasks

So, to answer more specifically the question "What do the scorers want?" we should look at test questions, much like the ones on the test.

Understanding What the Questions Are Asking

It is impossible to write a successful response to a question unless you thoroughly understand the question. Often test takers jump into their written response without taking enough time to analyze exactly what the question is asking, how many different parts of the question need to be addressed, and how the information in the accompanying charts, tables, or graphs needs to be addressed. The time you invest in making sure you understand what the question is asking will very likely pay off in a better performance, as long as you budget your time and do not spend a large proportion of the available time just reading the question.

Examine the overall question closely, then identify what specific questions are being asked, mentally organize your response, and outline your key themes. Leave yourself plenty of time to write your answer. If you think out your response beforehand, your essay will be stronger.

Sample Question

To illustrate the importance of understanding the question before you begin writing, let's start with a sample question:

> A 4-liter, thin-metal can with its screw-top lid removed contains 100 milliliters of water. It is heated until the water boils. The can is then removed from the heat and its lid firmly replaced. Describe what will happen to the can as it cools and why.

Identifying the Key Components of the Question

- What will happen to the can as it cools?

- Why does this happen?

Organizing Your Response

Successful responses start with successful planning, either with an outline or with another form of notes. By planning your response, you greatly decrease the chances that you will forget to answer any part of the question, and you increase the chances of creating a well-organized response, which is something the scorers look for. Your note-taking space also gives you a place to jot down thoughts whenever you think of them—for example, when you have an idea about one part of the question while you are writing your response to another part. Planning your response is time well invested, although you must keep track of the time so that you leave sufficient time to write your response.

To illustrate a possible strategy for planning a response, let us focus again on the sample question introduced above. We analyzed the question and found that it asked for a two-part response. You might begin by jotting down those parts on your notes page, leaving space under each. This will ensure that you address each part when you begin writing.

Sample Notes—Main Parts to Be Answered

Here you start by identifying each part of the question:

What will happen as the can cools?

Why does this happen?

You then might quickly fill out the main ideas you want to address in each part, like this:

Sample Notes—Ideas Under Each Main Part

What happens to the can as it cools?

— the sides of the can will collapse

Why does this happen?

— temperature changes cause a change in air pressure

Now look at your notes and add any ideas that would address these characteristics. Notice the additions that are made below.

Sample Notes—With Added Ideas

This is where you use your knowledge of physical science. What you put here depends on how much you know. The following are some possible responses:

What happens to the can as it cools?

— the sides of the can will collapse

Why does this happen?

— the air inside the can is displaced

— when removed from the heat, the vapor condenses back into liquid and because the lid was airtight, a lower pressure is created inside the can

— less air inside therefore the can collapses until pressure equalizes

You have now created the skeleton of your written response.

Writing Your Response

Now the important step of writing your response begins. The scorers will not consider your notes when they score your paper, so it is crucial that you integrate all the important ideas from your notes into your actual written response.

Some test takers believe that every written response on a Praxis test has to be in formal essay form—that is, with an introductory paragraph, then paragraphs with the response to the question, then a concluding paragraph. This is the case for very few Praxis tests (e.g., Writing). The *Middle School Science* test does **not** require formal essays, so you should use techniques that allow you to communicate information efficiently and clearly. For example, you can use bulleted or numbered lists, a chart, or a combination of essay and chart.

What follows is an actual response by a test taker.

Sample Response that Received a Score of 3

The sides of the can will start to collapse inward until the point of equilibrium is reached between the pressure inside the can, the pressure outside the can, and the strength of the can's walls.

This is caused by the liquid water being heated enough to turn to vapor. This vapor then displaces the air molecules inside. When the can is taken off of the heat source, the vapor then condenses back into liquid, and because the lid was airtight, this creates a lower pressure inside the can than outside, since there are less air molecules in the same space. Thus the can collapses until the pressure inside the can equals that outside.

Commentary on Sample Response that Earned a Score of 3

The examinee received a score of 3 for this response because the answer given demonstrates a thorough understanding of the most significant parts of the stimulus material provided and responds appropriately to all parts of the question. The examinee correctly explains that the sides of the can would collapse until equilibrium of air pressure is attained. Further, there is a strong explanation that is well supported by relevant evidence. The examinee explains that the increase in temperature causes displacement of air molecules and that the subsequent change in temperature causes air pressure to change and the can to collapse in order to equalize that pressure. The examinee has demonstrated a strong knowledge of the concepts, theories, and facts relevant to the question.

Sample Response that Received a Score of 1

> When the water in the can starts to boil, air escapes and water evaporates.
> Not much, because you'll remove it immediately and cover with the lid. As the
> can starts to cool, the can will produce sweat drops on the outside of the
> can. Being a thin metal can and tightly covered with a lid, the can will slowly
> alter. The sides will recede and pull inward as the cooling continues.

Commentary on Sample Response that Earned a Score of 1

The examinee received a score of 1 for this response because the answer given demonstrates a misunderstanding of significant aspects of the stimulus material provided. The response also fails to respond appropriately to all parts of the question. The examinee indicates that some change will occur as water starts to boil but uses vague and inaccurate terminology. (i.e. the sides of the can will "recede and pull inward.") Further, the examinee provides a weak explanation that is not well supported by relevant evidence. The examinee has demonstrated a weak knowledge of the concepts, theories, and facts relevant to the question.

In Conclusion

Whatever format you select, the important thing is that your answer be thorough, complete, and detailed. You need to be certain that you do the following:

- Answer all parts of the question.

- Give reasons for your answers.

- Demonstrate subject-specific knowledge in your answer.

- Refer to the data in the stimulus.

It is a good idea to use the practice test in the next chapter to help you develop a plan for how you will take the test on the actual testing day, especially if you tend to get nervous or freeze up in a testing situation. Some test takers prefer to start with the question where they feel most comfortable. Remember to consider your time so that you may give appropriate consideration to all three essay questions. Stay within the framework of the question. Some test takers feel a need to elaborate with examples even when no example is requested. Be sure that any example given is correct and relevant to the question. An incorrect example can cause the reader to question the examinee's complete understanding of a concept. Whatever format you select for your essay, the important thing is that your answer be thorough, complete, and detailed.

Chapter 15

Practice Questions for the *Middle School Science* Test

▶ ▶ ▶ ▶ ▶ ▶ ▶ ▶ ▶ ▶ ▶ ▶

Now that you have studied the content topics and have worked through strategies relating to multiple-choice and constructed-response questions, you should take the following practice test. You will probably find it helpful to simulate actual testing conditions, giving yourself a set amount of time to work on the questions. If you wish, you can cut out and use the answer sheet provided to answer the multiple-choice questions and write your responses to the constructed-response questions on the lined answer pages.

Keep in mind that the test you take at an actual administration will have different questions, although the proportion of questions in each area and major subarea will be approximately the same. You should not expect the percentage of questions you answer correctly in these practice questions to be exactly the same as when you take the test at an actual administration, since numerous factors affect a person's performance in any given testing situation.

When you have finished the practice questions, you can score your answers to the multiple-choice questions, see sample scored responses to the constructed-response questions, and read explanations of the answers and responses in Chapter 16.

Note: If you are taking these practice questions to help you prepare for the *Middle School: Content Knowledge* test, you should keep in mind that the test you take at the actual administration will have 120 multiple-choice questions, with 30 questions in each of the four content areas. You will be allowed 120 minutes to complete the test. The test does not contain any constructed-response questions.

Professional Assessments for Beginning Teachers ®

TEST NAME:

Middle School Science

68 Practice Questions

Approximate time for the whole practice test—95 minutes

Suggested time for Part A (multiple choice)—65 minutes

Suggested time for Part B (constructed response)—30 minutes

(**Note:** At the official administration of this test, there will be 90 multiple-choice questions and 3 constructed-response questions. You will be allowed 120 minutes total to complete the test. The sections of the test will not be timed separately, though it is recommended that you spend 90 minutes on the multiple-choice questions and 30 minutes on the constructed-response questions.)

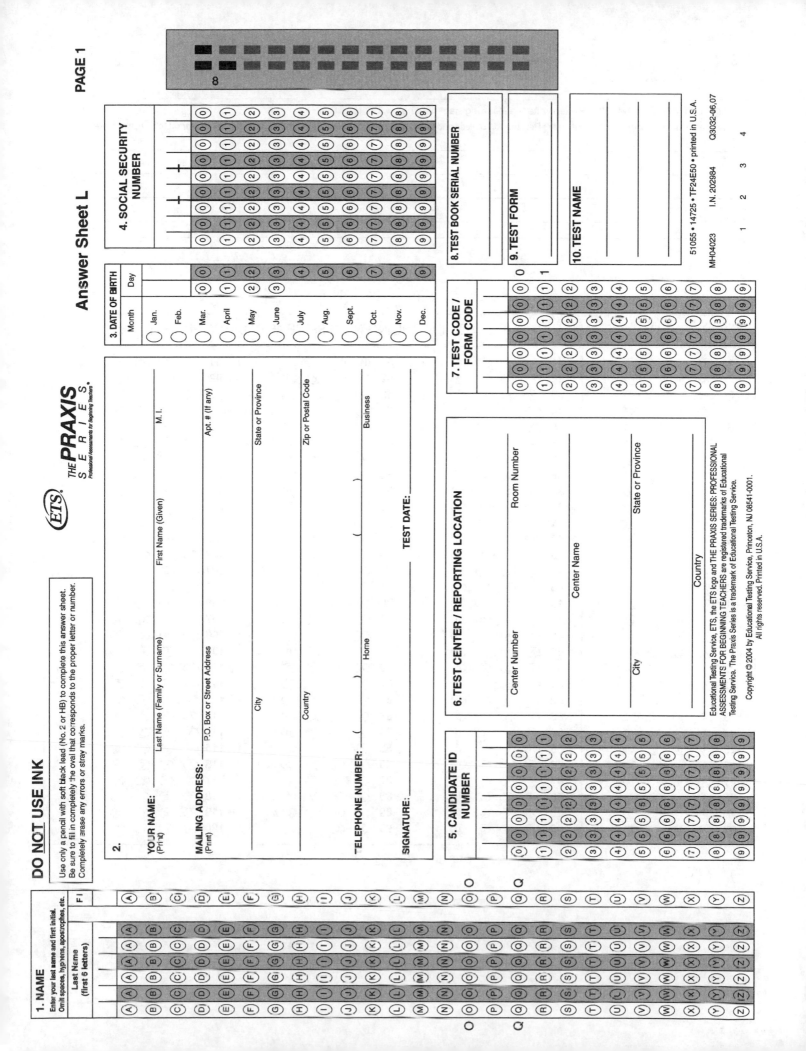

PAGE 2

CERTIFICATION STATEMENT: (Please write the following statement below. DO NOT PRINT.)
"I hereby agree to the conditions set forth in the Registration Bulletin and certify that I am the person whose name and address appear on this answer sheet."

_____

_____

_____

SIGNATURE: _____ DATE: _____ / _____ / _____
                                                                          Month   Day   Year

---

BE SURE EACH MARK IS DARK AND COMPLETELY FILLS THE INTENDED SPACE AS ILLUSTRATED HERE: ● .

1 Ⓐ Ⓑ Ⓒ Ⓓ	31 Ⓐ Ⓑ Ⓒ Ⓓ	61 Ⓐ Ⓑ Ⓒ Ⓓ	91 Ⓐ Ⓑ Ⓒ Ⓓ
2 Ⓐ Ⓑ Ⓒ Ⓓ	32 Ⓐ Ⓑ Ⓒ Ⓓ	62 Ⓐ Ⓑ Ⓒ Ⓓ	92 Ⓐ Ⓑ Ⓒ Ⓓ
3 Ⓐ Ⓑ Ⓒ Ⓓ	33 Ⓐ Ⓑ Ⓒ Ⓓ	63 Ⓐ Ⓑ Ⓒ Ⓓ	93 Ⓐ Ⓑ Ⓒ Ⓓ
4 Ⓐ Ⓑ Ⓒ Ⓓ	34 Ⓐ Ⓑ Ⓒ Ⓓ	64 Ⓐ Ⓑ Ⓒ Ⓓ	94 Ⓐ Ⓑ Ⓒ Ⓓ
5 Ⓐ Ⓑ Ⓒ Ⓓ	35 Ⓐ Ⓑ Ⓒ Ⓓ	65 Ⓐ Ⓑ Ⓒ Ⓓ	95 Ⓐ Ⓑ Ⓒ Ⓓ
6 Ⓐ Ⓑ Ⓒ Ⓓ	36 Ⓐ Ⓑ Ⓒ Ⓓ	66 Ⓐ Ⓑ Ⓒ Ⓓ	96 Ⓐ Ⓑ Ⓒ Ⓓ
7 Ⓐ Ⓑ Ⓒ Ⓓ	37 Ⓐ Ⓑ Ⓒ Ⓓ	67 Ⓐ Ⓑ Ⓒ Ⓓ	97 Ⓐ Ⓑ Ⓒ Ⓓ
8 Ⓐ Ⓑ Ⓒ Ⓓ	38 Ⓐ Ⓑ Ⓒ Ⓓ	68 Ⓐ Ⓑ Ⓒ Ⓓ	98 Ⓐ Ⓑ Ⓒ Ⓓ
9 Ⓐ Ⓑ Ⓒ Ⓓ	39 Ⓐ Ⓑ Ⓒ Ⓓ	69 Ⓐ Ⓑ Ⓒ Ⓓ	99 Ⓐ Ⓑ Ⓒ Ⓓ
10 Ⓐ Ⓑ Ⓒ Ⓓ	40 Ⓐ Ⓑ Ⓒ Ⓓ	70 Ⓐ Ⓑ Ⓒ Ⓓ	100 Ⓐ Ⓑ Ⓒ Ⓓ
11 Ⓐ Ⓑ Ⓒ Ⓓ	41 Ⓐ Ⓑ Ⓒ Ⓓ	71 Ⓐ Ⓑ Ⓒ Ⓓ	101 Ⓐ Ⓑ Ⓒ Ⓓ
12 Ⓐ Ⓑ Ⓒ Ⓓ	42 Ⓐ Ⓑ Ⓒ Ⓓ	72 Ⓐ Ⓑ Ⓒ Ⓓ	102 Ⓐ Ⓑ Ⓒ Ⓓ
13 Ⓐ Ⓑ Ⓒ Ⓓ	43 Ⓐ Ⓑ Ⓒ Ⓓ	73 Ⓐ Ⓑ Ⓒ Ⓓ	103 Ⓐ Ⓑ Ⓒ Ⓓ
14 Ⓐ Ⓑ Ⓒ Ⓓ	44 Ⓐ Ⓑ Ⓒ Ⓓ	74 Ⓐ Ⓑ Ⓒ Ⓓ	104 Ⓐ Ⓑ Ⓒ Ⓓ
15 Ⓐ Ⓑ Ⓒ Ⓓ	45 Ⓐ Ⓑ Ⓒ Ⓓ	75 Ⓐ Ⓑ Ⓒ Ⓓ	105 Ⓐ Ⓑ Ⓒ Ⓓ
16 Ⓐ Ⓑ Ⓒ Ⓓ	46 Ⓐ Ⓑ Ⓒ Ⓓ	76 Ⓐ Ⓑ Ⓒ Ⓓ	106 Ⓐ Ⓑ Ⓒ Ⓓ
17 Ⓐ Ⓑ Ⓒ Ⓓ	47 Ⓐ Ⓑ Ⓒ Ⓓ	77 Ⓐ Ⓑ Ⓒ Ⓓ	107 Ⓐ Ⓑ Ⓒ Ⓓ
18 Ⓐ Ⓑ Ⓒ Ⓓ	48 Ⓐ Ⓑ Ⓒ Ⓓ	78 Ⓐ Ⓑ Ⓒ Ⓓ	108 Ⓐ Ⓑ Ⓒ Ⓓ
19 Ⓐ Ⓑ Ⓒ Ⓓ	49 Ⓐ Ⓑ Ⓒ Ⓓ	79 Ⓐ Ⓑ Ⓒ Ⓓ	109 Ⓐ Ⓑ Ⓒ Ⓓ
20 Ⓐ Ⓑ Ⓒ Ⓓ	50 Ⓐ Ⓑ Ⓒ Ⓓ	80 Ⓐ Ⓑ Ⓒ Ⓓ	110 Ⓐ Ⓑ Ⓒ Ⓓ
21 Ⓐ Ⓑ Ⓒ Ⓓ	51 Ⓐ Ⓑ Ⓒ Ⓓ	81 Ⓐ Ⓑ Ⓒ Ⓓ	111 Ⓐ Ⓑ Ⓒ Ⓓ
22 Ⓐ Ⓑ Ⓒ Ⓓ	52 Ⓐ Ⓑ Ⓒ Ⓓ	82 Ⓐ Ⓑ Ⓒ Ⓓ	112 Ⓐ Ⓑ Ⓒ Ⓓ
23 Ⓐ Ⓑ Ⓒ Ⓓ	53 Ⓐ Ⓑ Ⓒ Ⓓ	83 Ⓐ Ⓑ Ⓒ Ⓓ	113 Ⓐ Ⓑ Ⓒ Ⓓ
24 Ⓐ Ⓑ Ⓒ Ⓓ	54 Ⓐ Ⓑ Ⓒ Ⓓ	84 Ⓐ Ⓑ Ⓒ Ⓓ	114 Ⓐ Ⓑ Ⓒ Ⓓ
25 Ⓐ Ⓑ Ⓒ Ⓓ	55 Ⓐ Ⓑ Ⓒ Ⓓ	85 Ⓐ Ⓑ Ⓒ Ⓓ	115 Ⓐ Ⓑ Ⓒ Ⓓ
26 Ⓐ Ⓑ Ⓒ Ⓓ	56 Ⓐ Ⓑ Ⓒ Ⓓ	86 Ⓐ Ⓑ Ⓒ Ⓓ	116 Ⓐ Ⓑ Ⓒ Ⓓ
27 Ⓐ Ⓑ Ⓒ Ⓓ	57 Ⓐ Ⓑ Ⓒ Ⓓ	87 Ⓐ Ⓑ Ⓒ Ⓓ	117 Ⓐ Ⓑ Ⓒ Ⓓ
28 Ⓐ Ⓑ Ⓒ Ⓓ	58 Ⓐ Ⓑ Ⓒ Ⓓ	88 Ⓐ Ⓑ Ⓒ Ⓓ	118 Ⓐ Ⓑ Ⓒ Ⓓ
29 Ⓐ Ⓑ Ⓒ Ⓓ	59 Ⓐ Ⓑ Ⓒ Ⓓ	89 Ⓐ Ⓑ Ⓒ Ⓓ	119 Ⓐ Ⓑ Ⓒ Ⓓ
30 Ⓐ Ⓑ Ⓒ Ⓓ	60 Ⓐ Ⓑ Ⓒ Ⓓ	90 Ⓐ Ⓑ Ⓒ Ⓓ	120 Ⓐ Ⓑ Ⓒ Ⓓ

FOR ETS USE ONLY	R1	R2	R3	R4	R5	R6	TR	TCR	RS	CS

PERIODIC TABLE OF THE ELEMENTS

1	2	3	4	5	6	7	8	9	10	11	12	13	14	15	16	17	18
1 **H** 1.0079																	2 **He** 4.0026
3 **Li** 6.941	4 **Be** 9.012											5 **B** 10.811	6 **C** 12.011	7 **N** 14.007	8 **O** 16.00	9 **F** 19.00	10 **Ne** 20.179
11 **Na** 22.99	12 **Mg** 24.30											13 **Al** 26.98	14 **Si** 28.09	15 **P** 30.974	16 **S** 32.06	17 **Cl** 35.453	18 **Ar** 39.948
19 **K** 39.10	20 **Ca** 40.08	21 **Sc** 44.96	22 **Ti** 47.90	23 **V** 50.94	24 **Cr** 52.00	25 **Mn** 54.938	26 **Fe** 55.85	27 **Co** 58.93	28 **Ni** 58.69	29 **Cu** 63.55	30 **Zn** 65.39	31 **Ga** 69.72	32 **Ge** 72.59	33 **As** 74.92	34 **Se** 78.96	35 **Br** 79.90	36 **Kr** 83.80
37 **Rb** 85.47	38 **Sr** 87.62	39 **Y** 88.91	40 **Zr** 91.22	41 **Nb** 92.91	42 **Mo** 95.94	43 **Tc** (98)	44 **Ru** 101.1	45 **Rh** 102.91	46 **Pd** 106.42	47 **Ag** 107.87	48 **Cd** 112.41	49 **In** 114.82	50 **Sn** 118.71	51 **Sb** 121.75	52 **Te** 127.60	53 **I** 126.91	54 **Xe** 131.29
55 **Cs** 132.91	56 **Ba** 137.33	57 *****La** 138.91	72 **Hf** 178.49	73 **Ta** 180.95	74 **W** 183.85	75 **Re** 186.21	76 **Os** 190.2	77 **Ir** 192.2	78 **Pt** 195.08	79 **Au** 196.97	80 **Hg** 200.59	81 **Tl** 204.38	82 **Pb** 207.2	83 **Bi** 208.98	84 **Po** (209)	85 **At** (210)	86 **Rn** (222)
87 **Fr** (223)	88 **Ra** 226.02	89 †**Ac** 227.03	104 **Rf** (261)	105 **Db** (262)	106 **Sg** (263)	107 **Bh** (262)	108 **Hs** (265)	109 **Mt** (266)	110 § (269)	111 § (272)	112 § (277)						

§Not yet named

*Lanthanide Series

58 **Ce** 140.12	59 **Pr** 140.91	60 **Nd** 144.24	61 **Pm** (145)	62 **Sm** 150.4	63 **Eu** 151.97	64 **Gd** 157.25	65 **Tb** 158.93	66 **Dy** 162.50	67 **Ho** 164.93	68 **Er** 167.26	69 **Tm** 168.93	70 **Yb** 173.04	71 **Lu** 174.97

†Actinide Series

90 **Th** 232.04	91 **Pa** 231.04	92 **U** 238.03	93 **Np** 237.05	94 **Pu** (244)	95 **Am** (243)	96 **Cm** (247)	97 **Bk** (247)	98 **Cf** (251)	99 **Es** (252)	100 **Fm** (257)	101 **Md** (258)	102 **No** (259)	103 **Lr** (260)

TABLE OF INFORMATION

Electron rest mass	$m_e = 9.11 \times 10^{-31}$ kilogram
Proton rest mass	$m_p = 1.672 \times 10^{-27}$ kilogram
Neutron rest mass	$m_n = 1.675 \times 10^{-27}$ kilogram
Magnitude of the electron charge	$e = 1.60 \times 10^{-19}$ coulomb
Bohr radius	$a_0 = 5.29 \times 10^{-11}$ meter
Avogadro number	$N_A = 6.02 \times 10^{23}$ per mole
Universal gas constant	$R = 8.314$ joules/(mole $\cdot$ K)
	$= 0.0821$ L $\cdot$ atm/(mole $\cdot$ K)
Boltzmann constant	$k = 1.38 \times 10^{-23}$ joule/K
Planck constant	$h = 6.63 \times 10^{-34}$ joule $\cdot$ second
	$= 4.14 \times 10^{15}$ eV $\cdot$ second
Speed of light	$c = 3.00 \times 10^8$ meters/second
Vacuum permittivity	$\epsilon_0 = 8.85 \times 10^{-12}$ coulomb^2/(newton $\cdot$ meter^2)
Vacuum permeability	$\mu_0 = 4\pi \times 10^{-7}$ newton/ampere^2
Coulomb constant	$1/4\pi\epsilon_0 = 8.99 \times 10^9$ newtons $\cdot$ meter^2/coulomb^2
Universal gravitational constant	$G = 6.67 \times 10^{-11}$ newton $\cdot$ meter^2/kilogram^2
Acceleration due to gravity	$g = 9.80$ meters/second^2
1 atmosphere pressure	$1 \text{ atm} = 1.0 \times 10^5$ newtons/meter^2
	$= 1.0 \times 10^5$ pascals (Pa)
Faraday constant	$\mathscr{F} = 9.65 \times 10^4$ coulombs/mole
1 atomic mass unit	$1 \text{ amu} = 1.66 \times 10^{-27}$ kilogram
1 electron volt	$1 \text{ eV} = 1.602 \times 10^{-19}$ joule

For H_2O:
heat of fusion	3.33×10^2 joules/gram
heat of vaporization	2.26×10^3 joules/gram
mean specific heat (liquid)	4.19 joules/(gram $\cdot$ K)

Volume of 1 mole of ideal gas at 0° C, 1 atmosphere	22.4 liters

PRAXIS MIDDLE SCHOOL SCIENCE

Part A

65 Multiple-choice Questions
(Suggested time—65 minutes)

Directions: Each of the questions or incomplete statements below is followed by four choices (A, B, C, and D). Choose the <u>best</u> response to each question and fill in the appropriate space for that question on your answer sheet.

$$^{6}_{3}\text{Li} + ^{1}_{0}\text{n} \rightarrow ? + ^{4}_{2}\text{Li}$$

1. Bombardment of $^{6}_{3}\text{Li}$ with neutrons, as shown above, will yield which of the following atoms?

   (A) $^{11}_{5}\text{B}$

   (B) $^{9}_{4}\text{Be}$

   (C) $^{4}_{2}\text{He}$

   (D) $^{3}_{1}\text{H}$

2. Tritium, a radioactive isotope of hydrogen, has a half-life of about 12 years. The fraction of a sample of tritium that remains undecayed after 50 years is closest to

   (A) $\dfrac{1}{4}$

   (B) $\dfrac{1}{8}$

   (C) $\dfrac{1}{12}$

   (D) $\dfrac{1}{16}$

3. Which of the following subatomic particles has a negative charge?

   (A) Electron
   (B) Proton
   (C) Neutron
   (D) Neutrino

4. Which of the following is the number of neutrons in $^{23}_{11}\text{Na}^{+}$?

   (A) 10
   (B) 11
   (C) 12
   (D) 23

5. In cold weather, it is more difficult to make people comfortable in a room with a high ceiling than in a room with a low ceiling primarily because

   (A) cold air is more dense than warm air
   (B) humid air is more dense than dry air
   (C) convection currents do not occur in rooms with a high ceiling
   (D) evaporation occurs more rapidly in a room with a high ceiling than in a room with a low ceiling

6. The Celsius temperature scale is based on the freezing point and boiling point of

   (A) alcohol
   (B) water
   (C) carbon
   (D) mercury

7. A 100.0 mL sample of water has an initial temperature of 20.0°C. The water is heated, and after 5.00 minutes its temperature is 50.0°C. Approximately how much energy was absorbed by the water? (The specific heat of water is 4.18 J/g·°C.)

   (A)   20.9 J
   (B)   418 J
   (C)   6,250 J
   (D) 12,500 J

8. An alkaline battery converts which of the following forms of energy into electrical energy?

   (A) Heat
   (B) Kinetic
   (C) Chemical
   (D) Mechanical

9. Which of the following is an example of a chemical change?

   (A) Glass shattering
   (B) Wood burning
   (C) Water boiling
   (D) Salt mixing with sugar

10. A magnet could be most easily used to separate a mixture of sulfur and

    (A) salt
    (B) iron
    (C) sugar
    (D) silicon

11. The volume of 1 g of liquid water at a temperature of 4°C and a pressure of 1 atm is

    (A) $0.1 \ cm^3$
    (B) $1 \ cm^3$
    (C) $3 \ cm^3$
    (D) $10 \ cm^3$

12. Which of the following is a balanced chemical equation?

    (A) $Cl_2 + NaBr \rightarrow Br_2 + 2 \ NaCl$
    (B) $Cl_2 + 2 \ NaBr \rightarrow Br_2 + NaCl$
    (C) $Cl_2 + 2 \ NaBr \rightarrow Br_2 + 2 \ NaCl$
    (D) $2 \ Cl_2 + NaBr \rightarrow 2 \ Br_2 + NaCl$

13. Barium reacts with oxygen gas to form barium oxide, BaO. Which of the following is produced in a similar reaction with oxygen gas?

    (A) KO
    (B) SO
    (C) PO
    (D) SrO

14. Which of the following best explains why a rubber raft that is slightly underinflated with air when in the shade is observed to be more fully inflated when placed in sunlight?

    (A) The rubber becomes more porous and allows more air to enter.
    (B) The rubber softens and collapses, causing the air inside the raft to become denser.
    (C) The temperature of the air inside the raft increases, causing the pressure to increase.
    (D) The air molecules inside the raft increase in size.

15. Which of the following is an organic compound?

    (A) Copper sulfate
    (B) Iron oxide
    (C) Calcium chloride
    (D) Sucrose

16. Which of the following compounds contains iron in the +3 oxidation state?

    (A) FeO
    (B) $FeCl_2$
    (C) Fe_2O_3
    (D) Fe_2O_4

17. Which of the following is a strong acid?

    (A) $NaHCO_3$
    (B) NH_3
    (C) HCl
    (D) $HC_2H_3O_2$

18. A student pours a sample of a saturated aqueous solution of a salt into a test tube and seals the tube. There is an air space above the liquid and no undissolved solids in the tube. When the temperature of the tube is lowered, some solid appears in the tube. What is the most reasonable explanation for this occurrence?

(A) The evaporation rate of water increases as the temperature decreases.
(B) The evaporation rate of water decreases as the temperature decreases.
(C) The amount of salt that needs to be dissolved to make a saturated solution increases as temperature decreases.
(D) The amount of salt that needs to be dissolved to make a saturated solution decreases as the temperature decreases.

19. Which of the following bodies exerts the greatest gravitational attraction at a distance of 5 million kilometers from the center of the object?

(A) A planet
(B) A star
(C) A meteor
(D) A moon

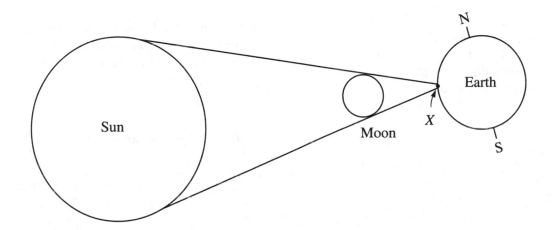

20. When the Sun, the Moon, and Earth are aligned as shown above, which of the following could probably be observed at point X on Earth? (Note: Figure is not drawn to scale.)

(A) The Moon passing through Earth's shadow
(B) A solar eclipse
(C) The Moon in its full phase
(D) The Sun setting below the horizon

21. Which of the following planets in the solar system takes the greatest number of Earth days to revolve around the Sun?

    (A) Venus
    (B) Mars
    (C) Neptune
    (D) Saturn

22. Which of the following correctly lists the first appearance of organisms in the fossil record from earliest to most recent?

    (A) Reptiles, fish, birds, amphibians
    (B) Fish, amphibians, reptiles, birds
    (C) Amphibians, reptiles, birds, fish
    (D) Birds, reptiles, fish, amphibians

23. Which of the following principles states that the processes observed at work on Earth today can be used to explain geologic evidence from the past?

    (A) Uniformitarianism
    (B) Second law of thermodynamics
    (C) Conservation of energy
    (D) Convergent evolution

24. In what country does the largest number of tornadoes occur?

    (A) Russia
    (B) United States
    (C) China
    (D) Indonesia

25. Which of the following statements best describes the general direction of movement of weather systems affecting the continental United States?

    (A) Most weather systems move according to no particular pattern.
    (B) Most weather systems move from south to north.
    (C) Most weather systems move from east to west.
    (D) Most weather systems move from west to east.

26. Which of the following types of precipitation forms when water vapor changes directly from a gas to a solid in the atmosphere?

    (A) Snow
    (B) Sleet
    (C) Hail
    (D) Freezing rain

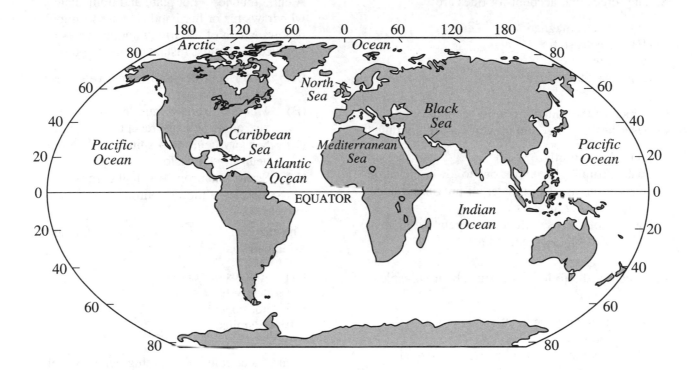

27. Which of the following labels for bodies of water is in the INCORRECT position on the map above?

(A)   Caribbean Sea
(B)   Black Sea
(C)   Mediterranean Sea
(D)   North Sea

28. The forces that account for tides are

    (A) electromagnetic
    (B) electrostatic
    (C) magnetic
    (D) gravitational

29. Which of the following most accurately describes the direction in which all rivers flow?

    (A) From north to south
    (B) From higher elevations to lower elevations
    (C) From areas of greater air pressure to areas of lower air pressure
    (D) From areas with dense vegetation to areas with sparse vegetation

30. Which of the following is true about volcanic activity on Earth?

    (A) It usually occurs at tectonic plate boundaries.
    (B) It is rarely associated with earthquake activity.
    (C) It produces only metamorphic rocks.
    (D) It produces lava with a temperature below the flash point of wood.

31. Which of the following is an example of asexual reproduction?

    (A) The growth of an oak tree from an acorn buried by a squirrel
    (B) The earthworm's use of sperm stored in its body to fertilize eggs that are produced by the earthworm
    (C) The formation of a new *Hydra* by budding from the parent *Hydra*
    (D) The transfer of pollen between flowering plants by foraging worker bees

32. The loud chirping noises made by crickets serve as the primary means by which crickets

    (A) maintain the correct rate of oxygen intake
    (B) locate food sources
    (C) control their metabolic rate
    (D) attract mates

33. A child touches a hot plate and immediately withdraws his or her hand. The nerve impulse follows which of the following pathways to produce the almost instantaneous response?

    (A) Motor neuron → spinal cord → sensory neuron → muscle
    (B) Motor neuron → muscle → sensory neuron → sensory receptor
    (C) Sensory neuron → spinal cord → motor neuron → muscle
    (D) Sensory neuron → spinal cord → muscle → motor neuron

34. The enzymes found in living organisms serve principally as

    (A) sources of energy
    (B) catalysts
    (C) hormones
    (D) vitamins

35. Some water containing both green plant cells and bacteria that are attracted to oxygen is placed on a glass slide, and the drop is sealed with a coverslip having grease around the edges. The bacteria will move toward the plant cells if which of the following parts of the plant cells are subjected to light?

    (A) Nucleus
    (B) Central vacuole
    (C) Chloroplast
    (D) Mitochondrium

36. A scientist collects a sample of a green material from the surface of a rock and wishes to determine whether it is living or nonliving. In making this determination, the scientist should study all of the following EXCEPT

    (A) the photosynthetic capability of the material
    (B) the presence of calcium in the material
    (C) evidence that the material is composed of cells
    (D) the capability of the material to reproduce

37. The Gram stain is used to distinguish between types of

    (A) protists
    (B) bacteria
    (C) viruses
    (D) fungi

Clover → Grasshopper → Quail → Hawk

38. In the food chain shown above, the tertiary consumer is which of the following?

    (A) A carnivore
    (B) A herbivore
    (C) A producer
    (D) A parasite

---

39. A certain species of plant has bright red flowers. Which of the following most likely explains how the red color is adaptive?

    (A) The plant is pollinated by hummingbirds, which can see red very well.
    (B) The red color protects the plant from predators.
    (C) Producing red flowers requires more energy expenditure than producing flowers of other colors.
    (D) Red pigments in the flower petals can not absorb the light needed for photosynthesis.

40. True statements about sickle-cell anemia include which of the following?

    I.   It is characterized by abnormal hemoglobin in red blood cells.
    II. It is an inherited disease.
    III. It can be a life-threatening disease.
    IV. It can be permanently cured with prompt treatment.

    (A) I and II only
    (B) II and III only
    (C) I, II, and III only
    (D) I, II, III, and IV

41. One of a woman's X chromosomes carries the recessive allele for a sex-linked trait. Her other X chromosome carries the dominant allele for the trait. Which of the following is true about the woman and her sons?

    (A) She will express the trait, and her sons may or may not express the trait.
    (B) She will not express the trait, but her sons will express the trait.
    (C) She will not express the trait, and her sons may or may not express the trait.
    (D) Neither she nor her sons will express the trait.

42. The method most often used by commercial plant growers to stimulate plants to bloom at a particular time during the year is to control the

    (A) amount of water the plants receive each day
    (B) concentration of fertilizer the plants receive each day
    (C) type of soil in which the plants are grown
    (D) lengths of the light and dark periods to which the plants are exposed

43. Which of the following is NOT a function of the root system of flowering plants?

    (A) Conducting water
    (B) Absorbing mineral
    (C) Anchoring the plant in the soil
    (D) Absorbing carbon dioxide

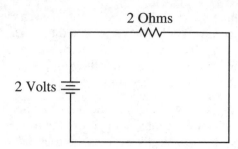

2 Ohms

2 Volts

44. In the circuit shown above, what is the current in the resistor? (Assume that the battery and the connecting wires have negligible resistance.)

(A) $\frac{1}{4}$ ampere

(B) 1 ampere
(C) 2 amperes
(D) 4 amperes

A

⊕   B   ⊕

C

45. Two identical positive electric charges are located as shown in the diagram above. At which of the points shown would a negative charge have no tendency to move due to electrical forces exerted on it by the two positive charges?

(A) A
(B) B
(C) C
(D) There will be a tendency for the negative charge to move no matter where it is placed.

46. Which of the following diagrams correctly shows the magnetic field lines resulting from an electric current flowing in a coil of wire?

(A)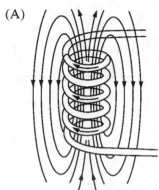

(B)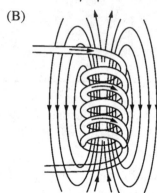

(C)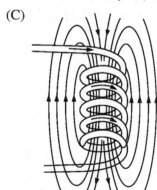

(D)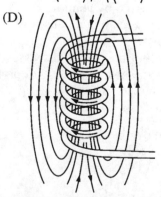

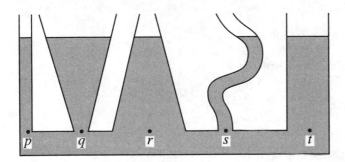

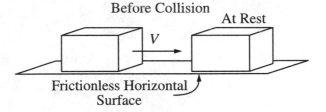

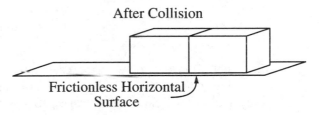

47. An open container is filled with a liquid to the level shown in the diagram above. Which of the following statements is true of the pressure at the lettered points shown?

(A) The pressure is least at p.
(B) The pressure at r is greater than the pressure at s.
(C) The pressure at q is the reciprocal of the pressure at r.
(D) The pressure is the same at each of the lettered points.

48. Four solid metal balls of the same size are dropped simultaneously from the top of a tall building. Each ball is made of a different metal: aluminum, gold, iron, or lead. If air resistance is ignored, in what order will the balls land on the ground, from first to last?

(A) Lead, gold, iron, aluminum
(B) Gold, lead, iron, aluminum
(C) Iron, lead, gold, aluminum
(D) They will all land at the same time.

49. A block moves to the right on a frictionless horizontal surface at a constant speed V, as shown above. The block collides with a second block, which is at rest but free to move. The two blocks stick together upon colliding. If no external horizontal forces act on the blocks, then after the collision the two blocks will move to the right with

(A) steadily decreasing speed
(B) a constant speed V
(C) a constant speed less than V
(D) a constant speed greater than V

50. Refraction, the bending of light rays, is the fundamental property underlying the operation of all of the following EXCEPT

(A) a magnifying glass
(B) a pair of binoculars
(C) an incandescent light bulb
(D) a motion-picture projector

51. The pitch perceived by a musician listening to a sound is analogous to which of the following wave properties?

(A) Frequency
(B) Speed
(C) Amplitude
(D) Intensity

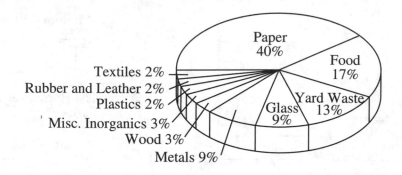

52. Assume that every day, on average, each person in the United States throws away 4.0 pounds of trash. The pie chart above shows the breakdown of this trash by weight. If paper, glass, metals, and plastics are recycled, the weight of an average person's daily throw-away trash will be reduced by most nearly

    (A) 1.6 lb
    (B) 2.0 lb
    (C) 2.4 lb
    (D) 3.0 lb

---

53. The basic function of a photovoltaic cell is to

    (A) perform photosynthesis
    (B) store photographic images
    (C) convert light energy directly into electrical energy
    (D) convert electrical energy into a beam of light

54. Which of the following results as a by-product of the fission process in a nuclear power plant and is of serious environmental concern?

    (A) Carbon monoxide
    (B) Radioactive wastes
    (C) Acid rain
    (D) Methane gas

55. When heat radiated from Earth's surface gets trapped by gases in Earth's atmosphere and cannot escape back into space, the process is referred to as

    (A) the greenhouse effect
    (B) ozone depletion
    (C) thermal inversion
    (D) acid rain

56. Which of the following is LEAST likely to result from excessive withdrawal of water from an aquifer?

    (A) The water table is lowered.
    (B) The ground subsides.
    (C) There is salt-water intrusion of aquifers near the coast.
    (D) The recharge area increases.

57. Which of the following practices generally does NOT result in increased soil erosion?

    (A) Logging
    (B) Growing crops in a previously empty field
    (C) Irrigating a field
    (D) Overgrazing

58. Which of the following diseases is caused by bacteria?

    (A) Chicken pox
    (B) Measles
    (C) Mumps
    (D) Tuberculosis

59. Which of the following is a safe laboratory procedure?

(A) Preparing a dilute acid solution by adding a small amount of concentrated acid to water in a flask

(B) Using a flame to heat an open beaker of alcohol

(C) Storing volatile liquids in containers with loose lids

(D) Flushing all waste chemicals down the laboratory sink with large amounts of water

60. Light travels at 3×10^8 meters per second in a vacuum. Approximately how long after a huge flare erupts on the Sun's surface is the flare seen on Earth, which is 1.5×10^{11} meters away?

(A) 8 milliseconds
(B) 8 seconds
(C) 8 minutes
(D) 1 hour

61. Four experiments were done with a metal wire. In each experiment, the resistance of the wire at a low and a high temperature was measured more than once. Which experiment gives the strongest evidence that resistance increases as temperature increases?

RESISTANCE (ohms)

		Low Temperature 600K	High Temperature 800K
(A)	Experiment A	4.1	4.4
		4.4	4.1
(B)	Experiment B	4.2	4.4
		4.3	4.5
(C)	Experiment C	4.0	4.5
		4.0	4.5
		4.1	4.4
		4.0	4.5
(D)	Experiment D	4.3	4.3
		4.2	4.4
		4.0	4.2
		4.2	4.2

62. All of the following represent the same length EXCEPT

    (A) 1 meter
    (B) 10 kilometers
    (C) 100 centimeters
    (D) 1,000 millimeters

63. A student placed 20 radish seeds on a damp paper towel in a petri dish and placed the dish under a fluorescent light. After 48 hours, all the seeds had germinated. In order for the student to draw a valid conclusion about the effect of water on seed germination, which of the following should also have been included in the investigation?

    (A) A second dish should have been placed in the dark.
    (B) A second dish should have been placed in a refrigerator.
    (C) A second dish with a dry, rather than damp, paper towel should have been used.
    (D) A second dish with a dry, rather than damp, paper towel should have been placed in direct sunlight on a windowsill.

64. Marie and Pierre Curie were awarded the Nobel Prize for their work with which of the following elements?

    (A) Magnesium
    (B) Radium
    (C) Barium
    (D) Calcium

65. Which of the following characteristics is most important in demonstrating that a hypothesis should be called a theory?

    (A) It interprets an observation.
    (B) It states a conclusion supported by an experiment.
    (C) It summarizes the most recent work of a scientist.
    (D) It provides an explanation for the results of many experiments.

Part B

3 Constructed-Response Questions
(Suggested time—30 minutes)

General Directions for Questions 66-68: There are three constructed-response questions below. Write your answers to these questions in the space provided in the lined pages following the questions. If a question has more than one part, be sure to answer each part of the question.

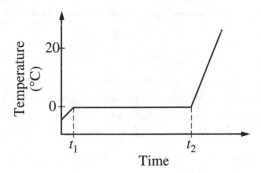

66. The graph above shows the temperature of a sample of water (initially in the form of ice) as heat is added to it at a constant rate.

- Describe what happens to the piece of ice during the time period t_1 to t_2 shown on the graph. In terms of energy, explain why the temperature remains constant during this time period.

- On the diagram provided in your response book, graph the changes you would expect to occur as heat continues to be added at a constant rate until the sample reaches a temperature of 100°C at time t_3, and then a temperature of 110°C at time t_4. Describe what happens to the sample of water during this time period.

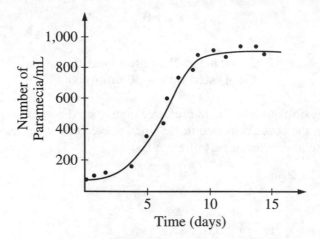

67. A population of the microorganism *Paramecium caudatum* is allowed to grow in a flask. A constant but limited amount of food is supplied daily, and the growth medium is replenished on a regular basis in order to eliminate the accumulation of metabolic wastes. The number of paramecia in a 1 mL sample taken from the flask is determined each day. The results are shown in the graph above.

  ● Explain how the growth rate of the paramecium population changes over the first 10 days of the experiment and why these changes occur.

  ● Explain what change has occurred in the growth rate of the population between day 10 and day 15 of the experiment and why this change has occurred.

  ● Briefly discuss how this model of population growth may have implications for the growth of human populations.

68. In the Cascade Range on the Pacific Northwest coast of the United States, a string of volcanoes runs parallel to the coast. This chain of volcanoes includes Mount St. Helens and Mount Rainier in Washington and Mount Hood in Oregon.

- According to plate tectonic theory, explain what is happening at this part of the North American plate by describing the type of boundary that exists and the geologic processes that are responsible for the formation of these volcanoes.

- Identify the major geologic feature that would be expected to be found on the seafloor of the northwest coast of the United States and explain how it would be created by the geologic processes occurring there.

Begin your response to Question 66 here.

(Question 66 continued)

_____
_____
_____
_____
_____
_____
_____
_____
_____
_____
_____
_____
_____
_____
_____
_____
_____
_____
_____
_____
_____
_____

(Question 66 continued)

_____

_____

_____

_____

_____

_____

_____

_____

_____

_____

_____

_____

_____

_____

_____

_____

_____

_____

_____

Begin your response to Question 67 here.

_____

_____

_____

_____

_____

_____

_____

_____

_____

_____

_____

_____

_____

_____

_____

_____

_____

_____

_____

_____

_____

(Question 67 continued)

_____

_____

_____

_____

_____

_____

_____

_____

_____

_____

_____

_____

_____

_____

_____

_____

_____

_____

_____

_____

_____

(Question 67 continued)

_____

_____

_____

_____

_____

_____

_____

_____

_____

_____

_____

_____

_____

_____

_____

_____

_____

_____

_____

_____

_____

_____

Begin your response to Question 68 here.

_____

_____

_____

_____

_____

_____

_____

_____

_____

_____

_____

_____

_____

_____

_____

_____

_____

_____

_____

(Question 68 continued)

_____

_____

_____

_____

_____

_____

_____

_____

_____

_____

_____

_____

_____

_____

_____

_____

_____

_____

_____

_____

_____

_____

_____

(Question 68 continued)

Chapter 16

Right Answers and Sample Responses for the *Middle School Science* Practice Questions

▶ ▶ ▶ ▶ ▶ ▶ ▶ ▶ ▶ ▶ ▶ ▶ ▶ ▶

The first part of this chapter contains right answers and sample responses to the multiple-choice practice questions for the *Middle School Science* test. The second part of this chapter contains scored sample responses to the constructed-response practice questions, along with explanations for why the responses received the scores they did.

Part One: Right Answers and Explanations for the Multiple-Choice Questions

Now that you have answered all of the practice questions, you can check your work. Compare your answers to the multiple-choice questions with the correct answers in the table below.

Question Number	Correct Answer	Content Category	Question Number	Correct Answer	Content Category
1	D	Atomic and Nuclear Structure	35	C	The Cell
2	D	Atomic and Nuclear Structure	36	B	Diversity of Life
3	A	Atomic and Nuclear Structure	37	B	Diversity of Life
4	C	Atomic and Nuclear Structure	38	A	Ecology
5	A	Heat and Thermodynamics	39	A	Evolution
6	B	Heat and Thermodynamics	40	C	Genetics
7	D	Heat and Thermodynamics	41	C	Genetics
8	C	Matter and Energy	42	D	Plants
9	B	Matter and Energy	43	D	Plants
10	B	Matter and Energy	44	B	Electricity/ Magnetism
11	B	Matter and Energy	45	B	Electricity/ Magnetism
12	C	Chemical Reactions	46	B	Electricity/ Magnetism
13	D	Chemical Reactions	47	D	Mechanics
14	C	Kinetic Theory and States of Matter	48	D	Mechanics
15	D	Mole and Chemical Bonding	49	C	Mechanics
16	C	Mole and Chemical Bonding	50	C	Waves
17	C	Solutions/Solubility	51	A	Waves
18	D	Solutions/Solubility	52	C	Mathematics, Measurement, and Data Manipulation
19	B	Astronomy	53	C	Science, Technology, and Society
20	B	Astronomy	54	B	Science, Technology, and Society
21	C	Astronomy	55	A	Science, Technology, and Society
22	B	Historical Geology	56	D	Science, Technology, and Society
23	A	Historical Geology	57	B	Science, Technology, and Society
24	B	Meteorology	58	D	Science, Technology, and Society
25	D	Meteorology	59	A	Laboratory Procedures and Safety
26	A	Meteorology	60	C	Mathematics, Measurement, and Data Manipulation
27	B	Oceanography	61	C	Mathematics, Measurement, and Data Manipulation
28	D	Oceanography			
29	B	Physical Geology	62	B	Mathematics, Measurement, and Data Manipulation
30	A	Physical Geology			
31	C	Animals	63	C	Methodology and Philosophy
32	D	Animals	64	B	Methodology and Philosophy
33	C	Animals	65	D	Methodology and Philosophy
34	B	The Cell			

Explanations of Right Answers

1. The correct answer is (D). Let $_Z^A X$ denote the unknown element X with atomic number Z and mass number A. The atomic numbers on both sides of the reaction must balance, and so must the mass numbers. Balancing the atomic numbers gives the equation $3 + 0 = Z + 2$, or $Z = 1$. An atomic number of $Z = 1$ corresponds to the element hydrogen, H. Balancing the mass numbers gives the equation $6 + 1 = A + 4$, or $A = 3$. Thus, the unknown atom is $_1^3 H$.

2. The correct answer is (D). The 50-year time period is slightly more than 4 half-lives of tritium. For each half-life, the amount of tritium decreases by $\frac{1}{2}$. The fraction remaining after 4 half-lives is

$$\frac{1}{2} \times \frac{1}{2} \times \frac{1}{2} \times \frac{1}{2} = \frac{1}{16}.$$

3. The correct answer is (A). Of the particles listed, only the electron has negative charge. The proton has positive charge, and the neutron and the neutrino have zero charge.

4. The correct answer is (C). The notation $_Z^A X$ denotes an element X with atomic number Z and mass number A. For $_{11}^{23} Na^+$, $Z = 11$ and $A = 23$. Now, $Z =$ the number of protons and $A = Z +$ the number of neutrons. Thus, the number of neutrons $= A - Z = 23 - 11 = 12$.

5. The correct answer is (A). Since cold air is more dense than warm air, convection currents will develop, with warmer air rising to the ceiling and cooler air dropping toward the floor. When the ceiling is high, there will be a greater temperature difference between ceiling and floor, thus making it more difficult to make people comfortable. (B), (C), and (D) are false.

6. The correct answer is (B). The Celsius temperature scale is based on a freezing point of 0°C and a boiling point of 100°C for water at 1 atm pressure.

7. The correct answer is (D). Assuming that 100.0 mL of water has a mass of 100.0 g, the amount of energy absorbed by the water is found from 100.0 g $\times 4.18$ J $g^{-1}{}^\circ C^{-1} \times (50 - 20)^\circ C = 12{,}540$ J, or 12.54 kJ.

8. The correct answer is (C). An alkaline battery consists of two electrodes (the anode and the cathode) separated by an ionically conductive electrolyte. Oxidation-reduction reactions occur at the two electrodes, causing chemical energy to be converted into electrical energy.

9. The correct answer is (B). Wood burning is the only process listed that involves a change in the composition of the substance. The resulting ashes, smoke, and invisible gases that are produced when the wood burns have different composition than the wood.

10. The correct answer is (B). Since iron is a magnetic material and sulfur is not, they can be separated by a magnet. The materials listed in (A), (C), and (D) are not magnetic materials.

11. The correct answer is (B). The volume of 1 g of H_2O at 4°C and 1 atm is 1 mL or 1 cm^3.

12. The correct answer is (C). In (C), the reactants and the products each contain the same number of each kind of atom, Cl, Br, and Na. (A), (B), and (D) are not balanced, as can be seen in the following:

	Reactants	Products
(A)	2 Cl, 1 Na, 1 Br	2 Cl, 2 Na, 2 Br
(B)	2 Cl, 2 Na, 2 Br	1 Cl, 1 Na, 2 Br
(C)	2 Cl, 2 Na, 2 Br	2 Cl, 2 Na, 2 Br
(D)	4 Cl, 1 Na, 1 Br	1 Cl, 1 Na, 4 Br

13. The correct answer is (D). Sr reacts with oxygen to form SrO because, like barium, it commonly has a +2 oxidation state in its compounds. (A) is not true, since K_2O should form. (B) is not true since SO_2 or SO_3 should form. (C) is not true since P_4O_{10} or P_4O_6 should form.

14. The correct answer is (C). The pressure is directly proportional to the Kelvin temperature. As the temperature of the air increases in the raft exposed to sunlight, the pressure increases, thus exerting more pressure on the material of the raft. (A) is not true, since if anything, more air would escape through pores as pressure increases. (B) is not true, since the raft would expand with the increasing pressure. (D) is not true, since temperature increases do not cause the size of individual molecules to increase.

15. The correct answer is (D). Organic compounds are those that contain the element carbon, with some exceptions, such as CO_2, CO, CS_2, $NaHCO_3$, which are normally classified as inorganic compounds. Sucrose is classified as organic since its formula is $C_{12}H_{22}O_{11}$. (A), (B), and (C) do not contain any carbon atoms.

16. The correct answer is (C). The oxidation state of Fe in (A) is $+2$; in (B) it is $+2$; in (C) it is $+3$; and in (D) it is $+4$.

17. The correct answer is (C). A strong acid is a compound that dissociates almost completely in aqueous solution, producing H_3O^+ ions. (C) is a strong acid, since HCl dissociates almost completely as follows:

$$HCl\ (aq) + H_2O(l) \rightarrow H_3O^+(aq) + Cl^-(aq).$$

(D) is a weak acid that only partially dissociates, producing $H_3O^+ + C_2H_3O_2^-$, while much of the $HC_2H_3O_2$ is undissociated. (B) is a base. (A) is a basic salt that reacts with water to produce some OH ions and is thus a basic salt, as follows:

$$NaHCO_3(aq) + H_2O(l) \rightarrow Na^+(aq) + OH(aq) + H_2CO_3(aq).$$

18. The correct answer is (D). Since some solid appeared, this indicates that some of the dissolved salt precipitated, due to a lower solubility for this salt at the lower temperature. The solution is saturated with a smaller amount of dissolved salt at this temperature. (A) is a false statement and (B), while being a true statement, would not result in a decrease of water and thus should not lead to precipitation of salt. If (C) were true, no solid would appear.

19. The correct answer is (B). The greatest gravitational attraction, at a given distance, is exerted by the object with the greatest mass. Of the four objects listed, a star has the greatest mass.

20. The correct answer is (B). The diagram shows that the Moon is directly between the Sun and point X. To an observer at point X, the Moon would cover the Sun and there would be a solar eclipse. A lunar eclipse occurs when Earth is directly between the Sun and the Moon and the Moon passes through Earth's shadow. The Moon is in its full phase when Earth is between the Sun and the Moon but not in the perfect alignment necessary for a lunar eclipse.

21. The correct answer is (C). The farther away a planet in our solar system is from the Sun, the longer it takes the planet to complete one orbit. Of the four planets listed, Neptune is the farthest away from the Sun.

22. The correct answer is (B). According to the fossil record, fish were the first of the four organisms listed to appear. Amphibians appeared in the late Devonian, reptiles in the Carboniferous, and birds in the Jurassic.

23. The correct answer is (A). According to the principle of uniformitarianism, the geologic processes operating today have acted in the same manner and with roughly the same intensity over geologic time.

24. The correct answer is (B). Although tornadoes occur in many different areas of the world, more occur in the United States than in any other country.

25. The correct answer is (D). The general pattern of air circulation in the midlatitudes of the Northern Hemisphere is from west to east, and weather systems tend to move with this flow.

26. The correct answer is (A). Snow results from the growth of ice crystals from water vapor. The crystals aggregate to form snowflakes. Sleet and hail form in the atmosphere from freezing water. Freezing rain is rain that freezes upon contact with cold surfaces.

27. The correct answer is (B). The body of water labeled the Black Sea is the Persian Gulf. The Black Sea is north of the eastern end of the Mediterranean Sea.

28. The correct answer is (D). The forces that account for tides are the gravitational forces exerted by the Moon and, to a lesser extent, by the Sun.

29. The correct answer is (B). All rivers flow from higher elevations to lower elevations. Although many rivers in the United States flow from north to south, there are many rivers worldwide that do not.

30. The correct answer is (A). Most volcanoes are located at tectonic plate boundaries. There are exceptions to this: for example, volcanoes in Hawaii formed over a "hot spot." Volcanic eruptions are typically associated with seismic activity. Lava cools to form igneous rock (e.g., basalt), not metamorphic rock.

31. The correct answer is (C). Asexual reproduction is a method of reproduction that enables organisms to produce offspring that are genetically identical to themselves. There is only one parent, so the offspring are essentially clones of the parent. *Hydra* can reproduce sexually or asexually. The example given, budding of a new *Hydra* from cells of one parent, is an example of asexual reproduction. In budding, a clump of mitotically dividing cells of the parent forms into a new *Hydra,* which separates from the parent organism.

32. The correct answer is (D). Crickets are insects that are related to grasshoppers. Males of these insects can make loud chirping noises by rubbing their wings together. The chirping noises are used to attract mates and vary in different species, and thus are species-specific.

33. The correct answer is (C). When the child touches the hot plate, the stimulus must first be received. The stimulus, or the sensation of extreme heat, is received by a sensory neuron, then transmitted to the spinal cord, then to a motor neuron, which can cause a response in a muscle—in this case the removal of the child's

hand from the hot plate. In many responses, the information received by the sensory neuron is carried to the brain before being integrated and a signal is sent via the motor neuron. Some reflexes, such as the "knee-jerk" response, are so automatic that the brain is not involved.

34. The correct answer is (B). Enzymes are proteins found in living organisms that catalyze reactions. A catalyst is an agent that lowers the energy of activation of a reaction; in other words, the catalyst enables the reaction to occur more easily. Enzymes catalyze reactions by various means; among others, they can put stress on chemical bonds or orient a molecule to maximize its chances of reacting.

35. The correct answer is (C). Contained in the water drop are green plant cells and bacteria that are attracted to oxygen. Oxygen is a product of photosynthesis, so if the green plant cells are producing oxygen, the bacteria should be attracted to them. The plant organelles responsible for photosynthesis are the chloroplasts. So, if a light is provided for the chloroplasts to undergo photosynthesis, then oxygen will be produced and the bacteria will move toward the oxygen source.

36. The correct answer is (B). In order to determine that a substance is living, it must be shown to possess the characteristics of living organisms. Living organisms are composed of cells, are capable of reproduction, respond to stimuli, are composed of organic molecules, and can undergo metabolic reactions, among others. If the material can perform photosynthesis, that would be evidence of metabolic reactions; if the material is composed of cells, that would be evidence that it is an organism; and if it can undergo reproduction, then that is further evidence that it is an organism. The presence of calcium is not a characteristic of living organisms, although many do contain calcium.

37. The correct answer is (B). The Gram stain is a procedure devised more than a century ago to identify bacteria. To Gram stain, a sample of bacteria on a slide is soaked in a violet dye

Study Guide for the Middle School Tests   303

and then treated with iodine. The slide is then rinsed with alcohol and stained with a pink dye. Bacteria can be identified as either gram-negative or gram-positive, depending on how the dyes are absorbed.

38. The correct answer is (A). In the food chain shown, the clover is the producer, and the grasshopper is the primary consumer eating the grass and thus is a herbivore. The quail is the secondary consumer and eats the grasshopper, so it is a carnivore, and the hawk eats the quail, so it is the tertiary consumer and also a carnivore.

39. The correct answer is (A). Bright red flowers in plants typically indicate that the plant is pollinated by another organism, and notably one that is attracted to the color red. The most likely pollinator would be a bird, as birds see colors well and hummingbirds are especially attracted to red flowers.

40. The correct answer is (C). Sickle cell anemia is a genetically based disorder of the red blood cells, or erythrocytes. It is characterized by abnormal hemoglobin, which is the molecule in red blood cells that carries the oxygen in the blood stream. It is inherited and can be a life-threatening disease. There is no permanent cure, as the genetic condition will persist throughout the person's lifetime and can be passed on to the next generation. It can, however, be treated.

41. The correct answer is (C). The woman is heterozygous for the trait; that is, she has one dominant allele and one recessive allele. Because the allele is carried on a portion of the X chromosome that has no corresponding locus on the Y chromosome, the trait is sex-linked. Males will have only one allele for the trait, as they have only one X chromosome. Thus, males will express whichever allele they have and exhibit either the dominant or the recessive condition of the trait. Since the woman can pass either of her X chromosomes to a son, her sons have a 50 percent chance of receiving the dominant allele and not expressing the trait and a 50 percent chance of receiving the recessive allele and expressing the trait.

42. The correct answer is (D). Flowering in plants is regulated by the amount of light and dark that the plant is exposed to. Different plants have different requirements, such as short-day and long-day plants. Short-day plants need long dark periods to flower, and long-day plants need long light periods and short dark periods to flower. Commercial plant growers can "force" flowering in plants by adjusting the regimen of light and dark periods.

43. The correct answer is (D). The root system of flowering plants has many functions. The roots help to anchor the plants, obtain and conduct water, obtain some nutrients, such as minerals, from the soil, and may store food for the plant for later use. The roots do not absorb carbon dioxide; that is the function of the leaves.

44. The correct answer is (B). The current I in a resistor of resistance R can be determined from Ohm's law, $V = IR$, where V is the voltage in the circuit. Thus,

$$I = \frac{V}{R} = \frac{2 \text{ volts}}{2 \text{ ohms}} = 1 \text{ ampere.}$$

45. The correct answer is (B). A negative point charge placed at either point A or point C will move toward point B. A negative point charge placed at point B will not move, since it experiences equal but opposite forces from the two positive charges.

46. The correct answer is (B). The coil of wire can be considered to be made up of many circular loops. The net magnetic field of the coil is then equal to the vector sum of the magnetic fields due to all of the loops. For a given circular loop, the right-hand rule can be used to determine the direction of the magnetic field: by placing the thumb of the right hand in the direction of current flow; the fingers will wrap in the direction of the magnetic field. Only (B) is consistent with the right-hand rule.

47. The correct answer is (D). For a liquid at rest in a container, all points at the same depth in the liquid are at the same pressure. Although the container is shaped differently above each of the five points $p, q, r, s,$ and t, it is evident that each point is at the same depth below the surface of the liquid. Thus, all five points are at the same pressure.

48. The correct answer is (D). In the absence of air resistance, all four balls will fall freely. Near the surface of Earth, freely falling objects all have the same downward acceleration g, regardless of mass, where g is the acceleration due to gravity. Thus, all four balls will land on the ground at the same time.

49. The correct answer is (C). There are no net external forces acting on the system, so the total linear momentum is conserved. Let M_1 denote the mass of the block moving with speed V before the collision, M_2 the mass of the block at rest, and V_{final} the speed of the two blocks after the collision. Since the horizontal surface is frictionless, V_{final} is a constant. To determine the magnitude of V_{final}, conservation of linear momentum can be used to give the equation:
$$M_1V = (M_1 + M_2)V_{final} \text{ or } V_{final} = \frac{M_1}{M_1 + M_2}V.$$
Thus, $V_{final} < V$.

50. The correct answer is (C). Refraction is the fundamental property underlying the operation of (A), (B), and (D), because they all involve the use of lenses to focus light. The fundamental property underlying the operation of an incandescent lightbulb is the phenomenon of incandescence—the emission of visible light by a hot body.

51. The correct answer is (A). The perceived pitch of a sound is the ear's response to the frequency of the sound wave. In a practical sense, pitch and frequency are the same.

52. The correct answer is (C). Recycling will reduce the weight of an average person's daily throwaway trash by the following amount:
$$\left(\frac{40}{100} + \frac{9}{100} + \frac{9}{100} + \frac{2}{100}\right) = 0.60$$
and $0.60 \times 4.0 \text{ lb} = 2.4 \text{ lb}$

53. The correct answer is (C). Photovoltaic cells convert light energy directly into electrical energy. A typical photovoltaic cell consists of a two-layer semiconductor material ($p-n$ junction). When light is incident on this material, it produces a potential difference, or voltage, between the two layers that can be used to provide a current to an external electrical circuit.

54. The correct answer is (B). Nuclear fission occurs when a heavy nucleus splits into smaller nuclei, resulting in the release of a relatively large amount of energy. The products of the fission process are long-lived, highly radioactive isotopes. This radioactive waste is of serious environmental concern, because it must be disposed of in a way that does not contaminate the environment.

55. The correct answer is (A). The greenhouse effect refers to the process described. Ozone depletion refers to the chemical destruction of the ozone layer by ozone-depleting substances. Thermal inversion refers to a region in the atmosphere in which warmer air lies above colder air. Acid rain refers to rain that has picked up oxides released into the atmosphere by the burning of fossil fuels.

56. The correct answer is (D). The water table is the surface of a body of groundwater. When excess water is removed from an aquifer, the water table is lowered. Removing water from pore spaces reduces the support given to the overlying material and can cause the ground to subside. In coastal areas, there is a wedge of salt water beneath the freshwater (salt water is denser than freshwater), being closer to the surface nearer the coast. When freshwater is withdrawn, the lower boundary of the freshwater rises in that area, and saltwater moves in to take its place. The recharge area is the area where water that eventually makes its way into the aquifer is absorbed into the ground. There is no reason for excessive withdrawal of water to increase the recharge area.

57. The correct answer is (B). Plants generally help reduce soil erosion. Roots help hold soil particles in place, and vegetation helps protect the soil from rain and wind. Logging and overgrazing reduce the amount of plant material, and irrigation can carry soil away.

58. The correct answer is (D). Of the diseases listed, only tuberculosis, or TB, is caused by bacteria. The others are caused by viruses. The tuberculosis-causing bacteria can attack any part of the body but usually attack the lungs. TB is spread from one person to another

through the air—the infected person coughs or sneezes and the bacteria become airborne.

59. The correct answer is (A). Concentrated acid should be added to water. (B) is unsafe because alcohol is flammable. (C) is a poor procedure because the volatile liquids will evaporate. (D) is not a safe practice, since many chemicals will contaminate waste water, no matter how much water is added, and because some chemicals that may become mixed can react with each other and produce harmful products, including gases that can disperse into the laboratory.

60. The correct answer is (C). The time t it takes for light to travel a distance d is given by the equation $t = \dfrac{d}{c}$, where c is the speed of light.

Thus, $t = \dfrac{d}{c} = \dfrac{1.5 \times 10^{11} \text{m}}{3 \times 10^8 \text{m} / \text{sec}} = 500 \text{ sec} \times$

$\dfrac{1 \min}{60 \sec} \approx 8 \min.$

61. The correct answer is (C). In experiment A, one pair of low-high measurements shows the resistance decreasing with temperature. In experiment D, two pairs of low-high measurements show no increase of resistance with temperature. In experiments B and C, all pairs of low-high measurements show resistance increasing with temperature. However, experiment C provides more evidence than experiment B, because more data points are involved.

62. The correct answer is (B). Answer choices (A), (C), and (D) are all equal to the same length of 1 meter, because 100 centimeters = 1 meter and 1,000 millimeters = 100 centimeters = 1 meter. Answer choice (B) is equal to 10,000 meters, because 10 kilometers = 10 × 1 kilometer = 10 × 1,000 meters = 10,000 meters.

63. The correct answer is (C). This question presents an experimental situation. The student wishes to determine the effect of water on seed germination. In order to determine this, there must be a control situation in which there is no water but everything else remains the same, to see if the presence of water made a difference. (C) is the only choice in which everything remains the same except the presence/absence of water.

64. The correct answer is (B). Marie and Pierre Curie discovered the element radium in 1898 by extracting it from pitchblende, a uranium ore. The elements radon and uranium were discovered by other scientists. X-rays are a type of electromagnetic radiation.

65. The correct answer is (D). A hypothesis is a tentative explanation for a set of observations. Further experiments are conducted to test the validity of the hypothesis. If the hypothesis survives many experimental tests, it may be referred to as a theory. (A) is not true because a hypothesis does not interpret an observation, but rather, attempts to explain the observation. (B) is somewhat true of a hypothesis, but it must be supported by many experiments before it can be called a theory. (C) is also not correct because, while observations, experimental procedures, and hypotheses may be involved, they represent only recent work; a theory must be based on work over a period of time.

Part Two: Sample Responses to the Constructed-Response Questions and How They Were Scored

This section presents actual scored sample responses to the constructed-response questions in the practice test in chapter 15 and explanations for the scores they received.

As discussed in chapter 4, each constructed-response question on the *Middle School Science* test is scored on a scale from 0 to 3. The general scoring guide used to score these questions is reprinted here for your convenience.

Praxis *Middle School Science* General Scoring Guide

Score	Comment
3	■ Demonstrates a thorough understanding of the most significant parts of any stimulus material presented
	■ Responds appropriately to all parts of the question
	■ Where required, provides a strong explanation that is well supported by relevant evidence
	■ Demonstrates a strong knowledge of concepts, theories, facts, procedures, or methodologies relevant to the question
2	■ Demonstrates basic understanding of the most significant aspects of any stimulus material presented
	■ Responds appropriately to most aspects of the question
	■ Where required, provides an explanation that is sufficiently supported by relevant evidence
	■ Demonstrates a sufficient knowledge of concepts, theories, facts, procedures, or methodologies relevant to the question
1	■ Demonstrates misunderstanding of significant aspects of any stimulus material presented
	■ Fails to respond appropriately to most parts of the question
	■ Where required, provides a weak explanation that is not well supported by relevant evidence
	■ Demonstrates a weak knowledge of concepts, theories, facts, procedures, or methodologies relevant to the question
0	■ Blank, off-topic, or totally incorrect response; rephrases the question

Constructed-Response Question 1—Sample Responses

We will now look at three scored responses to the first constructed-response question and see comments from the scoring leader about why each response received the score it did.

Sample Response 1: Score of 3

Between times t_1 and t_2 the ice is at a constant temperature. This is due to the phase change of ice (solid water form) to the liquid form of water. Whenever a substance changes phase, it must either absorb energy or give off energy. As an increase in temperature is noted, this example shows that water, (in solid form, or ice), is absorbing heat energy to change phase to liquid. <u>While absorbing this energy, all of the energy is used to change phase, while none is used to increase temperature of the substance, until after the phase change is complete.</u> The energy absorbed during this step goes towards breaking molecular bonds and counteracting those forces holding the ice in a solid lattice, allowing individual molecules to interact with each other more.

During the period between t_3 and t_4 the liquid water is changing phase to gaseous water, or steam. The temperature plateaus again during the phase shift as the energy goes towards the shift itself, rather than increased temperature. After the last of the water is converted to steam, the temperature of the steam begins to increase again to point t_4. It will continue to increase afterwards, provided it is given more energy.

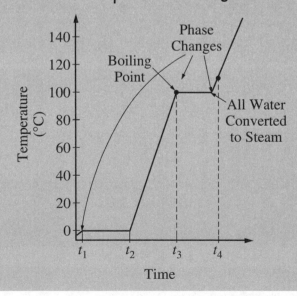

Commentary on Sample Response That Earned a Score of 3

The response demonstrates a clear understanding of the temperature and phase changes that occur to water as heat is added. Both parts of the prompt are answered with clear, well-developed explanations and descriptions. The answer clearly and accurately describes the phase change from solid to liquid that occurs during the time period t_1 to t_2, and from liquid to gas that occurs during t_3 to t_4. The response goes on to describe the need for added heat (latent heat of fusion) to create the phase change (i.e., energy used to break molecular bonds). The graph is accurate and clearly labeled, indicating changes that would occur as heat is added (plateauing at 100°C and then ascending to 110°C).

Sample Response 2: Score of 2

A certain amount of energy is needed in order for the ice to change phases. There is no increase in temperature from t_1 and t_2 to because the energy being applied to raise the temp. enough to change from a solid to a liquid is being applied but the temp. remains constant until enough of that energy is applied to cause a phase change.

Over time the temp will gradually increase until the temp. reaches 100°C which is the boiling point of water, again the temperature of the liquid will stay constant until enough energy is applied to the water to cause a phase change from a liquid to a gas.

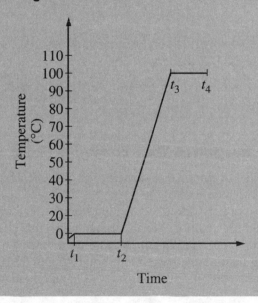

Commentary on Sample Response That Earned a Score of 2

The response demonstrates an adequate understanding of the temperature and phase changes that occur to water as heat is added. Both parts of the prompt are answered, but the explanations given are brief and general. The answer demonstrates an understanding of the phase changes that occur between t_1 and t_2 and between t_3 and t_4 but fails to discuss the change in molecular structure caused by increased heat. The graph is generally correct with some minor inaccuracies: a plateau is present but t_4 is misplaced—it should correspond to a temperature of 110°C instead of 100°C.

Sample Response 3: Score of 1

During the Period t_1 and t_2 and as heat is added the ice slowly begins to dissolve. The temperature of the ice cube will remain constant until it has completely dissolved to water and begins to boil due to the heat that is being added.

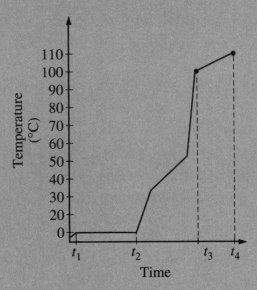

As the heat increases the water begins to reach its boiling point and the temperature of the water increases.

As the more heat is added the water begins to reach its boiling point and the temperature of the water increases.

Commentary on Sample Response That Earned a Score of 1

The response demonstrates a limited or minimal understanding of the temperature and phase changes that occur to water as heat is added. Only one part of the prompt is answered accurately. The piece of ice during the time period from t_1 to t_2 is inaccurately described as dissolving instead of melting and no mention is made of phase changes or the need for additional heat to accomplish this change in molecular structure. The response does recognize that there is a plateau in temperature until the water is completely "dissolved," but gives no further mention of this at the phase change from liquid to gas. The graph given is completely inaccurate. Temperature does not increase gradually from t_2 to t_3, and no plateau is indicated at 100°C.

Constructed-Response Question 2—Sample Responses

Sample Response 1: Score of 3

> Initially, in the flask, the amount of P. caudatum is no where near the carrying capacity of the ecosystem. There is plenty of food and not much competition (because of the low number of organisms). Therefore the population grows at an exponential rate over the first ten days. Between 10-15 days, the population is nearing the carrying capacity and competition for the limited resources increases. Also, space becomes a limiting factor since there is only so much room in the flask. The population growth levels off.
>
> Humans should recognize that space and natural resources can become limiting factors for us. Our population is expected to double by 2050. (From 6.2 billion to $\cong$ 12 billion people on earth). As more humans live longer and as we reproduce, resources and food become more scarce (competition increases also). We would need to continue to find other resources and more space in which to live or we will exceed the carrying capacity of the earth.

Commentary on Sample Response That Earned a Score of 3

The response demonstrates a clear understanding of the logistic model of population growth and the concept of carrying capacity. All parts of the prompt are answered with clear, well-developed explanations and discussions that use some of the appropriate terminology. The answer demonstrates an accurate description of the exponential growth rate over the first ten days: environmental conditions favor reproduction rate over death rate. The response demonstrates an understanding that population growth "levels off" or approaches zero as carrying capacity is reached. An appropriate discussion of the implications of this model to human populations if they exceed resources is included.

Sample Response 2: Score of 2

> In the first 10 days there was enough food to support the growing colony of parameciums. Also during this time the amount of waste generated was not too great as to affect the health of the colony before being replenished. At about day 10 through day 15, growth leveled off to a point that the number in the colony could be sustained by the environment. The population reached an equilibrium with the environment.
>
> This model is directly applicable to any population but especially for humans. In the environment, the population of a species fluctuates, based on available food, space, disease, predators, etc. but over time it will get into equilibrium with its habitat. Human populations grow with little consideration for how the environment can support them. Humans are polluting their environment, reducing the amount of food that can be

Sample Response 2: Score of 2 (continued)

> produced, safe places to live. The planet is quickly reaching its saturation point where it can no longer support the human population. At that point as with other animals, starving and disease may result to bring the world population down to sustainable levels.

Commentary on Sample Response That Earned a Score of 2

The response demonstrates an adequate understanding of the logistic model of population growth and the concept of carrying capacity. Both parts of the prompt are answered, but the explanations and discussions provided are brief and general. A general description of why growth occurs is given, with no mention made of exponential growth. While the response recognizes that the growth rate levels off after 10 days, there is little discussion of the environmental influences which may cause the change in growth rate. The implication of this model to human population growth is given in a brief and generally accurate description of the need for humans to be more conscious of their environment.

Sample Response 3: Score of 1

> The growth rate of the paramecium population changed because the amount of food supplied daily was limited. Although the food was given on a constant basis. Then the growth medium was replenished on a regular basis to eliminate the accumulation of metabolic wastes. The growth rate changed with a good food supply and a good clean environment to grow.
>
> The growth rate between day 10 and day 15 has become constant. I think the paramecium has reached its full growth size and there is no more room for growth. So the population will remain at a constant level.
>
> The model can show how humans development on the coarse of years. Humans have their greatest development within the first 15 years. Then in a human teenager years, he/she some what begin to grow into an adult. Which starts to become constant for the next few years.

Commentary on Sample Response That Earned a Score of 1

The response demonstrates a limited or minimal understanding of the logistic model of population growth and the concept of carrying capacity. The response indicates that the growth rate changed as food and a clean environment were provided but does not accurately explain why the growth rate changed during the first ten days and then remained at a constant level during days 10 through 15. The third portion of the prompt has clearly been misunderstood: the response seeks to explain pressures on human growth and development during the first 15 years of a person's life. The response demonstrates no understanding of the influences of environmental pressures on human population growth.

Constructed-Response Question 3—Sample Responses

Sample Response 1: Score of 3

> The type of boundary that exists along the Pacific Northwest coast of the United States is a convergent boundary (two plates collide into one another). When an oceanic plate collides with a continental plate the oceanic plate sinks under the continental plate. This forms a trench and will also cause new rock to be pushed up—forming mountains. Deep beneath the continental plate a magma chamber exists. When oceanic crust sinks beneath the continental plate it is melted into molten material in the magma chamber. When pressure reaches its peak, magma will be forced to the Earth's surface as lava.
>
> The major geologic feature found on the seafloor of the northwest coast of the U.S. is a trench. This is formed when an oceanic plate collides (converges) with a continental plate. The ocean plate sinks beneath the continental plate forming a trench.

Commentary on Sample Response That Earned a Score of 3

The response demonstrates a clear understanding of the tectonic plate boundaries, the geologic features, and processes involved at the boundary that exists in the Cascade Range of the Pacific Northwest coast of the United States. Both parts of the prompt are answered with clear, well-developed explanations and descriptions. The cause of such formations is clearly stated as a convergent boundary. The response accurately describes the subduction of the oceanic crust under the continental crust and the subsequent formation of volcanoes. A description of the geologic processes necessary to create the trench is also included in the response. The response contains no major inaccuracies.

Sample Response 2: Score of 2

> First, you have oceanic crust and continental crust converging on each. The oceanic crust is dipping down under the continental crust. This process increases the heat & pressure to a point in which, deep beneath the surface (Continental crust the rock begins to melt (molten). As it heats up it begins to rise, thus pushing up the continental crust above it. At a certain point, the molten rock can force its way to the surface in a violent explosion (MT ST Helens).

Sample Response 2: Score of 2 (continued)

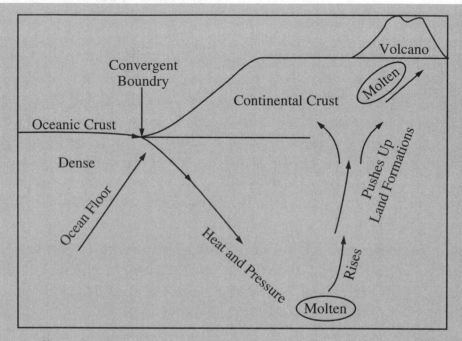

   The ocean floor in this area would be constantly changing. At certain points you would find faults (Transform) since the boundaries are not such that they meet as described in the illustrations. Some pass each other causing seismic activity. Basic processes of pressure and time and crust density (Thickness) create the features found. Igneous extrusive and igneous intrusive rocks are prevalent in the area. Once the volcanoes erupted (Mt St Helens) obsidian can be located found. Igneous intrusive is also found in these areas. Lastly, I would suppose, as the oceanic crust converges on the continental plate, old fossils would be found. This is based on the direction of travel and time to move such distance.

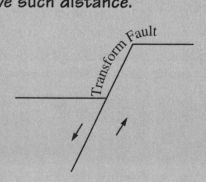

   Plate Tectonics—convergent, divergent plates, transform fault create the world we live in. Similar geologic activity is occurring on the west side of South America. Volcanoes, and seismic activities.

Commentary on Sample Response That Earned a Score of 2

The response demonstrates an adequate understanding of the tectonic plate boundaries, the geologic features, and processes involved at the boundary that exists in the Cascade Range of the Pacific Northwest coast of the United States. Both parts of the prompt are answered with explanations and descriptions that are accurate but brief and only general in their development. A very general discussion of the movement of these plates is given but specific terminology regarding convergent boundaries and the process of subduction is omitted. Faults are incorrectly identified as the major geologic feature that would be expected to be found on the seafloor.

Sample Response 3: Score of 1

Where this string of volcanoes exists there are two plates colliding together. One plate is continental and the other plate is oceanic. Where the two plates are colliding is causing an uplifting. There is an upward force, which is causing a volcano to be formed when these plates collide the molten from the center of the earth comes up and is released. There may also be a seafloor volcano where the plates are colliding. It would be the base of the volcano. As the plates collide/shift past each other, a large change is occurring. The plates are being uplifted and pushed against each other causing a lot of force. This in turn will form volcanoes.

Commentary on Sample Response That Earned a Score of 1

The response demonstrates a limited or minimal understanding of the tectonic plate boundaries, the geologic features, and processes involved at the boundary that exists in the Cascade Range of the Pacific Northwest coast of the United States. A limited response to one part of the prompt is provided; no response is provided for the other part of the prompt. The response describes the movement of one plate into another but only vaguely identifies these plates and does not describe subduction. A limited discussion of volcano formation is also included. A major geologic feature that one would expect to find on the seafloor of the northwest coast of the United States is not mentioned.

Chapter 17
Preparing for the *Middle School: Content Knowledge* Test

▶ ▶ ▶ ▶ ▶ ▶ ▶ ▶ ▶ ▶ ▶ ▶

The *Middle School: Content Knowledge* test is designed to measure the knowledge and higher-order thinking skills of prospective middle school teachers. The 120 multiple-choice questions focus on Literature and Language Studies, Mathematics, History/Social Studies, and Science.

There is not a separate section in this study guide containing preparation information and practice questions for the *Middle School: Content Knowledge* test. That's because the *Middle School: Content Knowledge* test covers the four content areas discussed in detail in chapters 5 through 16 of this book.

To use this study guide to help you prepare for the *Middle School: Content Knowledge* test, you may want to start by reviewing the Study Topics listed in chapters 5, 8, 11, and 14. The *Middle School: Content Knowledge* test covers nearly all of the topics mentioned in those subject-specific chapters but not always with the same degree of depth and breadth.

Then, to test your knowledge, answer the multiple-choice practice questions in chapters 6, 9, 12, and 15. Remember that at the actual test administration, you will have 120 minutes to answer 120 questions, with 30 questions in each of the four categories. Try to pace yourself accordingly while answering the practice questions.

Chapter 18

Are You Ready? Last-Minute Tips

▶ ▶ ▶ ▶ ▶ ▶ ▶ ▶ ▶ ▶ ▶

Checklist

Complete this checklist to determine whether you're ready to take the test.

❏ Do you know the testing requirements for your teaching field in the state(s) where you plan to teach?

❏ Have you followed all of the test registration procedures?

❏ Do you know the topics that will be covered in each test you plan to take?

❏ Have you reviewed any textbooks, class notes, and course readings that relate to the topics covered?

❏ Do you know how long the test will take and the number of questions it contains? Have you considered how you will pace your work?

❏ Are you familiar with the test directions and the types of questions for the test?

❏ Are you familiar with the recommended test-taking strategies and tips?

❏ Have you practiced by working through the practice test questions at a pace similar to that of an actual test?

❏ If you are repeating a Praxis Series Assessment, have you analyzed your previous score report to determine areas where additional study and test preparation could be useful?

The day of the test

You should have ended your review a day or two before the actual test date. And many clichés you may have heard about the day of the test are true. You should

- Be well rested

- Take photo identification with you

- Take a supply of well-sharpened #2 pencils (at least three)

- Eat before you take the test

- Be prepared to stand in line to check in or to wait while other test takers are being checked in

You can't control the testing situation, but you can control yourself. Stay calm. The supervisors are well trained and make every effort to provide uniform testing conditions, but don't let it bother you if the test doesn't start exactly on time. You will have the necessary amount of time once it does start.

You can think of preparing for this test as training for an athletic event. Once you've trained, and prepared, and rested, give it everything you've got. Good luck.

Appendix A
Study Plan Sheet

Study Plan Sheet

See Chapter 1 for suggestions about using this Study Plan Sheet.

STUDY PLAN						
Content covered on test	How well do I know the content?	What material do I have for studying this content?	What material do I need for studying this content?	Where could I find the materials I need?	Dates planned for study of content	Dates completed

Appendix B
For More Information

▶ ▶ ▶ ▶ ▶ ▶ ▶ ▶ ▶ ▶ ▶ ▶

Educational Testing Service offers additional information to assist you in preparing for The Praxis Series Assessments. *Tests at a Glance* booklets and the *Registration Bulletin* are both available without charge (see below to order). You can also obtain more information from our Web site: **http://www.ets.org/praxis/index.html.**

General Inquires

Phone: 800-772-9476 or 609-771-7395 (Monday-Friday, 8:00 A.M. to 7:45 P.M., Eastern time)

Fax: 609-771-7906

Extended Time

If you have a learning disability or if English is not your primary language, you can apply to be given more time to take your test. The *Registration Bulletin* tells you how you can qualify for extended time.

Disability Services

Phone: 800-387-8602 or 609-771-7780

Fax: 609-771-7906

TTY (for deaf or hard-of-hearing callers): 609-771-7714

Mailing Address

ETS—The Praxis Series
P.O. Box 6051
Princeton, NJ 08541-6051

Overnight Delivery Address

ETS—The Praxis Series
Distribution Center
225 Phillips Blvd.
Ewing, NJ 08628